Durkheim: essays on
morals and education

By the same author
Durkheim on religion

Edited and with
Introductions by

W. S. F. Pickering

Translations by
H. L. Sutcliffe

Durkheim:

essays on morals

and education

Routledge & Kegan Paul

London, Boston and Henley

First published in 1979
by Routledge & Kegan Paul Ltd
39 Store Street, London WC1E 7DD,
Broadway House, Newtown Road,
Henley-on-Thames, Oxon RG9 1EN and
9 Park Street, Boston, Mass. 02108, USA

Set in Compugraphic English Times
and printed in Great Britain by
Ebenezer Baylis & Son Limited
The Trinity Press, Worcester, and London

British Library Cataloguing in Publication Data
Durkheim, Émile
  Durkheim
    1. Ethics   2. Moral education
    I. Pickering, W S F
    170'.8   HM216   79–41002

ISBN 0 7100 0321 8

Contents

Acknowledgments

What would seem to be straightforward work entailed in a volume such as this calls for the help of those with specialized knowledge. As a consequence we are grateful for the aid that has been given in reading parts of the manuscript or in offering advice of various kinds. In particular, our appreciation extends to Philippe Besnard, Mohamed Cherkaoui, Norman Dennis, Andrew Fairbairn, Victor Karady, Steven Lukes, Mary Midgley, and Michael Stant. A word of appreciation also goes to Tony Evans for contributing to the bibliography in the section on education.

Not least we should like to thank our ever enthusiastic typist, Annemarie Rule, who offered us not only great technical skill, but also encouragement to press on with the work when sometimes it approached the laborious.

The editor and publisher would like to thank the following for permission to reproduce copyright material: from *Émile* by Jean-Jacques Rousseau, translated by Barbara Foxley. An Everyman's Library Edition. Reprinted by permission of the publisher in the United States, E. P. Dutton; and by kind permission of the publisher in the United Kingdom, J. M. Dent & Sons Ltd, London.

Finally, we mention with gratitude an initial research grant given by the University of Newcastle upon Tyne, which allowed us to launch the project.

W.S.F.P.
H.L.S.

The translations

On the whole, a literal approach has been adopted in the task of translating Durkheim. For the reader's sake, it was considered preferable to sacrifice embellishments of style to fidelity to the original. Changes have nevertheless proved necessary, for the most part in punctuation and in coping with occasional very long sentences such as occur, for instance, in the transcripts of the discussions.

As is the custom amongst translators of Durkheim, certain words for which there is no precise and unambiguous English equivalent have been left in the original. Among such cases one might instance *conscience* (which may mean consciousness, conscience, morality), *représentation* (idea, sentiment, volition), *moeurs* (custom, habit, social norm). In this category one might also include those words whose translation varies somewhat according to the context, but for which it was felt the reader should know the original French, despite the English word being used, such as *éducation*, *culture*, *enseignement*, and *morale*.

Where Durkheim quotes extensively from Rousseau's *Émile ou de l'Éducation*, it was judged best to use Foxley's Everyman translation, whilst indicating any discrepancies in page references or renderings which became apparent.

It is in fact Durkheim's lecture notes which presented the greatest challenge, since the French, as one might expect from notes, is skeletal and telegrammatic. No attempt has been made, however, to reflate the original text and thus provide it with meanings which Durkheim may never have intended.

Where emendations of footnotes were essential, or where the text was ambiguous, as in a number of places in the piece on Rousseau, this fact has been indicated by means of notes bearing the initials of the translator or the editor.

H.L.S.

Notation and bibliographies

In references in the Introductions and in certain notes to the translations, the shorthand sign for the name of a book or article is the date which follows the author's name. The title of the item, its publisher, date, and so on, can be found under the author's name in the Bibliography (which lists the works of Durkheim and those of other authors on Durkheim himself) or in the short reference sections at the end of each Introduction. The numbers which follow the date refer to the pages of the item. The prefix t. before the date indicates that the item is a translation of that date. The prefix r. before a date means that a previous item is reproduced in a book or article of the date which follows the prefix.

The actual combination of dates and letters of works by Durkheim is that of Steven Lukes (1972) and subsequently brought up to date by W. S. F. Pickering (see *Études durkheimiennes, Bulletin d'information*, June 1978, no. 2, pp. 9–14).

The items in the two sections are presented in the order of the date of their publication, though this does not necessarily mean that they were written at the time of the date specified. Where there is a large discrepancy between the date of composition and publication, an explanatory footnote will be found or reference made to the fact in the Introductions.

The bibliographies of the books and articles by other writers on Durkheim's approach to morals and education is a selection and is in no way exhaustive.

Many of the articles and other items by Durkheim are reproduced in V. Karady (ed.), *Émile Durkheim. Textes*, 3 vols, Les Éditions de Minuit, Paris, 1976.

W.S.F.P.

Abbreviations

AJS	*American Journal of Sociology*
AS	*L'Année sociologique*
ASR	*American Sociological Review*
BJS	*British Journal of Sociology*
BSFP	*Bulletin de la Société Française de Philosophie*
MF	*Mercure de France*
PR	*Philosophical Review*
RB	*Revue bleue*
RFS	*Revue française de sociologie*
RHPR	*Revue d'histoire et de philosophie religieuses*
RIS	*Revue internationale de sociologie*
RMM	*Revue de métaphysique et de morale*
RP	*Revue philosophique*
R de P	*Revue de philosophie*
SR	*Sociological Review*

Preface

This book consists of translations of essays and other items by Émile Durkheim (1858–1917) which have not been translated into English before.* As a revival of interest in this great French sociologist is taking place, the work of translation continues, encouraged by such developments.

The translations which are presented here relate to the two connected subjects of morality and education, which were crucial to the thought of Durkheim in general and more particularly to his social theory. It has not been thought necessary to reproduce English translations which have already been made, be they chapters taken from Durkheim's books, articles, or reviews. The work of translation is arduous, and, because there is still much to be done, it was thought undesirable to attempt any retranslations. What has been translated up to now on morality and education can be gleaned from the Bibliography.

As in a previous volume (W. S. F. Pickering (ed.) 1975 *Durkheim on Religion*, Routledge & Kegan Paul, London and Boston) we have presented items in their entirety and have avoided reproducing in translated form fragments of books or articles published for some *ad hoc* purpose. It is to be hoped, therefore, that this volume will contribute to the growing corpus of translations of Durkheim, in which each book, article or review by him stands in its own right. However, unlike the previous volume, there are cases in which a certain amount of editorial excursion has had to be made and this relates to items which consist of reports of academic discussions in which Durkheim took part. Such debates were associated with the Société Française de Philosophie, which met regularly in Paris

* Just at the time of going to press it was learnt that one item, 'Introduction à la morale' (1920a), will probably appear in translation before the publication of this book (see M. Traugott (ed.), *Émile Durkheim on Institutional Analysis*, University of Chicago Press, Chicago and London, 1978). Also, another piece, 'La Grandeur morale de la France: l'école de demain' (1916c), has very recently been discovered in translation in a somewhat obscure American book published in 1919 (see Buisson and Farrington, 1919, in the Bibliography).

and published the proceedings in its *Bulletin*; and with another group, the Union pour la Vérité, whose debates were published in the *Libres entretiens*. The contributions which Durkheim made on these occasions were important, not only for what he said but also for the criticisms that were levelled at him and against which he had to defend himself. By reason of the incisive and sometimes brilliant exchanges that took place between him and other members of the groups, his own position is often clarified and the issues sharpened. The discussions as reported were frequently lengthy and this raises a practical problem. One attempt has been made before to use Durkheim's contributions to a debate, which was in *Sociology and Philosophy* (1924a/t.1953b), but here Durkheim's speeches were extracted from their context. Such a procedure loses what atmosphere is created by the complete French text. However, to translate the whole of the debate would be of doubtful merit. The practical solution is to make a selection of the relevant parts of the discussion in which are located Durkheim's specific contributions. This procedure has been recently adopted by Victor Karady (see Notation and bibliographies). In order to try to recreate something of the situation in which Durkheim was speaking, we have in certain cases translated the speeches which preceded his and sometimes those which followed. Where the intermediate speeches were long, a summary is sometimes offered. If the contribution of a discussant was closely argued, it was felt best to translate the speech in full. On the subjects of morals and education, it so happened that the number of discussions and debates in which Durkheim took part was fairly numerous. A selection has been made of what might be said to be the most important discussions (see 1908a(2); 1909a(2); 1910b; 1911a; 1912b).

Morality and education were closely linked in Durkheim's mind: with justification it could be said that they were to him as theory and practice. We have nevertheless attempted to make a fairly clear-cut distinction between them. Certain items do, however, relate to both subjects and it has not been easy to place them in one section rather than the other. The problem of drawing a line of demarcation is particularly difficult in his famous lectures on *Moral Education* (1925a/t.1961a), which deal with basic problems about morality and yet are at the same time concerned with the problems of teaching not only morality but other aspects of education as well. Problems of locating items in this volume become apparent in the Introductions where there are many cross references. Furthermore, as might be expected, certain books and articles appear in the bibliographies of both sections.

In the selection of items on the subject of morality, attention is drawn in particular to 'Introduction à la morale' (1920a), which is of considerable interest for an understanding of Durkheim's theoretical and systematic approach to the subject, and which was one of the last things he wrote shortly before he died. However, Durkheim was very much concerned with practical morality in such areas as the family, divorce, suicide, sexual behaviour and so on, and items relating to some of these subjects have been included in both the section on morals and education. The only major article on morals that now remains untranslated, apart from reviews, is Durkheim's account of 'scientific' morality which he wrote in his early days as a result of a visit to Germany, a year before he started teaching in the University of Bordeaux in 1887. It is 'La Science positive de la morale en Allemagne' (1887c). The article is long – over sixty pages – and refers in detail to a number of now rather obscure German philosophers and psychologists. Although it is of much importance to the scholar, keen to trace the origins of Durkheim's concept of morality, it represents the work of the youthful and emerging sociologist, and to have included it in its entirety in this volume would have created a certain amount of imbalance.

In the case of education, and bearing in mind the specific nature of the French situation, it was decided that the selection of items should be of as wide a general interest as possible. For this reason items whose subject was university education, which calls for treatment in its own right, were excluded. None the less, in the bibliography on education, references to items on French university life have been given. With the translations made in this volume, nearly all the pieces Durkheim wrote on non-university education are now available in English. Within the selection, the reader's attention is drawn to the major item – again one edited or compiled at the end of his life – namely his notes on Rousseau's *Émile* (1919a). But there does remain perhaps one possible gap in the work of translation on the subject of education and it is the notes taken by students attending Durkheim's lectures on education and morality. They are Lenoir's 'De l'Enseignement de la morale à l'école primaire' (1968a(1-12)); Davy's 'La Morale' (1968c); and Cuvillier's

'La Morale' (1968d). As indicated, some of the items relate as much to morality as to education. Whilst the notes are well worth studying, their accuracy and veracity have been questioned (*RFS*, XVII, 1976:196). In the light of the limitations set by this volume, it was thought undesirable to translate the notes.

At the end of each item translated, certain notes will be found which have been added by the editor or translator and are enclosed in square brackets. These notes arise from an attempt to clarify points in the text which seemed to require elucidation. They also cover brief descriptions of French philosophers and sociologists whose names appear in the text. Notes appearing in parentheses are those which are printed in the French text. In the texts themselves, not in the notes, parentheses are used where the French text employs them and are also reserved for French words of the original, where it is thought readers would appreciate knowing the actual words used by Durkheim and others.

W.S.F.P.

Part I **Morals**

Introduction
by W. S. F. Pickering

Durkheim's sociological approach to morals and moral systems has always aroused considerable interest, be it by way of criticism or praise. Two notable contributions to the subject have recently appeared in English, that of Ernest Wallwork, *Durkheim: Morality and Milieu* (1972), and relevant chapters in Steven Lukes's *Émile Durkheim* (1972). Mention should also be made of the work of the French philosopher, J. Henriot (1967). An introduction such as this cannot hope to emulate these and other commendable studies, or even offer résumés of them. Its purpose must be quite different. The subjects within the area of moral life which Durkheim raised were many and complex and provoked much discussion amongst both sociologists and philosophers. The items which have been selected for translation are intended to bring to the attention of readers certain aspects of Durkheim's sociology of morals, which need further documentation for the English-speaking world, or which have not received adequate attention up to now. Therefore, only those aspects of Durkheim's thought of which the items make mention will be dealt with, albeit briefly. The topics that will be covered are the definition of the subject matter, moral reality, the science of morality, the obligatory nature of moral facts, relativism, rationality, and so on. The intention is not to present a comprehensive or overall introduction to Durkheim's sociology of morals. The raising of these topics, it is hoped however, will provide an outline of much of Durkheim's moral thought, and at the same time will demonstrate the reason for the selection of the items which have been translated. They will not be considered individually, because certain topics are to be found in more than one item.

Having said that, the principle is momentarily broken by referring at the very outset, and again at the end, to the importance of Durkheim's 'Introduction to ethics' (1920a), which could be seen as the most significant item in this small collection. It is important for many reasons. It was amongst the last things that he wrote just before he died. In the face of alleged changes in his thought, one may conclude that it represents his mind at its most developed point, although, as the title suggests, it forms but part of an introduction to a comprehensive study of morals. Although the *Elementary Forms of the Religious Life* (1912a) stands as his masterpiece, his ambition was to crown it with something greater, something closer to his heart, a sociological study of moral behaviour. He was a wholly moral person and this fact projected into his academic interests, and as Davy, a close disciple of Durkheim, said, no one could understand his work unless he was seen as a moralist (1920:71–2). However, he had never written anything systematic on morality, but he had planned such a work. Marcel Mauss, his nephew, wrote: '*Morale* was the goal of his existence, the centre point of his intellect' (*AS*, 1925, n.s., I:9). The years 1914–18, which meant the redirection of his energies to more pressing, practical concerns in supporting France's war effort, prevented him from embarking on his quest. Accelerated by the death of his beloved son André, killed on the eastern front, his health began to fail and as the end drew near, all he could produce was the opening chapter of the introductory section of *La Morale*. In such circumstances Mauss described Durkheim's endeavours as 'a supreme act of faith' (ibid.). Durkheim wrote the introduction in Paris and in Fontainebleau during the summer before he died in 1917 at the age of only fifty-nine. He departed life a sad man, sad because of the loss of so many of his disciples who died in the war, sad perhaps at the apparent failure of that form of humanism in which he believed; and sad also, it might be said, by his unfulfilled ambition to write a definitive book on ethics.

Defining morality

There is merit in referring at the outset to Durkheim's 'Introduction to ethics' since nowhere else does he so clearly attempt to define the area covered by morality. As a conceptualist Durkheim was convinced that it was necessary to begin any systematic study with a statement of definition. According to him, the French word *morale* implies one of two possibilities – it means moral actions, decisions, judgments, virtues; but it also relates to reasoning and speculation about such actions, decisions, judgments and virtues. The contrast between the two meanings is to be seen in that the first is associated with what is spontaneous, whereas the second is reflective, involving rational principles and speculation, even a doctrine of man. Further, the moralist, working within the limits of the second meaning, may criticize moral actions and attitudes within the first meaning and may even suggest changes. In modern terminology, the first meaning might be said to correspond to descriptive ethics, based on observed action and attitude. The second roughly corresponds to traditional ethics, or as the French in Durkheim's day called it, *la morale théorique*. Today this might be subdivided into normative ethics related to reasoning about right action – what is moral and what is not; and metaethics which deals with the ultimate nature of moral action and discourse (see Nielsen 1967:118ff.).

Moral reality

There are also two major theses on which Durkheim's study of morals is based. The first is that there exists what is called moral reality; and second, that this reality constitutes the subject matter of a valid scientific analysis.

There is a moral reality, as indicated in the word *morale*, because it is generally agreed that in history, in everyday life, there are institutions, laws, customs, modes of behaviour and thought, individual and collective, which are associated with the word moral. They constitute a set of facts or data which have an existence and stand outside the individual (see 1905b, translated here). They do not have to be constructed or deduced by the moralist. Acts of honour, loyalty, duty, are in society for everyone to see. Since the point of commencement has to be with moral behaviour as it is actually practised, Durkheim saw that speculation about the ultimate nature of what is moral or what is desirable is never legitimate as a first stage of the enquiry (see 1920a; also 1925a: 133ff./t.1961a:116ff.). Morality has its own reality independent of any thories which might be used to justify it or describe its essence (1907a(3):356). It is little wonder therefore that Durkheim attacked every piece of abstract or platitudinous reasoning about morals.

Such arguments could form no basis to develop a study of moral facts of a given society because those who used the arguments never began at the point of action or fact. Durkheim's attitude in this matter is patently clear in the debates in which he was involved in the Société Française de Philosophie which have been translated in the pages ahead (see especially 1909a(2)). The point of commencement can never be moral action in general: but must be specific actions – practices as they are found in concrete societies. His attack was often levelled against idealist tendencies, such as appeared in the arguments of Delvolvé (ibid.). Likewise Durkheim supported critics of Guyau who put forward an approach to morals, in which he made much use of a basic concept, which was akin to poetic intuition, 'the principle of life' (1906f).

A scientific discipline

The other thesis, basic to Durkheim's analysis of morality, is that the reality circumscribed as moral should be the subject of scientific investigation. His commitment to science as a means of acquiring knowledge and understanding in the world of human and social behaviour, as much as in the physical world, hardly needs to be emphasized. It is apparent in many of the pieces translated here, as well as in nearly all his major works (see, for example, 1893b; 1895a). He saw science as a discipline armed with a superior method to that of philosophers, artists or theologians. So many of their conclusions, stemming from *a priori*, not empirical methods, turned out to be unsatisfactory. His commitment was epitomized in his vocation to sociology – a subject he so skilfully developed. His interest in applying the scientific method to morality has probably deep and complex roots but it may well have been strengthened when he visited Germany in the academic year 1885/6 and listened to the lectures of such thinkers as Wundt and Post, whose approach to ethics was of a positivist kind (see 1887c).

Durkheim's plea for a scientific approach to the study of morals was evident throughout his academic life but it reached its clearest expression in the important paper he gave to the Société Française de Philosophie, 'La Détermination du fait moral' (1906b (see also its close parallel to *L'Éducation morale* 1925a)). Durkheim held that the science of morality has a proper place within the province of sociology, since sociology itself consists of a scientific analysis of social facts, and moral facts are part of the category of social facts (see also 1895a). One of the difficulties Durkheim saw in applying the scientific method to morality, which raises more problems than in other areas of human behaviour, is that it contains a strong component of the 'ought'. The 'is' must always be dissociated from the 'ought', that is, what people actually do in the realm of moral behaviour must be rigidly differentiated from what they ought to do. The difficulty is that moral action and belief are impregnated with the concept of the 'ought'. The problem can be said to be largely of Durkheim's own making since by definition he held that morality was concerned with the 'ought'. But the main methodological point is that the sociology of morals, which concentrates on moral behaviour as it is practised, is to be contrasted with the more traditional discipline where the starting point is theoretical morality, or what traditionalists have sometimes called normative science, which for Durkheim was a contradiction in terms. Speculation about morality has its place, but philosophers are to be criticized because, at the very outset of their studies, they fail to liberate moral behaviour from sentiment and prejudice (1907a(3): 356). It must be said with great emphasis that support for upholding a scientific procedure is evident in Durkheim's thought in the items translated. At no point did he ever abandon what he held to be the necessity of an initial scientific approach to the study of moral and social behaviour.

All the items translated in this Part, except 'Introduction to ethics', were published between 1904 and 1910. They were years not only marked by great activity on the part of Durkheim but they also witnessed the publication of a number of books on the subject of positive ethics, which caused considerable academic stir. It should never be thought therefore that Durkheim was alone in propounding a scientific or sociological approach to morality. There were many writers in this period who were fully convinced that traditional ethics or *la morale théorique* was no longer tenable in the face of increasing knowledge and new ways of thought about the universe. For these reasons if for no other, they explored the possibility of positive ethics. Some of them attributed much of their thinking to Durkheim himself, having been influenced by his early works (see Bibliography, Durkheim on Morals). Reference should be made to A. Landry, *Principes de morale rationnelle* (1906); A. Fouillée, *Les Éléments sociologiques de la morale* (1905); articles by G. Belot, 'En Quête d'une morale positive' (1905–6) and later a book, *Études de morale positive* (1907). (See reviews by Durkheim, 1907a(3)(4)(5).) There was also the book by Albert Bayet, *La Morale scientifique: essai sur les applications morales des sciences sociologiques* (1905) (reviewed by Durkheim, 1906a(11), translated here). Pleased though Durkheim was that he had had such an influence on thinkers of the day, his point of criticism was that as philosophers, as indeed most of them were, they had failed to apply a rigorous scientific method to the subject on hand and that they had developed their thought in ways which were not in keeping with such procedure. In Britain the philosopher and sociologist, Edward Westermarck, perhaps influenced by Wundt, had written *The Origin and Development of the Moral Ideas* (1906) and this was also criticized by Durkheim for its lack of scientific rigour (see 1907a(10), translated here). Amidst other books which were published on the subject at the time, one stood out in Durkheim's view, and indeed if continued editions is a criterion, stands as a classic. It was Lucien Lévy-Bruhl's *La Morale et la science des moeurs* (1903). Lévy-Bruhl, then lecturer in philosophy at the Sorbonne, attempted to justify and develop the concept of a scientific and sociological approach to morals. In this he was much influenced by both Comte and Durkheim. However, there is another side to the coin, for Lévy-Bruhl in turn influenced Durkheim (see below). He was never one of Durkheim's close followers and disciples who helped in the production of the important journal *L'Année sociologique*. He was very sympathetic to the new sociological school which was developing at the time but stood no further than on its periphery. Durkheim's review of the book just mentioned (1904a(5), translated here) is of measured admiration, although at least one of Durkheim's disciples, Paul Fauconnet, was critical (1904). Durkheim used the opportunity of reviewing the book as an occasion not only of supporting Lévy-Bruhl but of expanding his own ideas and implying that they were similar to those of the author. Lévy-Bruhl had two specific aims – to challenge the legitimacy of theoretical ethics and to develop the idea of rational moral art (see below). But over and above such particularities he argued strongly for the rightness of a positive or scientific approach to the study of morality – *la science des moeurs* or a sociology of moral actions, habits, customs, norms, such as Durkheim advocated, and indeed he used such phrases as *la science des moeurs* or *le physique des moeurs*. The book gave rise to much contention, especially among philosophers some of whose names have just been mentioned, and the result was that Lévy-Bruhl was forced to defend himself publicly (1906). (For an analysis of Lévy-Bruhl 1903, see Gurvitch 1937b and 1939.)

Whilst the sociology of morals or *la science des moeurs* was the source of considerable debate, relatively little controversy waged over the actual application of the scientific method to moral reality in terms of comparative studies or particular societies (e.g. Parodi 1910:ch.2). Rather, the points at issue in France were more of a theoretical kind, dealing with the nature of moral reality – its definition and characteristics, along with the possible application of the findings of the science once they had been established. In passing it should be noted that Durkheim argued that his critics attacked him at the level of theory rather than in the way he approached specific issues in such works as *Division of Labour* (1893b) or *Suicide* (1897a). The commendability of science lies not in its theory or in its philosophy but in the results it achieves in practice in the understanding of the data with which it deals. (For Durkheim's methodology of morals, see 1907a(3).)

Moral forces and moral facts

To emphasize the fact that morals constitute a reality to which the scientific method could be legitimately applied, Durkheim frequently called components of society 'forces'. He was well aware of the dangers of trying to use too literally the concept of force, common enough in physics. Nevertheless he felt it was valuable to use the word, not least to demonstrate the existence in experience of the data to which he was pointing. On numberless occasions he referred to religion, morality, and law as exerting force. This is another idea that remained with him from beginning to end. In his notes on Rousseau's *Émile* (translated in the section on Education) which date from the same period as his 'Introduction to ethics', he wrote: 'If the citizen is to be natural, he must feel that he is under the sway of a moral force, comparable in strength to a physical force' (1919a). Durkheim stated that social forces of course could not be physical forces but were mental or moral ones, derived from *représentations* or states of *conscience* (1910b).

But if the concept of force within morals is open to criticism so is that of fact. Is it legitimate to refer to moral actions as facts? Belot, a philosopher within the rationalist school, disagreed with Durkheim over what constituted the data of the science of morals. Durkheim's insistence on facts, rather than say personal action, caused Belot to retort that facts were like dead things (1908a(2), translated here). Durkheim remained unmoved. To the very end of his days he held that 'a science of morality, if it is not to be other than a matter of mere common sense, can only be arrived at by the scientific study of moral facts' (1920a). He wished to hammer home two points – the importance of empirical data and that they should be related to the social. The focus on what is now called 'facticity' is borne out by what he wrote in his lectures, *L'Évolution pédagogique en France*: 'Ethics . . . operate in the realm of action, which either gets to grips with real objects or else loses itself in the void. To act morally is to do good to creatures of flesh and blood, to change some feature of reality' (1938a:240/t.1977a:207). Although one does not know the essence of the moral ideal or of reality, *les faits moraux* must form the base on which to build a study of morality. Only in this way can the nature of the moral be slowly revealed.

But in the beginning, how are moral facts to be recognized? For Durkheim they are a sub-division of social facts and to find the answer to the question, one naturally turns to *The Rules of Sociological Method* (1895a:ch.I).[1] Of the several characteristics Durkheim enunciates, one is underlined here, which is highly relevant to moral behaviour, namely, the notion of coercion. Social facts control or constrain ways of thinking and acting of the individual, in other words, they exert a force on man's behaviour. Durkheim constantly referred to this characteristic of social facts, particularly in the realm of religious belief and ritual, as in *The Elementary Forms of the Religious Life* (1912a). The problem, however, which cannot be discussed here, is to carefully differentiate a cluster of concepts such as constraint, coercion, obligation, and so on. For Durkheim the coercive force in moral action is obligation – demands made by society – rather than sanction – penalty and reward (see below). Despite difficulties in handling these concepts,

10

Durkheim never repudiated the primacy of obligation. In his 'Introduction to ethics' he still emphasized it as being 'inherent and indispensable' (1920a). (For a general criticism of the notion of constraint, the reader is referred to Lukes 1972:12–14.)

The emphasis on individualism and freedom of choice, current among philosophers at the time, encouraged many to reject from the moral all that was mechanical or habitual. With intention and motive as key characteristics, actions which might be labelled 'automatic' could hardly be counted as being within the realm of the moral. Bayet in his *La Morale scientifique* (1905) rejected the notion that duty constituted the moral, because for him duty was a sort of illusion. It could not be therefore a subject of scientific study. Bayet saw a concern for duty as the preserve not of philosophy, or science, but of art. It was something not to be developed or corrected but to be dispelled, as a kind of nightmare which has been an obsession and a source of anguish to humanity for centuries. Gaston Richard (1925a) held that Durkheim's review of Bayet's book was of great importance in understanding Durkheim's approach to morality in so far as he took the opportunity in the review to correct errors that positivists had made in their approach to morality (1906a(11), translated here).[2] Bayet, who was a disciple of Lévy-Bruhl, had in Durkheim's eyes misunderstood the notion of duty. Although morality, Durkheim held, was made up of ideas and sentiments, duties were very much within its realm. Indeed, morality could be seen as consisting of little more than a code of duties. Durkheim rejected the idea that sanction was the chief characteristic of duty (1907a(10); see also 1906b/r.1924a/t.1953b: 43). In another review he partly agreed with Westermarck that sanction was a sign or expression of duty. However, he criticized the English moralist who held that sanction alone was the basis of duty. What constituted duty for Durkheim was the notion of command, in other words, that of coercion, which fits in neatly with *The Rules*. The notion of duty had therefore to be fully understood and its origins discovered if any progress were to be made in the sociology of morality. Here and in other matters Durkheim showed certain affinities with Kant.[3] Elsewhere Durkheim argued that the concept of duty was unknown in Greek or Latin thought but was born in Christianity. It has however survived its progenitor. Above all, the concept indicated that man is to rise above his nature and this is what was absent in classical thought (1938a:242/t.1977a:209).

As is commonly realized, Durkheim clung to the notion of duty on a number of counts. He saw it almost axiomatically as being the main characteristic of morality, but also as a major component of discipline which is necessary in human life as the antidote of egoism (see, for example, 1897a: Book II, ch.VI; 1898c; 1925a:ch.IX).

Durkheim, it might be said, was never able to solve the dichotomy between the individual and the social, despite the fact that so many of his endeavours were centred on this problem. By virtually equating the moral with the social, linked by the notion of duty, the personal or individual is either disregarded or underplayed. According to Durkheim man is only moral if he is at one with the social. The 'individual' component does not have a place of any significance. Indeed, individual *représentations* are seen as profane, over and against the social which is held to be sacred. It must not be forgotten that Durkheim's basic position was, on his own declaration, one of opposition to the moral individualism of Kant and the utilitarians (see 1893b; 1901a(i)). On the other hand, Durkheim admitted that the individual today is not dominated by an 'automatic' sociality. As man advances the personal element becomes more important and is allowed a greater place by public conscience. An unreflective morality is now seen as an imperfect morality (1907a(9)).

Relativism

Moral data, which constitute the subject matter of the positive science of morals, not only cover man's present behaviour, they are also concerned with such behaviour in the past, and not only in one society but in societies around the world (see 1905b and 1907a(10)). History and ethnography are therefore handmaids to the science of morals. Such disciplines demonstrate at least one thing: that empirical morality is subject to a great deal of variation. As Durkheim wrote:

> It can no longer be maintained nowadays that there is one, single
> morality which is valid for all men at all times and in all places.
> We know full well that morality has varied. It has varied not
> only because men have lost sight of their true destiny, but also

because it is in the nature of things that morality should vary.
The moral system of the Romans and Hebrews was not our own,
nor could it be. . . . There is not just one morality but several
and as many as there are social types [1909a(2), translated here
in Part II, Education; see also 1910b].

This contradicts and was intended to contradict any explanation of
moralities in terms of underlying universal principles, such as love
or hatred (as in Westermarck's book, see 1907a(10)). The reasons
or justification for a particular moral system lie in the nature of the
society in which it is found (1910b), that is, each society has its own
rationality. As Durkheim said in his 'Introduction to ethics' the
morality of a nation, which consists of ideas about actions associated with the concept of obligation, fully expresses the society's
'temperament, its mentality and the conditions in which it lives'
(1920a). Thus, morality expresses man – something Durkheim
frequently stated. It also means that the study of morality is a key
to the understanding of a society.

Durkheim, in opposition to much traditional philosophy, in
which it is assumed that human nature is universally the same,
argued for relativism in connection with human nature (1904a(5)).
The nature of man, he suggests, varies with regard to time and
the type of society in which particular men live. Because early and
primitive types of morality preceded those of modern western
societies, it was necessary to study them in order to understand
contemporary morality and its accompanying doctrine of man and
nature. Durkheim's 'anthropological' approach emerges in his
statement: 'since man is the product of history, it is only through
comparative history that he can be understood' (ibid.). And elsewhere he wrote: 'if disregarding his historical context, we attempt
to see him (man) as fixed, static, and outside time, we only
denature him' (1920a). And these variations in man's nature are
not external or minor issues – but 'deep-seated, essential qualities,
ways of acting and basic patterns of thought' (ibid.). But precisely
what these qualities, acts and thoughts were, Durkheim did not
enunciate.

Since moral systems show such wide variations, a historical and
ethnographical approach undermines the notion that one particular
system is superior to another, either on the grounds of internal
criteria or because of divine revelation. Durkheim realized that in

principle science clearly separates the 'is' from the 'ought' and therefore it cannot pass judgment either by way of praise or criticism on specific moral systems. Ethical relativism is the inevitable consequence.

But what are the wider issues resulting from such relativism? Can one break out of the relativist circle? If all is relative, then there is nothing which is true in a universal sense. Relativism itself is only relatively true. But apart from such epistemological problems, why should any man want to accept a moral code that has only merit for his own society? In short, why should one trouble to be moral? Durkheim attempted to defend this weakness of the relativist's armour in a debate on the effectiveness of moral doctrines, which is discussed here in the Introduction on Education and which has been translated in this volume (1909a(2)).

At least the relativism of the kind supported by Durkheim is an acknowledgement of the fact of change, and this should not be forgotten by those who would charge Durkheim with the sin of examining societies in a static mode. The moral idea is always in the process of being formed, it 'is not immutable: despite the respect with which it is invested, it is alive, constantly changing and evolving' (1920a). These transformations come about through the agency of the moralist who prepares the ground for changes and indeed proposes them. This attitude is similar to the one he adopted in his essay, 'The determination of moral facts' (1906b; see below). But Durkheim will not go further. No philosopher can produce a new system of morals and no new moral theory has given rise to a revolution (1904a(5)). One wonders if Durkheim would have been prepared to change his views if he had been alive to witness the present growth of Marxism in one form or another. For Durkheim changes occur when the legitimacy of reasons for moral actions and commands are challenged or are no longer thought to be adequate. As is commonly said, he failed to produce an adequate theory of social change; and, as is to be noted in these translations, he referred to history in a somewhat vague and mysterious way (see 1910b).

Rationality

It is often assumed that Durkheim made little use of the concept of rationality within sociology; and it is true that he did not give the term as prominent a place in his thought as did, not only Max Weber, but also Vilfredo Pareto. For Durkheim the rational was frequently associated with science and its method: indeed, the two were often equated (see, for example: 1925a: ch. 1; and Lukes 1972:72-6). In these essays, we present two items in which rationality is the key subject, 'A discussion on positive morality' (1908a(2)) and 'A discussion on the notion of social equality' (1910b). The topic is raised in other items as well.

Durkheim refused to call himself a positivist because of the associations of the term with Auguste Comte, but he was happy enough to accept the word rationalist and was ready to be identified with those who would call themselves rationalists. He was opposed to a facile or naive rationalism – a rationalism that implied quickly acquired knowledge, but he, and all Frenchmen recalling their Cartesian heritage, must, to use his own words, 'remain impenitent rationalists' (1925a:304/t.1961a:265). He used this highly ambivalent word, as many people did and still do, both to the application of reason and the acceptance of what is reasonable. He also based his thought on what he held were the realities of existence, but this did not mean that reality was that which was determined by the senses. He would not countenance the lowering of reason to sense experience. Reason itself must always be paramount. In the realm of morality, rationality for Durkheim and other rationalists meant a rejection of the claims and traditions of Catholicism and Protestantism to create a morality based on religious foundations. In the place of a religious morality the wish was to establish a secular or rational morality. Through this, man is encouraged to create a system that is designed to function according to the principles of reason. Amongst the many affected by the enthusiasm of the times for such a morality was Gustave Belot, in some ways sympathetic to Durkheim's general outlook, who expounded his own approach to rational morality (*Études de morale positive* (1907)). Durkheim in turn supported Belot but observed that rationality is not only what is imposed on ethical behaviour or on a newly created system of ideas, but is inherent in a system already established (1908a(2)). It is thus legitimate to refer to a particular moral system as being rational, in contrast to other systems which are less rational or which are not rational at all. Progressive rational morality is a more human notion of morality based on the need for

15

man to be at harmony with himself (1910b). Durkheim calls this ideal rationality. It is a system invented by man which is claimed to be based on reason. But there is another concept of rationality, which is more fundamental and of greater interest to science. This is what might be called rationality in things as they are.[4] It does not have to be 'created' in the mind of the scientist, for he discovers it in the data themselves (1908a(2)). Such a definition of rationality Durkheim had given at a previous meeting of the Société Française de Philosophie when he chose as his subject 'La Détermination du fait moral' (1906b). With this notion in mind, it can be said that each moral system is rational in so far as 'at each moment of time', as it is observed, it 'constitutes a system of *intelligible data*' (1908a(2)). The claim is that there is here a direct parallel with the presuppositions of the natural sciences and the way they view phenomena. Morality is rational to the degree it can be translated into an intelligible system of rules and relationships. In another debate (1909a(2), translated in Part II, Education), Parodi preferred the term intelligibility to rationality in dealing with this concept. For Durkheim, rationality according to his second definition meant fundamentally a relation between two entities. Thus, an institution cannot be rational (therefore presumably irrational) in itself, it can only be rational in relation to the social milieu, in the 'entire series of historical conditions on which it depends' (1910b). Useful connections with other institutions thus determine whether or not an institution is rational. Similarly, an institution can only be irrational if it loses relations with other social institutions.

This notion of an inbuilt or inherent rationality in ethical systems leads once again to relativism, since 'all moral systems have their own rationality' (1910b). All of them are 'natural' and therefore there is no objective criterion of judging one to be superior to the other on grounds of rationality. Thus, rationalism is relative to the society in question. In the second discussion previously mentioned, Durkheim adopted such a position in connection with egalitarianism. He held that it was impossible to justify the contention that inequalities of caste and class, as they existed in the past, 'were less rational' than inequalities in his day (1910b). To the scientist all social systems must be equally rational. Parodi, attempting to break such relativism, spoke not only about the rationality of the scientist, but of the individual within the moral system, who was fully aware of its inequalities and weaknesses. Then as today, Durkheim's focusing on objectivity in explanation and at the same time adopting a relativist position raised the criticism that such an approach inevitably produced a conservative outlook and the rejection of reform. Durkheim's reply was interesting. History proceeds along its way, and it would seem in an inexorable fashion. As it proceeds it settles problems which beset man. New moral systems emerge which are brought about by changes in social conditions which are themselves the product of history (ibid.). It is quite remarkable that once again when the problem of change is raised, Durkheim falls back on such an unsociological or non-scientific defence, hiding within the mysteriousness of history.

Durkheim's criticism of Belot was that, although he implied both meanings, he did not clearly differentiate them in a way that Durkheim thought necessary, and in speaking of rationality in connection with morals, slid all too easily from one meaning to the other, thus introducing confusion. But it is not a confusion of communication which is at stake. Far more important is the fact that it is logically inadmissible to move from one meaning to the other. They must be rigidly isolated – fact cannot establish value. Belot tried to transcend the dichotomy by pointing to the unity of reason and claiming that moral progress had taken place in such a way that each stage of history had built on and surpassed the previous one. For Durkheim such a use of rationality was no answer to the dichotomy, and in many respects we see here another reason for Durkheim wishing to dissociate himself from Comte and the idea of progress, although admittedly Comte defined progress in different terms to those of Belot. However, Durkheim never hesitated to affirm that the moral ideal of contemporary western Europe was more humane than once it was (e.g. 1910b), but whether this was right for all mankind was a different matter. What is general is not in itself rational. Therefore, the moral ideal of his day could not be considered to be more rational than the ideal of other systems of morality because it was tending to become universal or was thought to be desirable for the whole of mankind.

But there is yet another issue which arises from the use of rationality within ethical behaviour. It is the contention that moral behaviour is rational when it is reflective, and therefore irrational when it is non-reflective.[5] This view attracted liberal-minded people

17

of Durkheim's day, such as Belot. Durkheim held that this was an example of ideal rationality, and he demanded to know on what rational grounds reflective morality was more rational than non-reflective morality. An example of the second was in action carried out in the name of duty – a subject we have already briefly considered. The position adopted by such thinkers as Belot, Durkheim argued, meant that in the last analysis very few actions could be labelled moral. He also doubted whether rational ethical behaviour in this sense was universal either with regard to time or culture. Of course, such behaviour existed, but it was the province of only a minority.

Moral art

Apart from providing knowledge about the present and the past, can science – can the sociology of morals – offer help and guidance about the future? In other words can scientific information lead to amelioration – can what is known help to establish what ought to be? These sorts of questions occupied a great deal of the attention of French moralists at the time, who supported or were challenged by a positivist approach to morality. Even today within the realm of sociology the issues are no nearer a solution. There were and are two extreme positions to adopt. One is to maintain a rigid line of demarcation between the 'is' and the 'ought' and to state that at no point can there be a movement from one to the other. The two remain in watertight compartments. Science can never determine ends of individual or social behaviour and until these are declared by philosophers, religious leaders or the state, scientific knowledge about morality must remain unto itself. Over and against what might be called this thoroughgoing rationalism, stands a positivism which maintains that science has an immediate application to the future because such an approach to morality can reveal the ends to which social and individual conduct ought to be directed. Even in its early days therefore science is an immediate handmaid to society. Between these two extremes stand both Lévy-Bruhl and Émile Durkheim who, rejecting the validity or immediate usefulness of traditional ethics, wanted to see the findings of the sociology of morals applied to the moral problems of society (see Karady

1970:99ff.). In this sense they were utilitarian. Durkheim argued that true knowledge cannot close in on itself and must serve future human activity; therein lies its essential destination (see preface to 1893b).

Critics have pointed to Durkheim's earlier works, such as *The Division of Labour* (1893b) and *The Rules of Sociological Method* (1895a), as indicating his attachment to a form of positivism that has just been mentioned. In these works there is considerable attention to the concepts of normal and abnormal in social conduct which would seem to be derived from scientific analysis. Without pursuing the arguments of this longstanding controversy, suffice it to say that such concepts refer to the past and the present of a society and do not relate to the future or to the problem of how science can be applied practically to social issues. Although Durkheim wanted science to have a full part in the study of morality, he set his face against a complete dominance or takeover by science. Science has its limitations and nowhere more so than in the area of values. The sociology of morals may well be able to account for changes and perhaps even the origins of values but it can do no more. It cannot formulate moral beliefs and invent values. A science can determine the goal or end of a particular moral system of the past or present and it is concerned with ends in a way that engineering and medicine are not (1920a). But when it comes to demonstrating new ends a society should pursue, or the adoption of new moral rules, science is forced to remain silent.

Bayet, in *La Morale scientifique*, stated that if ethics were to become a science of moral facts, it could inform man about the technical means whereby he could obtain moral ends. Man is indeed a social creature: he receives pleasure in being involved in a common life. If morality leads to sociability, it has to be admitted that morality will be based on such pleasure. And if life as it occurs in society imposes constraints in the name of duty, it is because society is imperfect. Hence the task of the sociology of morals has as its practical outcome ways of eliminating what is imperfect, that is the abolition of duty (1906a(11); see also Richard 1925a). Not surprisingly, Durkheim strongly opposed such reasoning as being a false application of sociology. There was in what Bayet and others like him were saying a confusion between moral truth and technique: they had nothing in common. Technique is something only known to the natural scientist. The notion of duty, which is at the base of morality, is not in the province of the engineer or the scientist.

In order to escape possible attacks by those of a positivist outlook and of certain rationalists, Durkheim chose art, moral art, as the area in which the findings of the sociology of morals could be legitimately applied to problems of future human behaviour.

It seems certain that Durkheim was not original in his use of the concept of moral art. He may well have seen the value of the idea from reading Lévy-Bruhl's book, mentioned earlier, where the possibility of applying the results of *la science des moeurs* within the area of what he called *l'art moral rationnel* (rational moral art) was one of the main themes (see Durkheim's review, 1904a(5)). Lévy-Bruhl held that like all sciences, the sociological study of morals could have application in dealing with practical problems. It stood in relation to rational moral art as biology and physics stood in relation to medicine and engineering. Lévy-Bruhl's rejection of *la morale théorique* to be substituted by *la science des moeurs* coupled with *l'art moral rationnel* gave rise to various kinds of attack that might be anticipated about the eternal issue of ends and means (see Bayet 1905; Belot 1905–6, 1907; Cantecor 1904; Fauconnet 1904; Fouillée 1905; Landry 1906; etc.).

Durkheim was given to arguing the case for the legitimacy of moral art on grounds of expediency. Science moves slowly. It is hoped that one day it will provide answers to many problems, but in the meantime man cannot wait for the answers to be produced. He has to face practical issues and make decisions. Hence the time comes when he must leave the realm of science and enter that of faith or art and so anticipate the future as best he can. This kind of movement applies as much to morality as it does to medicine (cf. Lévy-Bruhl). The moralist is thus forced to make the best judgments he can using such scientific knowledge as is available but realizing its limitations (1906a(11)). (The same order of reasoning is behind Durkheim's concept of educational theory (*pédagogie*) which is a combination of science and art. See Introduction on Education.) Art has to abandon the real since it is concerned with the future it seeks to anticipate. As with so many terms Durkheim uses, the word art is employed in various senses, even in a derogatory way (see Introduction on Education). Durkheim visualizes art based on imagination and not bounded by the limits of reason, as in the visual arts. However, moral art – and it would seem he would accept the term rational moral art (1904a(5)) – is, as he says in his 'Introduction to ethics', never without bounds, for it always has to presuppose the science of morals and this it cannot contradict. Similarly, science must be true to itself and maintain self-imposed boundaries. In the case of morality the 'ought' of the future is excluded from its concern.

Durkheim did not speculate about the extent to which moral art could in fact modify conduct. It is probable that he was in sympathy with Lévy-Bruhl who claimed for rational moral art only very limited changes, largely because the science on which it depended was itself in its infancy (1903:205). This cannot be said of biology in the help that it gives to medicine.

A change in Durkheim's thought?

It has long been the contention of commentators on Durkheim that his thought underwent significant changes in the course of its development (see, for example, Davy 1920:102–6; Parsons 1937: 441–50). We confine our attention strictly to the realm of morals and ethics. The material that has been translated does not prompt comment on Wallwork's contention that a complicated change in Durkheim's approach to morals occurred around 1893, when there was a move from ethical naturalism to a position in which society was seen as the goal of moral behaviour (1972:ch.VI). Rather, the argument which will be considered briefly might be stated along the following lines. In the early years – years associated with the publication of *De la Division du travail social* (1893b) and *Les Règles* (1895a) and for a short time afterwards – Durkheim visualized morality very much in terms of obligation, of rules, of discipline, of ends centred on society. Here morality could be easily recognized and its reality instantly agreed on. Certainly by the time he died a change appears to have occurred and he saw the key to the understanding of morality to be located in ideals and beliefs, about society and man, which underlay the moral superstructure. The 'Introduction' stands as an important piece of evidence in supporting or challenging such a transformation. Mauss and Davy held that the intended book, *La Morale*, pointed to a radical recasting of Durkheim's approach to morality. And Lukes

21

has said that in the 'Introduction' Durkheim took a further step in connecting the sociology of morality with the sociology of knowledge (1972:420). 'The moral idea is always strictly dependent upon the conception that men have of themselves and their place in the universe' (1920a). On the other hand, Mark Traugott has taken a position which would deny any serious change. He has recently written: 'I find nothing new in the outline of the book's prospective contents which represents a significant departure from the arguments Durkheim had made many times before' (1978:257 n.36).

Since no one knows the contents of the chapters of the long book Durkheim planned, it seems pointless to base arguments on such tentative data as chapter headings alone. As Lukes suggests, attention must be focused on the evidence of the 'Introduction' not on notes Durkheim appended to its conclusion.

Part of Lukes's case rests on the distinction he held Durkheim made in the 'Introduction', which was something new – a distinction between *morale* and *moeurs* 'which amounted to that between ideals, values and norms, on the one hand, and practices, or rule-governed behaviour, on the other' (1972:420). It is undeniably true that Durkheim does make a contrast between these terms, emphasized in a footnote where he writes: 'Opposition between *moeurs* and *morale*' (see note 15, English translation of 1920a, on p. 96). The reason for this can be seen in the second half of the 'Introduction' where Durkheim argues that although man lives by what he believes are moral truths, he does not understand their real nature. In dealing with the world in any of its dimensions, or in trying to understand his experience, man has made full use of *représentations*, by which data are portrayed, understood and accepted. Durkheim used by way of illustration man's thinking about the sun. He observed that man all down the ages had *représentations* of the sun. But these *représentations* are different from those the scientist uses to portray it. He employs other concepts and reaches his conclusions about the sun by different methods from those used by the man in the street. The scientist knows what the sun is – its reality – in a way the layman does not. Scientific inquiry starts with ignorance, of not knowing precisely the nature of the phenomena being studied, and in the case of morals, not knowing how moral ideas or moral behaviour are to be recognized or distinguished. There is no self-evident truth about morality, as indeed there is no self-evident truth in science. External

22

signs are used in the beginning of a study which reveal or indicate the reality which the scientist attempts to explain. Later, the outward signs are replaced by others, and when these are mastered it is possible to know the innermost characteristics of the reality. Nevertheless, Durkheim holds that certain characteristics can be stated initially, and in the realm of moral behaviour and moral ideals such characteristics are: every morality has an ideal, embedded in its institutions and traditions; moral ideals change; acts are directed by moral rules; morality as part of behaviour is concerned with ends; morality is part of a natural order; and so on. In the world of morality such arguments lead to the conclusion that the *représentations* which the common man has of morality are not adequate to gain a comprehensive understanding of moral behaviour. Thus, the scientific approach uses *représentations* and concepts that the common practitioner will not himself employ or know about. The actual morality that men indulge in is a reflection – a manifestation – and a poor one at that, of moral ideals (*morale*). Durkheim writes: 'It seems clear that the morality (*morale*) obtaining in a particular epoch is embodied in social norms (*moeurs*) though in a degraded form and reduced to the level of human mediocrity' (1920a). Man's motives are always mixed, including what is noble and vulgar. *Moeurs* therefore can be seen as *la morale vulgaire* – a term not actually used by Durkheim, but not unknown amongst moralists, and it certainly seems to fit what he is saying at this point. *Moeurs* is thus the area of everyday ethics, of norms which are the average way of applying the rules of morality (see Mauss 1925:9). *Morale* covers moral precepts 'in all their purity and impersonality' (1920a). It is morality *per se*, ideal morality above human misuse. These two well-defined areas within moral life give rise to two sciences. They are called *la science ou physique des moeurs* (the science of natural philosophy of social norms) and *la science morale* (the science of morality) or *la science des faits moraux* (the science of moral facts). These two disciplines would roughly correspond to descriptive ethics and to theoretical ethics, metaethics, mentioned earlier.

The two sciences stand side by side, not in a mutual relation, but in a hierarchical one, the nature of which is not altogether clear. But there seems no doubt that Durkheim sees the science of morality as a theoretical science over and against the phenomenal science or descriptive science of *moeurs*. He argues that for each area of social life, family, law, religion, specific moral issues are raised which have to be dealt with on their own, that is within the area of *moeurs*. Thus there emerges as it were a number of sciences of the moral life. However, the overall science, the pure or theoretical science, is not determined by a synthesis of the moralities of these specific areas. They tell us nothing about the fundamental nature of what moral life is. Quite clearly the science of morality (*morale*) has to use and above all integrate 'the science of areas of moral life'.

How far are these ideas new in Durkheim's approach to the study of moral life? Before that question is answered it is worthwhile to rehearse what has not changed. First, the starting point is that moral reality exists both in terms of the area of *moeurs* and that of *morale* – norms as well as ideals exist outside the individual observer. Second, the necessity is reiterated that to begin a discipline one must point to a number of assumptions and in the realm of morals these relate to the notions of obligation and duty. Third, and very strongly sustained, is the contention that the scientific method, as Durkheim sees it, is the only valid method. There is not the slightest hint that any reliance should be made on intuition, on metaphysics, or religion. Whether it is in fact possible to have a science of morality as Durkheim defined it is a different matter. Durkheim thought that it was. A matter which is less clear is the role of *la science des moeurs*. Has its importance been played down? Durkheim lectured on the subject frequently throughout his academic life (cf. 1950a) and it is not likely that he would now write it off as being of little or no value. It still has a valid place in his scheme and in the 'Introduction' he admitted that only relatively few people are working in the subject. He declared that he was planning to write the book on the science of morality, not on the science of social norms, and it would appear that he evaluates the former discipline as being more abstract and general than the latter, and in this way perhaps more important.

What one sees in the 'Introduction' is certainly no denial of a past position or the casting off of a former method. What is evident is a shift of focus from one area of study to another that is closely associated with it. Such a shift is parallel, it might be argued, with a change in his thinking about the nature of science and scientific procedure. Surely what he wanted to do in the book he was planning was to pursue the science of the moral life at a deeper level –

at a more theoretical level. The search was for scientific statements which would be more abstract and general and which would contain more information than those derived from sciences whose subject area was narrower. It might also be argued that just before the First World War Durkheim saw that sociology had made sufficient progress to be in a position to tackle more abstract areas and perhaps to contribute to knowledge which might in some cases be thought to border on the ultimate.[6] One should also recall in this respect his classic work, *The Elementary Forms of the Religious Life*, published in 1912, in which he dealt with religion and philosophical issues which bordered on the metaphysical and for which he was subsequently criticized. The change from the early article on religion, 'De la Définition des phénomènes religieux' (1899a(ii)), to that of the *Elementary Forms* shows a similar movement from his earlier works on morals, such as the *Division of Labour*, to the final 'Introduction to ethics'; that is, from a study of phenomena to a study of the essence of the phenomena themselves.

Durkheim's aims contained in the 'Introduction' give rise to a multitude of problems. For example, can one have a *science* of idealized morality so that the nature of the moral can be fully understood? Many would deny this. Gurvitch might see in Durkheim's aim but another example of what he pointed to in the earlier works of Durkheim, namely, that Durkheim was in fact not dealing with the sociology of *moeurs* but entering the field of metaethics (*métamorale*) concerned with the ultimate goal of moral action and belief (1937a). Posed in a slightly different way, what kinds of scientific procedure can be used to develop a science of morality? It seems difficult to suggest them. Again, the relation between the two areas *moeurs* and *morale* is problematic. How did the two emerge? And can the relation be understood by the mediation of society, so that society stands between the ideal and what is practised? If this is so, then Durkheim's concept of the role of society in morality would have to be changed. More puzzling still is Durkheim's equation of *la science de la morale* with *la science des faits moraux*. Are *les faits moraux* the same as those which are referred to in *The Rules of Sociological Method* (1895a)? Might they be seen as the results of *la science des moeurs* which would make some contribution to *la science de la morale*?

Since we have, unfortunately, only the opening pages of the book Durkheim was so keen to write, it is idle to speculate how far he would have forestalled such questions and criticisms had the book been finished. That which he hoped would make a contribution to the solution of moral problems must for ever remain hidden. Thus, while there are signs of a change of subject matter to which Durkheim wished to turn, the full extent of those changes and their consequences can never be known because of a lack of evidence.

A move of a different kind, which has not often been noted in his last works, is also associated with what we have suggested is a changed attitude to science. The point at issue is an élitism which surrounds the scientist. In the 'Introduction to ethics' he is seen as someone who stands above the rest of society as a somewhat superior being. By being able to use *représentations* not known to people at large, he possesses knowledge by which he is able to grasp the nature of the reality of his subject matter in a way others cannot understand. He is thus an unassailable specialist. The scientist working in morality is no exception. He comprehends the nature of the moral actions of the layman in a way the layman is unable to understand himself. Also, the moralist within the realm of moral art is accorded a special place in society. He has assimilated the findings of the sociology of the moral life and is capable of applying it to the future. In this way he too stands above the layman by reason of his superior knowledge and perspicacity. He is like the educational theorist who has the potential for bringing about change. He is thus a reformer, an agent of amelioration, an 'engineer'. There are signs in what Durkheim says – no more than that – that the 'moralist' is a manipulator of men with the power to bring about changes on which the layman is ignorant and over which he has little control. These ideas are not to be found in the earlier writings of Durkheim, though it might be possible to argue that they are present but hidden.

The neglected subject

It is remarkable that there is a dearth of classics in the sociology of morals. This is not the case in, say, the sociology of religion or criminal sociology. Morality is a field that has not attracted a large number of scholars devoted to sociology. Although French philosophers and sociologists continued to debate the scientific approach to morality after Durkheim's death, the subject made little head-way. Nor did those disciples of Durkheim who lived after him take up his great interest and supply the masterpiece on morality which still has to be written. Commentators from the 1920s onwards were pleased to write about his approach to moral science, often in a critical vein, but very little of a creative kind emerged. The lack of interest in the discipline is particularly the case amongst socio-logists in the English-speaking world, especially since the Second World War (see Lukes 1972:432 n.19). The reason is something of an enigma. That modern western man has rejected much tradi-tional morality and from time to time swum in the rivers of per-missiveness is hardly an answer. Sociologists of religion in the face of the decline of institutional religion are numerous and active in research. Is it that the subject contains certain internal charac-teristics that make it difficult to study scientifically, as Durkheim himself suggested? One thing is certain: anyone who ventures into the sociology of morals will have to take the contributions of Durkheim very seriously, fragmentary though alas they are.

Notes

1 It can be well argued that Durkheim defined moral facts in different ways. See, for example, Henriot 1967:40ff.
2 For information about Richard, see Pickering 1975:343–59; and 1979.
3 Kant's influence on Durkheim is treated in detail in various parts of Wallwork 1972.
4 Parallels with Durkheim's two concepts of rationality can be seen in the thought of two English philosophers, Michael Oakeshott and Peter Winch. See Winch 1958:54ff.
5 See also Oakeshott and Winch on this problem in Winch 1958:62ff. Cf. in this Introduction the section 'Moral forces and moral facts'.
6 Cannot one detect this kind of change reflected in the launching by Durkheim in 1908 of Travaux de l'Année sociologique, when the time had come for his group to publish books rather than articles in the journal, *L'Année sociologue*? See Durkheim's editorial note in C. Bouglé, *Essais sur le régime des castes*, Alcan, Paris, 1908, which was the first book in the new series.

References

(Nearly all the references relate to items to be found in the Bibliography. Those not specifically concerned with Durkheim's sociology of morals are listed below.)

FAUCONNET, P. 1904 'La Morale et la science des moeurs', *RP*, 57, pp. 72–87.

GURVITCH, G. 1937b *Morale théorique et sciences des moeurs*, P.U.F., Paris.

LÉVY-BRUHL, L. 1906 'La Morale et la science des moeurs. Réponse à quelques critiques', *RP*, 62, pp. 1–31.

NIELSEN, K. 1967 'Problems of Ethics', in *The Encyclopedia of Philosophy*, Macmillan and Free Press, New York.

PICKERING, W. S. F. (ed.) 1975 *Durkheim on Religion*, Routledge & Kegan Paul, London and Boston.

PICKERING, W. S. F. 1979 'Gaston Richard: collaborateur et adversaire'. *RFS*, XX pp. 163–82.

WESTERMARCK, E. 1906 *The Origin and Development of the Moral Ideas*, vol. I, London.

WINCH, P. 1958 *The Idea of a Social Science*, Routledge & Kegan Paul, London and Boston.

1

1904a(5)

Review '**Lévy-Bruhl**, *La Morale et la science des moeurs*, Alcan, Paris, 1903'[1]

First published in French in *L'Année sociologique,* VII, pp. 380–4.

In this work Lévy-Bruhl offers the reader an uncommonly skilful dialectical analysis of the idea which underlies all my work in this sphere, namely, that a positive science of moral facts does exist, and that it is upon such a science that the practical speculations of moralists must be based.

In order to establish this, the author begins with a critical assessment of the traditional conception of morality, showing how it is confused and incoherent. One can usually distinguish two parts – almost two distinct disciplines – in morality. On the one hand, theoretical, and on the other, practical morality. It is the former which is regarded as the scientific part. Lévy-Bruhl has no difficulty in showing that it does not in any way constitute a science. Its object is not in fact to express a given reality, but to determine the general principles of what ought to be done. Morality seeks to discover what goals man *should* pursue, and what the hierarchical relation of these goals *should* be with one another. The only function of sciences, whatever they are, is to discover what is, not to prescribe or legislate. It has been supposed that one could get round this objection by calling theoretical morality a normative science; but the linking of these two logically incompatible words merely expresses the contradiction inherent in the conception. It does not lessen it. A science can indeed reach conclusions which permit the establishment of norms, but it is not normative in itself. The notion of a theoretical morality is therefore a bastardization which lumps together genuinely scientific, theoretical considerations and the practical ones. And lastly, it is the latter which are far and away preponderant.

This confusion between theory and practice − the former being subordinate to the latter − is furthermore not peculiar to morality. It is encountered in the initial stages of all the social sciences. As necessities for action stimulate thought, so thought has always centred on practical aims. Only very slowly did it liberate itself, learn to pursue purely speculative aims, and to study things solely in order to understand them, with no concern for the possible applications of the theoretical results it obtained. But it was especially in the study of moral facts that this progress was to prove slow and arduous. For morality is distinguished by a religious characteristic which places it outside the bounds of truly scientific thought or, in other words, free thought. In the course of time, the morality which men have actually practised has taken on a kind of veneer of beliefs and symbols which have turned it into something sacred (*une chose sainte*) which cannot legitimately be approached with the usual procedures of the positive sciences.

Yet if theoretical morality is not a science of moral facts, what is it? It is quite simply a way of co-ordinating as rationally as possible the ideas and sentiments which comprise the moral *conscience* of a particular period. In actual fact, the moralist lays down the law less than he thinks; he is merely the mirror of his time. He simply reproduces the moral practices of his contemporaries, organizing them in such a way as to make them easier to grasp (*représentables*). This is why the moral speculation of philosophers has upset public opinion (*conscience*) far less often than the discoveries of science. There is no 'moral theory' which has ever produced a revolution in thinking comparable with what resulted from the teaching of Galileo, for example. This is because theoretical morality, far from dictating laws for practice, merely mirrors practice and conveys it in a more abstract language. It is just another aspect of moral reality. It is partly therefore the thing to be explained, without itself actually providing explanations. It is an object of science and yet not a science.

Furthermore, this co-ordination is based on postulates which are presented as truths, whereas in reality they are untenable. To enable them to construct a morality by deduction, moralists start by admitting the abstract notion of human nature, which is always the same everywhere and is sufficiently well known to make it possible to prescribe to man the type of conduct most suitable for him to pursue in the principal circumstances of life. What is more, since they take it upon themselves to create a system, they suppose that moral *conscience* normally possesses an inner unity and that the precepts it decrees are bound together in a relationship of un-challengeable logic. But both these hypotheses are contradicted by the facts. Human nature has varied in time. What it was yesterday is not the same as it is today. And it varies geographically. Human nature is not the same for the aboriginal Australian as it is for us. Such a notion cannot therefore be constructed from it just like that. The different types which have appeared in the past and which co-exist in the present would have had to be constituted first. And this diversity has sprung out of the diversity in human societies, of which the human type is a function. Consequently, since man is the product of history, it is only through comparative history that he can be understood. To achieve this, all kinds of research which have hardly yet been carried out are required. It is therefore not enough to borrow the notion of man in general from current psychology. Moreover moral *conscience* is made up of frequently quite heterogeneous elements precisely because it is a product of history, and because all the social forms of the past find their echo in the present.

The contradictory conception of a normative science must there-fore be abandoned and science must resolutely and definitively be dissociated from practice. Rather than using morality merely in order to dictate what man's duties should be, morality should first be studied. Or better, the various types of morality that have in fact been in use in the different societies should be studied for the sole purpose of understanding them, of learning how they are made up and what factors condition them. Each social type has its own parti-cular moral discipline. It is made up of maxims, customs and beliefs which are just as real as the other phenomena of nature and are therefore facts that are a subject for scientific study. They can be described and one can endeavour to explain them. The morality of a people at a given moment in its history does not have to be created. It exists: it is a reality. The old conception, according to which there is one natural morality and only one, to wit, the morality that is based on the human constitution in general is now no longer tenable. All the moral institutions one encounters in his-tory are equally natural, in so far as they are founded in the nature

31

of the societies which uphold them. There is only one particular morality that a society can have, given the way it is constituted. Its morality does not therefore come from the hands of some intellectual genius; it receives it with its very organization, which is to say, when it receives life. Viewed in this light, the science of moral reality is *the science of morals*, which the author contrasts sharply with the theoretical morality he began by criticizing. Since the causes and conditions on which every morality is dependent at all times are manifestly social, the science of morals is a branch of sociology.

Only such a science can provide a rational basis for practical applications. As the laws of moral reality become known, we will be gradually more in a position to undertake a rational modification of it, to say what it should be. Yet there will be little room for such systematic modifications, for morality does not have to be constructed from fundamentals. We do not have to create it completely. It exists and functions, and we have only to supervise its workings. There will of course always be numerous cases where science will not be able to provide us with the information we require to guide our action to useful effect. For it is only very slowly that science obtains results, and these are always only partial. But there is nothing in this which is peculiar to morality. Does it not happen constantly that the doctor becomes involved in problems for which physiology provides no solution? And what does he do then? He opts for the course of action which seems the most reasonable according to the present state of knowledge. Rational moral art will proceed likewise.

This circumspect reply will probably not satisfy those who clamour for absolutes, for whom the provisional and relative certainties of science cannot suffice. For them, the art of morality only appears true to itself if it decrees precepts as though they were infallible. Alas, every time one passes from general, theoretical propositions, however they may have been arrived at, to specific practical advice, one runs risks, try as one might, which no method can automatically eliminate. Only very vague approximations can be obtained and is it not best to become resolutely aware of this fact? In this respect, the abstract theories of the Kantian school or the Utilitarians have no advantage over the method advocated by Lévy-Bruhl. They do not give us any clearer picture of the end to strive for and the path to follow in the concrete circumstances of life. There is an enormous logical gap between the categorical imperative, once it has been admitted, and the question whether today we should or should not desire socialism, divorce, etc. The mind can only feel its way across this gap by resorting to procedures and methods which are far from being indisputable. Seen in this light, all possible methods are equally imperfect. This general and necessary imperfection makes it therefore impossible to object to any of them.

Note

1 [Lucien Lévy-Bruhl (1857–1939) was lecturer in the history of philosophy at the Sorbonne and, from 1908, professor. The book reviewed here by Durkheim caused a great deal of controversy. Lévy-Bruhl first became known to the English-speaking world through its translation, which was entitled *Ethics and Moral Science* (1905). Both Comte and Durkheim influenced his thought, not least in his call for the development of a *science des moeurs* or a science of moral facts. He hoped this would then help build up a rational moral art in the same way as science is used by medicine (for further details, see the Introduction to Part I). Lévy-Bruhl later turned to ethnology and his influence spread, especially amongst anthropologists and philosophers outside France, with the publication of *Les Fonctions mentales dans les sociétés inférieures* (1910), translated as *How Natives Think* (1926), and *La Mentalité primitive* (1922), translated as *Primitive Mentality* (1923). – W.S.F.P.]

2

1905b

Contribution to 'Morality without God: an attempt to find a collectivist solution'

First published in French in *La Revue*,
LIX, pp. 306–8.

Those who like myself regard morality as quite simply the vital element in collective discipline, naturally refuse to admit that it can only be taught by resorting to some sort of mystical method. As it is a human creation, fashioned by men and for men, one cannot see in what way or in what respect it could be shielded from the judgment of reason.

But it is important to pin down the exact meaning of words. When I say that it is a human creation, and that it is entirely the product of reason, I do not mean that we can construct it from nothing, in the silence of the study and by dint of pure understanding alone. All the dialectic constructs in which moralists usually delight are to my mind no more than the games of logicians, whose futility I have demonstrated elsewhere.[1] Morality is not geometry; it is not a system of abstract truths which can be derived from some fundamental notion, posited as self-evident. It is a complexity of quite a different order. It belongs to the realm of life, not to speculation. It is a set of rules of conduct, of practical imperatives which have grown up historically under the influence of specific social necessities. All peoples of the same type have at all stages of their development a morality which results from the way they are organized and which expresses their mentality, just as the nervous system results from and conveys the nature of the living being. The role of the moralist is thus not to create or invent morality as though it did not already exist: *it does exist* and must be recognized by him, just as it must be recognized by his contemporaries. But what he can, indeed what he must do, is to apply his reason to it with a view to reaching an understanding of it, and by procedures analogous to those employed by the physicist for learning and understanding the phenomena of the physical world. Through historical analysis and by utilizing the data provided by moral statistics, what one can legitimately do is to endeavour to discover which causes have given rise to the moral precepts which we practise and which sustain them. To discover, in other words, what the social needs, the ideas and the collective sentiments are from which these precepts result, and how these sentiments, ideas and needs are connected with and derive from the nature of society. This is the only method which will enable morality to be explained and rendered intelligible to the minds of men, and, consequently, which will enable it *to be taught in a rational way*.

For this to be achieved, a complete science is required which, rather than proceeding by vague syntheses, will weigh up one by one the principal maxims of morality in order to determine their conditions, to see what social states they result from, and what social ends they serve. It is to the development of such a science that I have devoted myself for twenty years or so.

The objection has been raised that morality as it has existed, or as it now exists, can indeed be explained but not judged; nor can one say what it must become. In fact, morality is not always all it ought to be; it must change so as to fit in with the new conditions of social life, which are constantly changing. Yet when the forms it currently displays have been explained, one has still not said what forms it should assume in the future. My reply to this is: (1) that a knowledge of the present and the past, in this as in all cases, is the only means available for predicting the future with the least margin of error. When one knows that a moral conception is dependent upon a particular condition of existence which has now disappeared, it can be declared with certainty that this conception must change, and furthermore it is by analogy with the past that it is possible to conjecture – one can do no more than that – what the change shall be. (2) I would add that in all events any method allowing one to make the principal precepts of the present morality understood, would very adequately meet the requirements of *popular teaching*.

A more serious objection, though of a provisional kind, might be raised with regard to the present state of the science I have just mentioned. So novel is it, that it has not yet emerged from infancy: this is quite certain. But if it is not yet able to provide a detailed explanation of the moral and legal institutions, it is none the less able even now to provide all the pointers required for elementary teaching of the kind which must be given at school, where the sole task is to make the children generally understand why they must be attached to their family, their country and to mankind. Moreover, what inspires me with a certain amount of confidence is that in fact this method is being applied today in the primary school and lycée by a number of my former pupils and it would not seem that this has produced any bad results.

Note

1 [The reference is to *The Division of Labour in Society* (1893b/t.1933b). See part of the introduction to the first edition, which was omitted in the second edition of 1902. It is reproduced in t.1933b:411ff. – W.S.F.P.]

3

1906a(11)

Review 'Albert Bayet, *La Morale scientifique: essai sur les applications morales des sciences sociologiques*, Alcan, Paris, 1905'[1]

First published in French in *L'Année sociologique*, IX, pp. 324–6.

Albert Bayet would like his book to be seen as an implementation of the principles which underlie my treatment of the science of morality. I can but express my gratitude for his careful and extremely sympathetic reading of my work. Yet honesty compels me to state that on several essential points I cannot accept the interpretation that he appears to give to my ideas, and the conclusions which he believes can be deduced from such an interpretation.

In common with Lévy-Bruhl[2] and myself, Bayet admits that in any speculation on moral matters it is necessary to make a distinction between science and the practical applications that can be drawn from it. He, too, considers that 'the role of science in the moral sphere . . . is the study of moral reality, which is to say, the study of moral facts and the laws pertaining to them. Sentiments, ideas, customs and morals must be considered as things and studied accordingly' (pp. 4–5). It would seem that once both this principle and the demand to remain consistent have been accepted, one would necessarily have to regard those beliefs or moral practices, which are observed at all times and in all kinds of society, as things and as normal, deep-seated realities. For if universality is not the mark of normality, then what is? If a fact, which is ubiquitous, is not an objective fact, then what does merit this term? Yet the author does not appear to have seen that this is the direct corollary of his basic postulate.

Morality appears everywhere to the observer as a code of duties. What is one to conclude from this, other than that morality is essentially just such a code, and that the idea of duty expresses its essential characteristic? And it must be the overall purpose of the science of morals to explain this notion, indicating how it is founded in reality. But the author, instead of proceeding along these lines, on the contrary admits that this idea of duty is a sort of illusion which has no objective basis. He does not consider it a subject for scientific research. It has been the exclusive preserve of art, not in order to develop it, nor to determine its precise nature, nor to correct it, but to dispel it, like a sort of nightmare which has been an obsession and a source of anguish to humanity for centuries. All ideas of this kind must be dispelled, as must the idea of responsibility and the principle which holds that intention alone has true moral value. The only reason put forward in justification of this attitude is that the arts corresponding to the physical sciences – the art of the engineer, of the doctor, etc. – produce 'machines and an abundance of appliances and products, but they do not generate the idea that it is a duty to employ these machines or products, nor the idea that there is anything to be gained by utilizing them or lost by disdaining them' (pp. 35–6).

It is, of course, indisputable that the art of the engineer or the agriculturalist does not involve anything akin to duties; but nor do the phenomena of mechanics and organic chemistry which the corresponding sciences cover contain anything resembling moral obligation. But because physical facts exclude all idea of duty, why should this also apply to moral facts? What entitles one to construct one portion of reality on the exact model of the other portion, without bothering about the differences which possibly always exist and even *a priori* probably do exist between the different domains? If we suppose that the phenomena of moral life are essentially duties, then it is with duties that moral art will have to be concerned, just as the science of morals: the one for the purpose of explaining them, the other to weigh up what form they should take. As I see it, the author has therefore no justification at all for proclaiming that an idea of such universality is invalid. And what actually prevents him from considering the obligations which are forced upon us as facts, which are as definite and real as the facts of material nature? It is a fact that we feel ourselves to be under an obligation – that we are obliged in this way or that. There is nothing that runs more contrary to the scientific attitude than the denial of a fact.

I have felt it necessary to explain exactly where I stand on this point in order to dispel certain misunderstandings which have arisen, and which I find very surprising. Let me add that in the rest of the work the author displays an exact feeling for the concrete and complex aspects of moral reality. He clearly demonstrates the inadequacy of the generalities moralists delight in using.

Notes

1 [Albert Bayet, born in 1880, was a prolific writer in philosophy, ethics and sociology. As well as the book critically reviewed here by Durkheim, he wrote *L'Idée du bien. Essais sur le principe de l'art moral rationnel* in 1908. He was a student of Lévy-Bruhl and, following in his steps, he attempted to apply sociology to morality. He stood opposed to what he saw as the conservative approach of Durkheim to morals. His later writings include *La Suicide et la morale* (1922), *La Science des faits moraux* (1925), and *La Morale des Gaulois* (1927–31). He became a member of the Année Sociologique group after the death of Durkheim – a group which tried to revive the journal of that name. – W.S.F.P.]
2 [See 1904a(5), n.1, on p. 33 – W.S.F.P.]

4

1907a(10)

Review 'Westermarck, *The Origin and Development of the Moral Ideas*, vol. I, London, 1906'

First published in French in *L'Année sociologique*, X, pp. 383–95.

This voluminous work, which is the product of extensive reading, is presented as an attempt to study moral facts scientifically. It is the author's aim, as it is my own, to trace the origins of moral facts from the perspective of history and comparative ethnography. And this affinity between the attitude of the author and mine is not the only example it has been my pleasure to note. The following analysis will show that, on particular issues, Westermarck's ideas are not dissimilar to those I have had occasion to express in this journal and in other works. He himself indicates some of these instances of agreement that I note, certainly not with the intention of claiming a vain right of priority which may very well be unfounded, but because such meetings of minds are still only too rare in this science of ours for them not to be pointed out when they do occur. Anything which enables one to hope that sociology will finally emerge from the philosophical subjectivism in which it has marked time for too long, cannot be overstressed. But at the same time, Westermarck's method and my own diverge in certain essential ways which naturally have a bearing on the detail of theories and whose examination will enable us to discuss important questions of method in a concrete way.

Westermarck is quite correct in stating at the very beginning of the work (p. 2) that the moral evolution of the human species will have to be taken in its totality if the way our moral ideas have formed and developed is to be reconstructed. He therefore draws on history and ethnography as a whole; and consequently there is an enormous array of facts in this work which cannot fail to be of use. But how is this material handled?

To trace the origin of our moral ideas is to seek to discover what causes have given rise to them. I shall not pause here to set out yet again the reasons which lead one to believe that the causes are essentially social; and this is, furthermore, an assumption that Westermarck will surely allow me to make. But to discover the causes and explain the variations which a moral rule has undergone, the varations will necessarily have to be considered in the context of the social milieux wherein the rule was elaborated and trans-formed. To separate the rule from the milieux is to separate it from the living springs from whence it flows: it is to render it impossible to understand. A study such as the one in question is thus based upon the assumption that one already possesses at least a pro-visional classification of the principal types of society and their individual characteristics. Given the present state of this science, there can, of course, be no question of establishing a completely methodical and systematic classification. But at the very least it ought to be possible from the confused mass of societies of all kinds, which have followed one another in succession through history, to extract some forms of organization which are suf-ficiently characteristic to serve as a point of reference against which some of the transformations can be measured, which the moral rules under consideration have undergone.

Unfortunately, Westermarck has remained quite oblivious to this necessity. He continues to be a loyal disciple of the method which both the German school of juridical anthropology and the English school of religious anthropology have used for so long. While he recognizes in principle that morality is essentially social (p. 122 *et seq.*), he believes that one should look to the most general and permanent dispositions of human nature for the mainsprings of this evolution. The account which follows will make this abundantly clear. To perceive the fundamental, universal tendencies, there is no need whatever to differentiate between the various forms each moral rule assumes according to the societies concerned, nor is there any need to relate each of these forms to the social milieu from which it issues. The differences that such a procedure may bring to light are of no more than minor interest. Rather than limiting and circumscribing the field of observations in such a way as to perceive what is specific to the facts, it should on the contrary be enlarged as much as possible and be made to include in vast syntheses all the information we possess on the moral life of mankind. The greatest possible number of peoples, however heterogeneous they may be, must be examined. One might even say that the more heterogeneous they are, the greater the chances will be of revealing the very general processes one is aiming to discover. And such is indeed the procedure adopted by Westermarck, following in the footsteps of Post and all the anthropological school. To substantiate every proposition he makes, he draws examples from the most disparate societies. He is chiefly concerned with the accumulation of facts, not with selecting those which are conclusive and cannot be contested. To establish, for instance, how domestic solidarity results in collective responsibility, he cites with tumultuous rapidity, the Aleuts, the peoples of the Gold Coast, Madagascar, China, Greece, etc. (pp. 45–6). One would think it was his aim to create an impression of quantity rather than leave the reader with distinct, definite ideas.

This shows all the shortcomings of the method, which produces only over-simplified results. What science needs above all else is relevant, perceptive analyses, and these are only possible if they are attached to more limited subjects. Anyone who deals with so many facts can only give a more or less vague impression of each of them. It is even impossible to carry out a critical examination of documents which are used in such a way. When one takes them from so many different sources, one is obliged to accept them as they are. It cannot be denied that this confused heaping together of imprecise facts did originally serve a purpose; this is where Post's work, for example, was useful. It was a way of exploring, of making a rough reconnaissance of the new territory which had opened up to science, of conveying a vague idea of its extent and of awakening the taste for new and more methodical explorations. But this work has now been accomplished and it would seem pointless to embark upon it again.

Yet it is best to see how the auther applies the method if one is to make a fair evaluation of it.

It is a general rule of method that the subject matter of a positive science must consist of facts which are immediately within its reach. Beginning with the given effects, science works back to the causes which are to be discovered. In morality, the directly observable facts are the rules of conduct and the judgments which represent an imperative expression of the way the members of a specific social group must behave in the different circumstances of life. If, therefore, morality is indeed a science of facts, it would seem that it has no alternative but to take such rules as the immediate object of its research, and then find out what causes they are dependent upon. And one might have expected Westermarck to follow this method, given the fact that he does indeed see an expression of moral ideas in the systems of rules which customs and laws constitute. Chapter VII is entitled 'Customs and Laws as Expressions of Moral Ideas'.

Yet his approach is very different. Feeling quite rightly that morality is not a logical construct, he refuses to regard the abstract concepts upon which the discussions of moralists usually centre – the concepts of good, duty, law, etc. – as truly primitive facts. For him, and we shall not take issue with him on this point, they are generalizations of simpler states of quite a different order. The immediate task he sets himself is to discover these original states. The aim of his first chapter, 'The Emotional Origin of Moral Judgments', is to demonstrate that they are emotional in nature; and the object of the following chapters is to indicate what particular kinds of emotions are involved. What is unusual about such an approach is clear. It is precisely because these emotional states lie at the root of moral facts that they will not immediately be revealed by observation. To discover them, one must begin with complex yet apparent and visible facts which are the product and expression of the former, thereafter working back from one cause and one condition to the next, until one reaches the deep-seated sources of moral life. It is not possible in the preliminary stages of the investigation, namely in the early chapters of the work, to determine the origins of our moral judgments. This is an ultimate question and it serves no useful purpose to tackle it until the end of the study. In no circumstances is it part of the introduction. If Westermarck has not scrupled to reverse the natural and logical order of the problems in this way, it is certainly under the influence of the principle I mentioned above. This is because, for him, the emotional process is essentially a very simple matter, consisting merely of very general sentiments that anyone can discover in himself through introspection.

And for Westermarck this mechanism does in fact consist essentially of two quite elementary emotions: in the first place anger, or the indignation we experience when confronted by an act of aggression of which we are the victims, and the resulting need to retaliate; in the second place, goodwill, or the liking we feel for anyone who has acted benevolently towards us, and the need to respond to such demonstrations of friendship by demonstrations of a similar nature. These two sorts of emotion are thus two varieties of one single kind; they are both *retributive*, but in opposite ways. The former is expressed in censure, stigma or even the material pain which is consequent upon an immoral act. The result of the latter is esteem, or the positive rewards attendant upon virtuous acts. The author, like myself, thus considers pain to be a 'reaction of a passionate nature', which conveys and relieves public indignation. And precisely because it is passionate, this personal reaction is not determined by utilitarian considerations. Its essential object is not to intimidate those who are ill-willed or to correct them. Its true purpose is to remind men 'what, in the opinion of society, they ought not to do' (p. 90). Admittedly, when it is considered from the historical perspective, repression is observed to take on a more introspective and less violently aggressive character; yet whatever one does, its nature cannot change.

These ideas are greatly akin to those I have set forth in my *Division du travail social* and elsewhere on the same subject. But, in Westermarck, the theory of pain is juxtaposed with another theory which diverges from the first in one essential point.

According to the author, the indignation provoked by the criminal act is principally aimed at the perpetrator, its chief purpose being to make him suffer within himself. And pain is essentially suffering inflicted upon a sensitive being in retaliation for the suffering he has himself caused. If moral anger is basically determined by the immoral act, if it serves no utilitarian purpose, it seems difficult to see how the agent could to such an extent be the object of it. These two conceptions do not fit well together. But above all, any number of facts make it clear that in a vast number of cases the object of public indignation is not the agent, but something quite different. Repression does of course always imply a violently destructive act of some kind; but it is often considered quite immaterial that the victim of such destruction is guilty, or, in the sense currently attributed to the word, innocent. Westermarck is as well aware of these facts as I am: he attempts to reconcile them to his thesis. But I cannot see how he succeeds. To explain the numerous cases of collective responsibility in which the victim of the pain is innocent and is recognized as such, he invokes domestic solidarity; but it is the very fact that the members of one group can be considered jointly responsible where errors or crimes are concerned, which implies that the social indictment does not necessarily fall upon the head of the perpetrator. Religious criminality provides yet more examples of the same fact. Westermarck's answer is that religious impurity is essentially contagious by nature. But this is still answering one question with another. The real question in fact is to find out exactly how it is that reprobation can be transmitted in this way as though it were contagious. It is because it is not attached so exclusively as is maintained to the person of the agent.

Whatever the case, it shows the extreme generality of the sentiments from which moral life supposedly stems; they are not even peculiar to mankind, but are found also in animals, for animals too know vengeance and gratitude. Such sentiments are quite amoral in themselves; there is nothing morally worthy in retaliation to satisfy purely selfish ends. If these sentiments are to play a moral role, they must therefore take on individual characteristics. Retributive emotions, to use the author's term, are not specifically moral; to merit this term they must, in addition, be disinterested and must possess at least 'apparent impartiality'. The author understands by this that, if in fact they are partial, then the partiality should not be conscious or felt to be so. And as a disinterested emotion can be felt by everyone, the criterion of moral emotion is, in short, 'a certain flavour of generality'. This is the Kantian criterion extended to include the affective forms of moral life.

Once the emotions from which moral life springs have been thus characterized, an explanation is required of how they come to present such distinctive characteristics, in other words, how it arises that the moral emotions properly speaking can be disinterested and impartial, etc. The author's reply is that this is because 'society is the birthplace of the moral consciousness; that the first moral judgments expressed, not the private emotions of isolated individuals, but emotions which were felt by the society at large; that tribal custom was the earlier rule of duty' (p. 117). Two or three pages are employed to illustrate the proposition with a number of facts. The reader will find the proof a little brief. I have certainly no reason to contest a principle which I hold myself, yet, as it is so important, I should like to see it more thoroughly proved. This is the very heart of the question, or rather questions raised by the scientific study of moral facts. Here and only here (on Westermarck's own admission) can an explanation of the distinctive properties of moral rules be found. It is therefore most surprising to see that the author solves a problem of such importance in a few words, as though the solution were simply a matter of course and of only secondary interest.

However this may be, once the author has determined what these emotions are, he believes that he has uncovered the inner source from which all essential moral ideas derive. This assertion is not a little surprising, for it is difficult to see how the origin of moral precepts can be discovered while nothing is known of their content, and so far there has been no question of this. The analysis I have just summarized in its general conclusions has shown that there are indeed some acts which moral *conscience* disapproves of and others which it praises in a positive way. However, we do not know what these acts are, or the ideas which they express and consequently it seems hard to understand how, at this point, one could say where these ideas originate. In point of fact, the entire first part of Westermarck's work consists simply of a theory of moral sanctions. There are some sanctions which are repressive and reprobative; there are others which are laudatory: that is an established fact. The author links them with certain emotional states. But a theory of sanctions is not a theory of moral ideas. The sanction merely expresses the way *consciences* react in the presence of the moral or immoral act but *consciences* do not directly convey the nature of the act itself and the *représentations* from which it derives. Furthermore, this theory of sanctions is put together in a somewhat sketchy manner, for the author did not begin by observing, describing and classifying the different kinds of sanction attached to moral rules, thereafter working back methodically to the emotional states of which they are the consequence. Yet it is these states that he claimed to have discovered right at the beginning. He considered that it was possible to find the causes without first undertaking a descriptive study of the effects.

So the method he employs to proceed from these basic emotions to the essential moral concepts is purely ideological. The chapter in which this question is discussed (pp. 131–57) is merely a series of introspective analyses and abstract deductions, practically devoid of any objective facts. It is those cardinal ideas which supposedly

govern all moral life and contain its whole essence that Westermarck terms 'the principal moral concepts', namely, the ideas of
duty, of law, of what is just and unjust, of good, or merit and
virtue. And certainly, these ideas are a long way from being so
completely lacking in reality that they should be swept disdainfully
aside. They express, or it is their aim to express, the most general
aspects of moral reality. But if they are to be a part of the science,
they must be scientifically constituted. And as they merely convey
the most general characteristics of moral life, it is from the analysis
of moral facts that they must progressively be derived. The method
adopted by Westermarck did not allow him to proceed along these
lines and he states the problem in the same terms as the ordinary
moralists. He does not elaborate these notions for himself through
a methodical and objective comparison of the numerous moral
rules of which these notions express only certain properties. He
accepts them ready-made, as they are given to the common *conscience* with all the vagueness and lack of precision which necessarily
accompany ideas which have developed in this way on a day-to-day
basis, according to the requirements of practice, with neither order
nor method. And he sets about linking them up with the two large
categories of retributive emotions which he has distinguished,
resorting to a wholly dialectic analysis to achieve it. Duty, law,
the idea of justice and injustice are considered as modalities of the
varied specifications of the emotion of disapproval, whereas the
ideas of good and of virtue are derived from the emotion of
approval.

The author proceeds to make these links as follows. The idea
of duty is the idea of a certain way of acting which, when not carried
out in the prescribed way, incurs censure (p. 135). Law is merely
the subjective aspect of the duties that other people have towards
ourselves and justice consists in respecting the law. Good is the
name given to any act which is praised in a positive manner. Lastly,
virtue is a constant disposition to act in a good way. It is plain to
see that we are completely in the realm of abstractions, and of
abstractions which are constructed without any great attention to
method. What could be more artificial than seeing duty as merely
the censure which ensues from a violation of duty? It is doubtless
legitimate to make use of the sanction which attaches to duty as a
convenient sign by which it can be recognized and distinguished
from the other precepts for action with which it might be confused.

But it is no more than a sign; it is not the essence. On the contrary, what constitutes the idea of duty is fundamentally something quite positive: it is the idea of command – of the imperative – and it is the notion of the imperative which must be analysed if the origins of the concept of duty are to be discovered. Then again, it is quite arbitrary not to admit that there is any link between duty and the emotion of approval. And what if it is said that as far as public opinion is concerned, the man who merely does his duty has no right to any retribution? This is one of those popular sayings whose meaning is easy to twist since they do not have a very clear one. Is it therefore without reason that Kant, interpreter of the public *conscience* on this as on so many other issues, declared that the only true moral good consists in doing one's duty? The second of these aphorisms is probably no less well founded than the first, and testifies to the fact that the question is not a simple one and that duty is not foreign to all ideas of approbation – far from it. The same applies to the notion of law. There are at the very least strong reasons for believing that law is a positive attribute of the moral personality and consequently that the bond by which it is linked to the duty of others is singularly artificial. At all events this is a very complex problem which cannot be solved in a few words by pure, ideological analysis.

Yet these very general notions are still completely formal. To create the science of moral phenomena, a study of the content of morality will eventually have to be undertaken, which is to say of the particular precepts which govern relations between men. The author embarks upon this study in the second part of the work[1] and intends to continue it in the following volume, where the shortcomings of his method will be perhaps still more evident.

As the author is unable to study all the ways of acting to which the rules of human morality apply or have applied in the past, he retains only the following modes of conduct for inclusion in his study:

1 Those which concern the interests of our fellow men (their lives, their health, freedom, property, their honour).
2 Those which concern the interests of the agent himself (the moral rules relating to suicide, temperance, asceticism etc.).
3 Those which concern sexual relations (this third group, on the author's own admission, partly overlaps with the two preceding groups).

4 Those relating to the lower animals.

5 Those relating to the dead.

6 Those relating to real or ideal beings which are conceived to be supernatural.

In the first volume, Westermarck studies only the first of these six groups of facts, and then only in part. He discusses the rules which protect human life (prohibition of homicide, of assault and battery), those which recommend that we should work to promote the material and moral welfare of others (charity, generosity, hospitality), rules which concern the freedom of individuals (on this point, it is the submissiveness of women to their husbands, of children to their fathers and slaves to their master, that is discussed).

I shall not dwell on the fact that this classification is not very rational. It is surprising that domestic, civic and contractual relations are not allotted a place apart in this list of moral relations. Each of these groups of facts constitutes a natural whole and needs to be studied in and for itself. As this is not the case, one is obliged to separate questions which are related and to consider together others which have no connexion at all. The question of the relations between husband and wife has nothing in common with the question of slavery but is, on the contrary, only an isolated case of conjugal morality, which is itself closely bound up with domestic morality.

Yet what is more remarkable still is the spirit in which these problems are discussed: it is here that the tendencies of this school are most clearly apparent. The author is constantly preoccupied with linking the different maxims of morality with some constitutional disposition of human nature in general. And only when he has shown that they are the result of certain ideas and sentiments which, save several differences of degree, are to be found everywhere where men are present, does he believe that he has accounted for this. For example, the prohibition pertaining to homicide is explained by a natural sentiment which inclines man to respect the lives of his companions, of those individuals among his fellow men who belong to the same social group as he does (pp. 328 *et seq.*). In the course of time this sentiment has become more refined; it has grown stronger, more widespread and generalized, but it was already present in the most primitive societies known to us. The same can be said of the sentiments of charity and generosity which are contemporaneous with mankind. The narrow circle within which they were circumscribed and which did not extend beyond the limits of the family, has just become progressively wider (pp. 527 *et seq.*). Similarly the authority of parents is founded 'in the first place' upon their natural superiority over their children, upon the feelings of affection and respect that the young have for their elders (pp. 618 *et seq.*). It is not that on occasion Westermarck does not introduce causes which are less universal and less permanent. There exist certain more temporary ideas and sentiments which have indisputably played a role in the genesis of moral ideas, either by preventing the fundamental causes from producing their full effect for a time or, on the contrary, by helping them do so by a sort of chance event. For example, the author shows us how certain superstitions (stemming from the practice of the vendetta or human sacrifices) or the bare necessities of primitive life, have long increased the number of homicides reputed to be legitimate. And on the other hand, how certain religious beliefs have stimulated the rapid development of charity and reinforced paternal authority. But in whatever way these influences have made themselves felt, they have never been other than secondary. They have merely slowed down or else speeded up the evolution of moral ideas, whose general progress depends upon more general and constant factors.

Hence it is easier to see now why Westermarck does not feel the need to link up the various systems of morality with the social systems of which they were, or still are, a part. This is because, for him, there is no such thing as qualitatively different types of morality, in harmony with equally different social milieux. But basically it is clearly his belief that there is one single morality, engraved upon the congenital nature of man and of which the types of morality that history and ethnography teach us are only progressive approximations. It is the same ideas and the same sentiments which are everywhere at work, except that according to the degree of civilization men have attained, they are asserted with varying degrees of clarity and force.

What an enormous simplification of the notion of moral evolution this is! Yet what a surprising contrast between the extreme simplicity of this conception and the vast accumulation of facts which are thought necessary to justify it! Was there really any need to draw so heavily upon both ethnography and history *in toto* in order to re-discover the principle which formed the basis of the ancient philosophy of natural law?

This illustrates the contradiction inherent in the idea held by Westermarck and the school to which he belongs, of morality and the way it should be studied. On the one hand they appreciate that it is complex and consequently see that to be understood it must be observed in its historical manifestations; hence the fact that they feel compelled to consult history. But on the other hand, and like the classical moralists, they believe that it is possible to reduce all this complexity to several very general and elementary ideas and sentiments. The result is that the erudition they display appears somewhat superficial and in any case unconnected with the very simple theoretical conclusions which are drawn from it. However, if moral reality is truly of such a kind that it can be understood by introspection alone, it would seem difficult to account for it by means of explanations derived from mere introspection.

If I have felt it necessary to criticize the method employed by the author, and his conception of the science of morality, it is only fair to pay tribute to his immense learning. He is incomparably well-read. The book represents a gargantuan labour and will therefore certainly be of great service. For each of the questions discussed, the reader will find a veritable abundance of references and useful information.

Note

1 A series of six chapters are intercalated between the section analysed above and the section I am about to discuss below. In these chapters (VII–XIII), the author discusses sanctions – principally or even exclusively penal sanctions – and the way they are applied to individuals, according to whether the criminal act is intentional or not, and according to the part played in this by the will, etc. As sanctions were already discussed with regard to moral notions, these chapters would apparently not seem to be quite where they belong. They break the continuity of the argument. It is for this reason that I have rejected the idea of analysing them and restrict myself to mentioning them only. The reader will find that they contain certain interesting facts concerning the question of responsibility.

5   A discussion on positive morality: the issue of rationality in ethics
1908a(2)

First published in French under the title 'La Morale positive: examen de quelques difficultés', séance du 26 mars 1908, in *Bulletin de la Société Française de Philosophie,* VIII, pp. 189–200.[1] (Belot's contribution, immediately below, starts on p. 188. – W.S.F.P.)

BELOT:[2] People like to separate the world into two distinct spheres: on the one hand social life, which is seen as a sort of extension of animality, and on the other, the superior life of the mind, reserved for the few. *Humanum paucis vivit genus* (the human species lives for the few). According to such a view pure moral life is a matter for a few philosophers, for whom society is only a more or less comfortable lodging place which one adapts to as well as one can, on whose upkeep one expends no effort, and within which one is engaged on a quite different kind of work. Other people limit their ambitions to well-being and security.

It is not simply that by virtue of its aristocratic and exclusive aspects, this conception is very ill-suited to meet the needs of the contemporary *conscience*, and the Christian *conscience* in particular, but – and in this I believe I am more spiritualistic than those who contrast their own spirituality with mine – but in my estimation, to confine reason to the work of pure thought does injury to it and arbitrarily restricts its sphere of influence. But I also believe that there is about the mind and the life of the mind something heterogeneous which is incommensurate with all the mechanical laws of matter. Yet I envisage the life of the mind beginning at a level far below that superior intellectuality in which it is enclosed. The wish to abandon the social world to the free play of needs and interests, to the automatism of tradition and routine is, in the name of pure reason, the wish to prevent reason from carrying out its tasks and from manifesting its creative power in human society.

52

Nor do I conceive of society as an extension of pure animality. I believe that society can and should increasingly become a true pro- duct of the mind which in any case it helps to develop. Instead of relegating morality to a peak inaccessible to the majority, and in- stead of making society into the insignificant instrument of a small number of privileged minds, I prefer, starting at the bottom, to link morality directly with society and to assign to it the task of rationaliz- ing and spiritualizing society, of turning it into a veritable co-opera- tive venture of free minds.

If furthermore the metaphysician chooses to consider not only that the mind is profoundly dissimilar to physical reality in its power to create and organize – and I agree that this is so – but that thereafter it extends far beyond the individual man and even beyond the social being, then I do not dispute that. In my view it is a matter of speculation not morality but, as I have said, I have by no means the arbitrary and insufferable pretension to close the door on the hypotheses and constructs of metaphysical thought. What I should like to see is that recognition be at least accorded to the necessity which is incumbent upon morality to seize the life of the mind in that part of its trajectory through the real which constitutes the development of human societies. Beneath this level it is still too obscure and concerns our knowledge rather than our will. Above that level, it is not perceptible to us. Only as the shooting star passes through the atmosphere does it shine. Grant me then that social morality as I have defined it, in which 'sociality' is characterized by the greatest degree of interpenetration of minds and contractuality between wills, truly encompasses the only region where Mind be- comes visible to us. And that if it continues to progress at a later date, in other words when the wills of all men are just and brotherly, when there is no more misery or ill-will, when peoples are united in a co-operative human effort involving the whole planet, then the moment will have come to ask ourselves whether morality has any other ends and whether mankind united as one can work towards some superior good. We have plenty of time to consider the matter!

DURKHEIM: I am very much inclined to state the problem in the same terms that Lachelier[3] has just employed. This duality is a fact which no one can fail to recognize. There is no moral system which does not imply it. It remains to be seen how it can be accounted for. Is it necessary, as Lachelier seems inclined, to posit an absolute in order to explain it, or is it not possible to get round the difficulty in another way? If one pictures things in the form of a linear series, the solution indicated by Lachelier is unavoidable, for one of the two terms of the duality would then have to be a means with regard to the other which can only be an end – an end in itself – and therefore an absolute. But the same no longer applies if things are in a circle, if one of the terms of the duality is the part (the individual) of which the other is the whole (society), for the whole is a function of the parts just as the parts are functions of the whole. In a sense it is the end of which they are the means, since it cannot exist without them; but in another sense they are themselves an end. Is it not said that the aim and fundamental purpose of society is to create the individual? So everything is a means and everything is an end, and there is no longer any need to posit an absolute.

But let me come to the questions I wished to raise with Belot.

The first concerns the notion of rationality. It seemed to me that he used the word in two different ways in turn.

The first of these is the meaning I myself gave to the word in the paper I presented here two years ago.[4] What we are faced with here is an objective rationality which is immanent in reality, a rationality which is given in things themselves, and in which the scientist *discovers* and *deduces* but does not *create*. In this sense, to say that morality is rational is simply to say that, at each moment of time, morality, as it is and as it can be observed, constitutes a system of *intelligible data*. It is in the same sense that the physicist and the chemist suppose the physico-chemical world that they study to be rational. I am in complete agreement with Belot on this sense attributed to the word.

But it would seem that in his book[5] the same word consistently indicated another kind of rationality, namely, one which has to be created and not simply registered by the mind. The question then is to introduce into morality a *sui generis* order, different from the one which is present in it naturally. These are two very different ideas and one cannot pass from one to the other without explaining how the transition is effected.

The difference is glaringly apparent in the very terms employed by Belot. Sometimes he speaks of morality as a reality which forces itself upon observation and which no one has either the right or the means to invent, or to create in his own way. At other times he speaks of *his own morality*, an expression which it is difficult to understand when one adopts the standpoint of objective and provable (*expérimentale*) rationality.

Similarly, when Belot declares that rationality is the necessary postulate of all moral research, as it is of all scientific study, I fully accept that. But one often has the impression that what is actually meant beneath the surface of this word, is something quite different from what one first thought. In fact, Belot concludes from this first observation that the more reflective and reasonable conduct is, the more moral it will be. But that rationality – if in fact one single word can serve to designate two different things – is not an objective, immanent, given rationality. It is an ideal rationality which is of our own making and which we introduce into our conduct in unequal amounts. What enables one then to conclude in favour of one rather than the other once the word has been divested of all its ambiguity?

Far from being unavoidable, this conclusion would rather appear to contradict Belot's first principle and his initial notion of rationality. Indeed, as far as the actual facts are concerned, one does not in any circumstances find that reflection has always been and is even today considered a necessary factor in morality. Never at any moment in history has the individual been capable of re-thinking the morality of his time as a whole. The philosopher probably does what he can to work it out: but he never succeeds other than in an incomplete, truncated way, and he is well aware of it. In any case, the overwhelming majority of people are content to accept passively the reigning morality as it is, without question-ing it and without even understanding it. And yet it is incontestable that, in fact, the public *conscience* does not refuse to admit that such non-reflective conduct has some moral character: otherwise scarcely any actions would be considered moral. Conduct which is thoroughly reflective is probably held to be morally superior, but a different form of conduct is judged to be neither immoral nor amoral. This example shows, it seems to me, the extent of the gulf between the two senses given to the word rationality.

BELOT: The question is a difficult one, and I cannot delude myself that I could solve it completely here. Yet it seems to me that Durk-heim's last few remarks contain within them a good answer to his objections. It has been conceded that morality is more perfect if it entails reflection and that it is only complete on that condition. This itself recognizes and acknowledges my right to introduce re-flection into morality. Once the *conscience* recognizes that it has to be autonomous, it forfeits the moral right not to be so.

But this indication is not enough for me and I wish to tackle the question from another angle. If I understand properly the distinction Durkheim is making, it amounts to separating: (a) that rationality which is the principal factor in determining the organization of the fact; (b) that rationality which governs what ought to be done, which governs everything that concerns human activity when it aims to bring into being that which does not yet exist.

DURKHEIM: That is not absolutely so: only a certain sense of what ought to be is involved.

BELOT: In any case, according to the principal meaning of the word, rationality is the scientific organization of the existing morality, of the morality which is observable as fact. And rationality, the way I use the word, has a different meaning, indicating the state in which the individual finds himself at the moment the action takes place, at the moment he makes his choice from among several working hypotheses. So what I call rationality is the mere fact that he attempts to think out his future conduct and consequently to organize it in a practical way, for one cannot think out one's future conduct without organizing it.

DURKHEIM: But one can do that. One can reflect upon and acquiesce in a rule without organizing morality as a whole: organization is only the highest form of acquiescence.

BELOT: Of course, I have never said that at the moment of acting the individual can organize morality as a whole or all his future life. But he will seek to perceive enough of it to justify in his own eyes what he is going to do. He attempts to embrace the next part of his conduct within an adequate framework.

I believe in the unity of reason, theoretical as well as practical, and in the homogeneity of the need for unity which, as far as the datum is concerned, is manifest in the form of scientific systematization and, in practice, in the form of the effort to organize the real. You ask me how I can make the transition from the rational organization of moral data to the rationality of the individual who creates reality. The simplest answer is this: when the scientist considers morality in the past, and in the stable present as a reality to be systematized, he cannot help but encompass in the reality that which promotes the progress of morality, everywhere where it has grown up. This is the idea of something better, of an effort to surpass each stage of the reality and the data. In morality, which is an object of science, experience and observation, the more or less conscious and reflective attitude of the moral agent, of the man of action, is always manifest. One cannot make an objective study of morality even from a wholly historical point of view, without acknowledging the presence of this rationality which organizes, without finding not only blind submission to transcendent rules in the men observed, but a renewed need for action, an effort to bring into being something better and to put into effect a superior ideal of society.

DURKHEIM: I do not see how the ideas which have just been expounded answer the question I put to you and which I repeat. You acknowledge that there is in moral facts an immanent rationality just as there is an immanent rationality in the various phenomena which are the subject matter of the positive sciences. But at the same time you distinguish another form of rationality. How do you pass from one to the other?

BELOT: I thought I had fully understood the question you put to me but it seems that this is not the case. Yet it appears that what you are asking me now is how it arises that rationality can determine the ends, the rules of action, other than those which are already present in the real. How does it arise that society can progress rather than simply being determined through the observance of existing social forms?

DURKHEIM: I am raising the objection which has often been made to me, and I should be happy to see whether you are better able than I am to reply to it.

BELOT: It is precisely in order to avoid the force of that objection that I have never wished to adopt the purely sociological point of view. My entire attitude is a response to the difficulty you have raised. I have tried going beyond purely external, descriptive observation to discover the social finality which generates all moralities, and I believe that I have found, in that finality, the dynamic and rational principle of their creation and continual development.

DURKHEIM: That is not the question, it seems to me. Again, it is not the content of morality which is at issue but a question of method. How can one pass from one rational order to another?

BELOT: As a matter of fact, I do not agree that there are *two* absolutely distinct rationalities. If, in observable moral systems, the moralist finds an element of that creative impulse – of that

57

power to go forward which explains them – then what is manifest in the past at all stages of morality will merely have to be extended to the present, and the moralist's very right to judge the given moralities and, in his turn, to propose his own ideal, will be understood. There is a connection between what you consider to be *two* different rational orders.

DURKHEIM: I wonder whether it would not be better for the sake of clarity to deal with the question of method I raised with you, leaving aside the results which the application of the method might produce. The question is certainly a difficult one. To state it using the terms in which it was put to me: how does the objective study of moral facts permit new ends to be determined which are different from those that the given morality assigns to conduct?

BELOT: But you see, the attitude I adopt enables me not to state the problem in that insoluble form. I am not *suddenly* introducing something completely new, and I am not passing from one kind of rationality to another. For I have not eliminated the second form of the rationality of science and sociological observation: I have discovered its presence in embryonic form. I therefore conceive of the separation of the two rationalities neither subjectively in the method nor objectively as regards subject matter. When the first form of rationality is used and applied to the moral datum, this more or less always reveals the action of the second form of rationality, which creates and organizes new rules and which, above and beyond each fact, tends to make it pass on to something else. We are only passing from a less to a more clearly conscious finality.

DURKHEIM: But you can do no more than establish that this tendency to create, to organize new rules, is a fact (we shall see whether the tendency is real or not in a moment). What permits you to make it into a law? To make it into a privileged tendency to which you accord a veritable priority as over the different or contrary tendencies which co-exist with it? How can the principle of a new moral orientation be created from even the complete systematization of moral data?

BELOT: I would reply yet again that I do not in fact believe that the complete systematization of the moral datum, observed in the past and in the present, is possible, because morality is not complete but by nature constantly aspires to completion. This need for something better, this dissatisfaction with the given, this dynamic principle, is a part of its very essence.

DURKHEIM: If the scientific systematization remains incomplete, the problem will only be more difficult still, and it will continue to exist. It was my supposition that science was intended to facilitate discussion: that was a hypothesis.

BELOT: Exactly, the hypothesis prejudges the solution. For one could never, in fact, deduce moral ends or lay down new rules, if societies *could* form the object of a complete and definite science. Men would no longer set themselves anything to do other than to make use of this reality which would be fixed and analysed for ever, and there would be no longer any morality. In a society which was immutably fixed or definitely organized – the second form of rationality, practical rationality – moral action would no longer have any conceivable meaning. I reply by rejecting the very way you state the question, which consists in supposing that social facts, considered in the past, are like dead *things* and are to be studied as such. Consequently, when one reaches the point in time which is the present – when the action will take place and will tend towards the future – one would find oneself confronted by a sudden novelty: and it would be impossible to form a link between this and the past. But that is creating a false methodology outside the real.

DURKHEIM: If the complete systematization of morality is impossible, in other words, if in principle the given morality cannot be translated into an intelligible system of notions and relationships, then it must be said that it is not rational, or not totally so; and in that case, it is objective reality, in the first sense of the word, that is being abandoned.

But if you wish, let us leave aside the question of method and come to the question of fact. What allows one to say that reflection – that rationality, in the second sense of the word – is an essential factor in morality?

BELOT: I have several reasons for presenting the notion of rationality alongside the notion of sociability and as its necessary complement. Among other reasons for doing so, I have had to take into account the fact of observation that certain theorists appear to neglect in a curious way, namely, that in social reality a moment almost always comes when individual *consciences* rebel against the collective imperatives, conceive new imperatives and create new *working hypotheses*.

In fact, all great minds who have initiated superior moral rules have thought along such lines. Sociological observation itself shows this individualism in action and in continual rebirth. One cannot disregard it or eliminate it from the concept of morality.

I have attempted to take the greatest possible account of the observation of social facts. I have defined morality by sociality and shown that to a very large extent morality is in fact comparable to a technique which uses the datum. But in the elaboration of a science of moral things, it would be quite extraordinary and most unscientific not to take account of those isolated movements of *conscience*, of that spontaneous rational effort which tends to re-organize the systems of rules and moral judgments, especially so, as these movements of *conscience* have spread out over a wide area, as they are the origin of a transformation of moral reality, as they virtually create the morality of an age to come, and as they thereby provide sociology in the last analysis with new material which would perhaps not have appeared without them. If we leave aside this attempt at improvement and rationalization, sociology would be reduced to no more than a collection of fragmentary studies on the various moral realities, which would be unable to grasp the link and the ceaseless relation between them.

DURKHEIM: There is no doubt that reflection tends to become an element of morality, but what has to be discovered is whether it is a necessary element, without which morality could not exist, which must enter into the definition of morality and which must be placed on the same level as its social character, as you propose to do.

BELOT: I confess I do not fully see the point in distinguishing such levels. If you posit two equally necessary conditions for a phenomenon, how are you to say which is the more 'essential' of the two? What I maintain is that on the one hand there is no morality, if we do not consider an action accomplished with a view to some social grouping, and it is this which defines the specific character of morality. And on the other hand, that we never allow that there is any morality where there is pure passivity of the agent, absence of all initiative and all reflection which organizes. Lastly, that the superior morality is distinguished by the development of this second characteristic. Is that not enough for us?

Now which of these two factors is essential I am quite at a loss to say.

DURKHEIM: If these two elements are necessary they are in fact both essential. But I contest the fact that they are both necessary. There is one which may be absent without morality ceasing to exist.

The fact you have raised does not seem at all accurate to me. Even today we do not go so far as to say that for an act to be moral it must be reflective. Otherwise take care lest morality becomes a thing of vanity and luxury. The vast majority of men carry out moral imperatives passively and the more cultivated men only partially reflect upon them. To be sure reflection raises and perfects morality but it is not the necessary condition of it.

BELOT: I think I understand the underlying reason for the objection which Durkheim is raising. It results from the fact that two things are being presented *in abstracto* and as absolutes when in fact they are not, and when it is only through each other that they have meaning and true purpose. Relativism alone can remove the last difficulty Durkheim has raised. He asks what would happen in the case of an individual deprived of all reflection and whether the acts of such an individual could be moral. Whether, furthermore, reflection could ever be applied to moral reality as a whole and the rules which are laid down for the individual. These are two borderline situations which, in fact, confirm my analysis. . . .

DURKHEIM: If you simply mean to say that there is no morality without *conscience* or without thought, if in the case of a mineral which is supposed to be unconscious, there is no morality, no one will contest what you say. But in that case, I do not see what bearing the fact thus conceded has on the particular case in point.

BELOT: What I am trying to say and what I wish people would understand is that there is not an absence of reflection at the lowest level and total reflection at the top, but that in fact there is an imperceptible, continuous transition between the fact of having *conscience* and the fact of reflecting.

DURKHEIM: That is stating the obvious. But the fact nevertheless remains that the simple *conscience* of which you are speaking now is one thing, and the 'considered acceptance of the rule' of which you speak in your book is another. The proof of this is the fact that in your book you anticipate the case where there would be no considered acceptance on the part of man and you say that, in such a case, the act could not be moral. It is therefore not present everywhere where there is thought. That and that alone is what I was referring to.

But there is one final question I wished to put to you. You say in your book, observation and induction seem to have provided a more plausible hypothesis about the nature of morality than most of those which have been suggested by hasty or abstract speculation. What is that hypothesis? It is that the moral act is that which is called for by social interest. I should like to ask you what works and what research bear out this hypothesis which for my part I cannot accept as it is, on account of its extreme generality.

BELOT: When one sets out to create a hypothesis, one does not normally have a proved fact in front of one.

DURKHEIM: All the 'Speculative hypotheses' of the moralists have this character and you condemn them.

BELOT: Yes, but you are comparing two absolutely different things. On the one hand, metaphysical hypotheses are created out of the air, without scientific method, without any basis in facts, as their authors admit. Furthermore, it is the property of such hypotheses to be perfectly sterile and it is impossible to derive any definite application from them or to verify their accuracy. The one I am proposing has, you will admit, quite opposite characteristics. It is founded on observation; it applies directly to reality. I do not think you wished to reproach me, as some have done, for not having 'provided a morality' in 500 pages. I should dearly like to know who has ever 'provided a morality'! At a pinch, the metaphysician might claim he could achieve this by being able to create a morality from his own mind. But that is certainly not my claim. You can neither attribute it to me, nor can you reproach me with having made it! It remains that in those 500 pages I think it was possible to distinguish a likely hypothesis, first directly induced from the observation of the most significant facts and then applied to a certain number of the particular and characteristic questions in which it seemed to work successfully. Naturally, it is not a complete science, but I surely have the right to call this hypothesis a likely one which deserves to be examined and put to the test by those people, in fact, who have the leisure to extend it and verify it against a more considerable number of facts.

DURKHEIM: I am not discussing the value of the hypothesis for the moment. I am only asking on what it is based. If it has no other basis than the few facts set out in your book, I cannot help but feel that there is a singular disproportion between the scope of such a hypothesis and the data which you use to support it.

BELOT: I do not fully understand this criticism. I see that a large number of facts is needed, and in a manner of speaking, all of them, to substantiate the claim that a hypothesis is proved. But how many facts are needed to suggest the hypothesis and make it worth putting to the test? Sometimes only one, if it is very characteristic. Moreover, did you yourself not believe that you could define the religious fact in twenty-eight pages?[6]

DURKHEIM: An argument *ad hominem* does not constitute a scientific argument, even if it is well founded. But in addition, in this particular case, the parallel you have just drawn appears to be based upon a confusion. In the article to which you have just alluded, it was not my aim to seek a formula which would express the fundamental nature of religion, but simply an initial, provisional definition, such as exists in the initial stages of all sciences, and which conveys only the external and most visible signs by which one can most easily recognize the phenomena one intends to study at a later date. I took care to explain myself on this point and in the most deliberate way in the work you have just mentioned. A definition of such a kind, which does not serve as a conclusion to research but on the contrary merely precedes and prepares the way for it, can and even must be made rather rapidly, for it is only preliminary and does not concern fundamentals.

The aim you set yourself is quite different. It is your belief, to use your own expression of a few moments ago, that you have gone beyond 'the purely descriptive and external observation of moral forms, and found the dynamic and rational principle of their creation and their continual development'. I cannot help but find that something else is needed to provide the beginnings of a proof for a principle of such importance, besides the three or four very fine studies contained in your book. Truly, the speculative hypotheses that you reject and that I do not defend have in the main at least as wide a basis.

Notes

1 [Belot (see n.2 below) presented some opening observations based on the criticisms of his book, *Études de morale positive* (1907). The critics had said of positive morality that its principles were inadequately demonstrated and that it lacked precision in practical application. Belot attempted to defend such objections. It was, however, Parodi (see 1910b, n.2 on p. 76) who introduced the discussion and who stated that Belot had presented a positive morality based on the notion of society in which

a large place was given to rationality. After a considerable discussion involving several members of the Société, Belot took up the theme described below. – W.S.F.P.]

2 [Gustave Belot was a philosopher by training who on the whole supported Durkheim but was nevertheless critical of his strictly sociological approach. (See comments which follow in the discussion.) Belot, whilst writing books and contributing to learned societies, was for most of his life in educational administration as Inspecteur général de l'instruction publique. He held in his book, *Études de morale positive* (1907), that sociology could deal with the facts of morality but it could not determine ends. – W.S.F.P.]

3 [Jules Lachelier (1823–1918) was a philosopher who taught at the École Normale Supérieure, who advocated the use of reflection in philosophy. He was opposed to certain kinds of empiricism and sceptical towards Kant's notion of experience. Basically he adopted a synthetic approach as in *Psychologie et métaphysique* (1885) in which he identified laws of thought with laws of being. – W.S.F.P.]

4 [A reference to 'La Détermination du fait moral' (1906b/r.1924a/t.1953b). – W.S.F.P.]

5 [Belot, *Études de morale positive* (1907). – W.S.F.P.]

6 [This refers to Durkheim's article, 'De la Définition des phénomènes religieux', in *L'Année sociologique*, II, pp. 1–28 (1899a(ii)/t.1975a), which was an initial attempt to approach religion systematically. – W. S. F. P.]

6
1910b

A discussion on the notion of social equality

First published in French under the title, 'La Notion d'égalité sociale', séance du 30 décembre 1909, in *Bulletin de la Société Française de Philosophie,* X, pp. 59–70.[1]

DURKHEIM: If I have understood Parodi[2] correctly, he has set himself a double aim. First, he wished to justify egalitarian ideas and then to base a certain conception of morality on this justification. I think it would be useful for the sake of clarity to reverse the order in which Parodi proceeded and start by examining his general conception of morality, for fundamentally it is from this conception that his particular theory of the idea of equality stems.

Parodi posits as a self-evident truth the fact that, historically speaking, morality has continued to become more and more rational with the passing of time. This assertion seems highly contestable. Every moral system has its own rationality. The reasons for the moral system of the Romans lay in Roman society, just as our own society has its reasons in the nature of contemporary European societies. To allow the postulate put forward by Parodi, one would, as he has done, have to reduce morality to no more than a system of abstract notions – to a certain kind of geometry. But this would, I believe, constitute a serious misunderanding of moral reality, which consists not in a system of concepts that might be constructed by a *sui generis* logic, but in a system of forces – surely not physical ones – but mental, moral forces, forces which derive all their power from action, *représentations* and from states of *conscience*.

I shall take an example from the realm of law, since this is the topic which is being discussed today. Janet[3] defines law somewhere as *a moral power*. Imagine a child, he says, asleep on the edge of

65

a precipice. There is in that child a force which is no less effective for being moral, since it prevents me from casting him into the abyss, even though this would be to my advantage. In fact forces of such a kind emanate from every human being and they forestall attacks or determine positive acts on our part. To give an account of morality is to give an account of such forces, of their origin and their workings. It can probably be presumed that they are not as we commonly imagine them, that they are not immanent in the individual they protect, but they are only the objective form of the sentiments which the individual inspires. But this is important. What is certain is that they are indeed forces since they have the property of either inhibiting or provoking movement.

If one supposes this to be true, I do not see how there can be any justification for saying that the morality of one country or one period is more rational than the morality of another country or another period. All moral systems have their own rationality. All moral forces have their reality. All of them are natural and consequently rational, like the rest of nature. We can express them in notions, in other words, we can create the science of them, as we create the science of physical forces. But there is no moral system which cannot thus be translated into concepts. In this respect one can make no distinction between the morality of today and that of times gone by.

I can see only two reasons that could lead to a belief in the progressive rationalization of morality.

(1) It is sometimes thought that rationality can be defined in terms of generality. Because our moral ideal is at present more humane than it formerly was, our morality is more impersonal, more abstract, freer from the contingencies of time and place. We conceive of it as valid for all mankind. The conclusion which is drawn from this is that it is more rational by virtue of this alone.[4] But that is to fail to recognize the fact that the general does not possess any virtues which are peculiar to it. It is merely an extract of the particular. It cannot therefore contain anything other than what is particular. If the latter is irrational, then the general will have the same irrationality.

(2) Nowadays we feel the need to be in harmony with ourselves more urgently than before. It is possible that this need exerts a greater influence upon moral life, but to what extent we have absolutely no idea. The contrary need remains active. Without it,

I do not know how morality would have been able to evolve, since for evolution and change to take place, the principle of identity should not be too staunchly respected. Now what is the respective proportion of these tendencies? This is rather difficult to say. There is, therefore, nothing here to justify the categorical thesis which serves as a postulate for Parodi.

Let us now try to see how these general considerations apply to the problem of egalitarian ideas.

We are told that the universal inequalities of caste or class, as they existed in the past, were less rational than our current inequalities. Why is this? In what respect? I cannot see what basis there is for such an assertion. Our present inequalities are founded on the nature of our present societies, as those of India are founded upon the nature of Hindu societies. The one is not more incomprehensible than the other. The biologist does not ask himself whether it is more rational to breathe with lungs than with gills.

Conversely, let us consider the relative equality towards which we are moving today. Can it really be attributed to a greater need for logical co-ordination and for a more perfect systematization in our societies today? But to begin with, if we are to be justified in accepting this paper, it should have been shown that the logical motive has indeed been the determining cause of egalitarian aspirations as they are evident in either law or the contemporary moral *conscience*. And I do not see that Parodi has attempted even the beginnings of a proof on this point.

However, in the absence of such a proof, let us consider the question from a purely dialectical point of view.

According to such a view, the need to classify peoples according to one single criterion predisposes us in favour of egalitarian concepts. As a hypothesis, a classification of such a kind would be purely logical and it would be a perfectly logical way of envisaging men. But the equality which has to be explained is a *moral equality*, which is to say, as I have shown above, *an equality of rights and powers*. Yet I cannot possibly see how Parodi passes from one classification to the other. It does not follow that, because it is convenient to classify men according to one single criterion, we should ascribe equal social value and the same power to all men.

Logic and rationality play such a small part in this question and our egalitarian practices fall so far short of meeting the need to bring about self-harmony that, as Parodi himself has indicated, they are in reality based on two contradictory conceptions.

On the one hand there is the conception which is expressed in the formula: 'To each according to his works' or else 'To each according to his merit', which claims equal treatment for men of equal merit, but different treatment for men of different value. But with respect to this principle there is another which demands that to a certain extent men should be equally treated despite their unequal value. This principle is not merely, as Parodi seemed to admit, the ideal and virtually utopian outcome of moral evolution. We are already practising it in part and it affects conduct at all times. Charity demands that we do good to those who suffer whatever their merit, at least up to a certain point. There was a time when heavy penalties were arranged in such a careful way as to graduate them so that they would correspond to the inequality of the crimes. We have abandoned such refinements and we no longer have a carefully graded hierarchy of tortures for all possible sorts of serious crimes. The reduction of penalties by simplifying the penal scale has meant that the various grades are much closer together. There is, therefore, a less exact correspondence between the gravity of the punishment and the seriousness of the crime. This conception is quite the opposite of the preceding one, yet it co-exists with it in our moral *conscience* and we are well aware that it has its place in it. For there are cases where people should be treated according to their value and others where their value must be disregarded. It is clear how small is the concern in all of this with satisfying speculative needs and ordering our ideas, since our attitude towards this practical problem is dependent on contradictory notions. The question should have been presented in quite different terms.

PARODI: It seems to me that Durkheim's remarks do not contradict what I have said, however much they may appear to at first sight. He admits that there exists in the individual a certain need to remain in harmony with himself or to achieve such harmony. From that point, why could this same need not also constitute a social force? The idea of equality seemed to me to be linked with all attempts at social classification, so can it be denied that, once social classes have become established, a sort of need to define them more accurately appears, which is the true task of law, and that in the course of time this need reacts upon them, and in fact helps to define them and to distinguish the social force more rationally? Is that not a positive element of collective evolution that the sociologist must not ignore? Furthermore, this in no way prejudices the importance of this factor compared with all others. It remains to see how effective it is and I have been careful not to claim that in such ways the power of logic was preponderant.

Furthermore, Durkheim asks what justification I have for declaring that universal distinctions or non-egalitarian organizations are less rational than others, since, just as much as the second, where they exist they are bound up with a set of social conditions which determine them, and which would not permit of any others. It seems necessary to make a distinction here. All social, egalitarian or non-egalitarian régimes are equally rational for the scientist, in so far as they are effects linked to causes which he has attempted to elucidate. They are rational in so far as they are explained or are explicable in sociological terms. But for the individual actually situated in a society of such a kind, and who seeks to comprehend the institutions by which he is surrounded, not by their determining causes which more often than not he does not know, but by their practical ends, such a justification cannot suffice. With the small amount of intellectual freedom available to him to ask the question, he will not judge that social distinctions which do not correspond to any real superiority are rational, or whose direct or indirect usefulness is not shown to him, and which the force of tradition alone demands should be accepted. But in any case, we cannot for our part judge that they are rational, when we attempt to evaluate the social order of which they form part, unless the argument of the traditionalists in favour of inequality and the defence of prejudice as such have seemed conclusive. In other words, I think that we can compare the various social types in such a way as to determine between them degrees of coherence, of adaptation and of finality, by virtue of a sort of ideal of rational order. I do not believe that it is possible to confuse completely the two ideas of *explanation* and *justification*. Or in other words, it is my view that there are two senses of the word rationality. There is scientific rationality, which I would be more inclined to call intelligibility and which consists in discovering how a social or material fact is determined and what laws govern it. And there is moral rationality, which is to say, a certain idea of order and organization. The first would correspond to the point of view of causality and the second to that of finality. And it is this second sort of rationality which alone seems to me to be capable of justifying an institution or a moral rule in the eyes of the person who has taken it upon himself to reflect upon it and evaluate it critically. It is also this second one which in fact seems to have achieved a higher degree of realization in egalitarian societies than in others, which seem to correspond to a higher degree of critical reflection, to a more conscious and pronounced demand for intelligible organization and finality.

Lastly, Durkheim raises the objection that the abstract notion of equality, as I have studied it, is so vague and so far removed from the facts, that I have been led to confuse arbitrarily within the notion two conceptions which are logically different and almost opposites. On the one hand, equality in competitive conditions between men, which is a sort of method for bringing to light natural differences between them, in merit or in skill: and on the other hand, equality as a tendency to treat all men equally, whatever services have been rendered or whatever superiorities are evident. My reply is that I have in no way identified these two conceptions, but that they did not seem contradictory to me. It would appear to me that one passes naturally and almost imperceptibly from the one to the other. To begin with, at the moment and doubtless for a long time to come, the two formulae 'To each according to his works', and 'To each according to his needs', lead us down the same path and can suggest or justify the same social reforms. Does a measure such as income tax, for example, not tend, according to one's point of view, either to establish greater economic equality between the fortunes of different individuals, or more effectively to equalize competitive conditions or the comparison of merits between them? Yet I admit that at a given moment the divergence between the two points of view may appear, for that divergence exists and I have not denied it. I have only tried to show the logical passage from one to the other. In the first conception, it is a matter of evaluating exactly the merit of each, so as to adapt the social sanctions to it. But here the practical difficulties increase and the complication grows infinitely. For what common measure can one establish between values or services which are quite heterogeneous? One has recognized both to be useful or necessary to social life, though in different ways – especially as the rarity of the one group is compensated for by its lesser urgency and vice versa. Can one not therefore come to regard as equal services which are very different but equally real, provided goodwill and effort are equivalent?

From the strictly moral point of view which feels able to take account of the intention only, one cannot see on what infallible scale one could weigh up the pure merit of each of them, and would strict justice itself seem thus to lead us to the extreme limits of charity? It therefore seems to me that one cannot say that there are really two conceptions here which are quite independent of equality, but rather two moments in the expansion of one idea, in the extension of one single sentiment.

DURKHEIM: Regarding the role played in our moral life by logical need, I simply meant to say that we are completely ignorant of what its importance was; and even that its role was in all probability rather limited. A theory, which rests on the opposite postulate, therefore seems to me somewhat hazardous.

But let me come to the two questions of fact which have been put to me.

First, scientific explanations of social institutions, says Parodi, may be valid for the man who observes the society in question from outside, but not for the individual who is part of that society and participates in its life. Why is that? He would probably, and quite justifyably, find that historical explanations were not relevant if they were limited to showing in what way the past weighs unreasonably on the present. But these institutions, and in this particular case, these inequalities, would not have persisted if they had not been founded in the nature of things. How therefore could they appear irrational to the individual who seeks to understand them, whether he considers them from inside or outside? Historical explanations are not simple assertions: in certain conditions they are justifications. The universal inequalities of caste and class were once realities. We are no longer at the stage of admitting that they could have become established and been maintained by artifice and ruse. They necessarily resulted from conditions of communal life. Societies have existed in which such inequalities were completely justified and had their *raisons d'être*. Why could these reasons not have been understood by the individual who lived in those societies, provided we supposed (which is doubtless an anachronism, though legitimate in this case) that he was sufficiently informed and enlightened? And how would he not have found that practices which he judged to be justified were rational? For the outcome to have been otherwise, one would have had to be able to establish that such inequalities did not correspond

71

to any need or any social necessity. And this flies in the face of all probabilities, given the generality and persistence of such inequalities.

In the second place, the two formulae – the two egalitarian conceptions I have mentioned above – are so contradictory that they form the basis of two opposite theories. One, 'To each according to his works', is the favourite principle of orthodox economists; the other, that of moralists and ascetics. One cannot at one and the same time disregard inequalities of value and stimulate them by means of rewards. Nor do I mean that it is necessary to choose between these two phrases and sacrifice one to the other. Each of them has its place in moral reality. The fact nevertheless remains that they point us in divergent and even contrary directions.

Moreover, how is it possible to justify egalitarian ideas by purely logical considerations? The role of logic is to help or oblige us to see things as they are. *But in fact we are unequal.* We have neither the same physical force, nor the same intellectual power, nor the same energy of will. The social services we render are of unequal importance and we are more or less easy to replace in the functions we carry out and we carry them out more or less well, etc. In spite of this, morality demands that to a certain extent we should be treated as though we were equal. It ascribes to us an equality which has no empirical foundation. Some powerful cause must therefore intervene which makes us see men other than what they are in tangible experience, which makes us see them in such a way that they appear equal to us, and which consequently transfigures them. So long as he has not explained how this transfiguration takes place, I fear that the problem of egalitarian ideas will remain completely unsolved.

PARODI: To start with, as regards the second difficulty that has been raised, I fully appreciate that in certain extreme cases, or in plans for the thoroughgoing reform of society, the two tendencies may find themselves in conflict. But it is my contention that for the most part they act in concert and in the same direction. We attempt to adjust social advantages to merit, but in order to achieve this we are put into the position of wishing to restrict inherited or unearned privileges, and we thus increasingly tend to place men in equal situations, which in turn may permit natural superiorities to reveal themselves all the more easily. Once again, can we decide if it is more directly from the first or the second tendency that inspiration comes for both a graded income tax and all restrictive measures on inheritance, such as the prohibition of the automatic handing down of wealth within certain degrees of kinship? Is it not true to say that the arguments used to support such measures are borrowed indiscriminately from both conceptions of equality? As for those cases where there would be a real choice between the demands of distributive justice and suggestions which are quite akin to it, they appear to be borderline cases or cases of *conscience*, perhaps even questions of degree and expediency, rather than revealing a fundamental rational incompatibility.

Furthermore, Durkheim asks me again whether the members of an unequal, caste-ridden society would not regard it as rational and would not accept it in its entirety, not because they were forced to do so but because they did it wholeheartedly. I do not deny this, but it would be in so far as the members were governed by the force of tradition or custom – in so far as it would never occur to them that things could be any different from the way they have always observed them – in so far as they would not wonder about the wherefore of the institutions they accept. The existing order of things would seem natural rather than rational and in actual fact the problem would not even occur to them. Or, if it did, it might be that inadequate reasons would be considered sufficient or that in the face of everything, they attempted to persuade themselves of it. We are well aware, historically speaking, what sophistic or infantile arguments not only the general mass of humanity, but also the 'thinkers', the philosophers have sometimes been content with, so as to give themselves the illusion that the régime which is favourable to them, or else the one in which they are accustomed to live, is just and reasonable. Let us call to mind the justifications put forward in support of slavery, not only in antiquity but as late as the sixteenth century, or else the arguments in favour of religious intolerance in periods which are still very close to us. And how few reasons are we ourselves prepared to accept in order to justify this or that social institution, whose basic inadequacy we are aware of and which we should reject if we pursued our thoughts to their logical conclusion, and if we were not held back by reasons of expediency or prudence. Yet finding inadequate reasons to justify oneself at least means that one feels the need to find reasons. If some people are able to accept them either from natural timidity or intellectual weakness, others in the same period, who are bolder or more logical, may reject them. One can only conclude, it seems to me, that the rational need does not exist, or that it is entirely devoid of force, whether because in certain cases, habit deadens or smothers it, or because in other cases, habit deceives and mystifies it.

But for Durkheim not only have non-egalitarian institutions been able to appear rational to the members of the societies in which they held sway, but were actually so, in so far as they were 'founded in the nature of things'. In other words, I think, they were required by the general state of society or by collective utility. In this case they may probably have seemed and perhaps still do seem justified to the enlightened critic, but not in and by themselves. It will only be so far as they are linked with the more general conditions that justify them, in so far as no means or reasons to modify the latter are observed. This is how one of our contemporaries might perhaps be opposed to the reforming of an institution which, though illogical in itself, will seem to him to belong to a whole established order of things, which it would be dangerous to interfere with; not a few will declare for instance that our system of direct taxation deserves respect because it has proved its value, even though he will admit that it is irrational or unjust in itself. It is thus one thing to admit the expediency or the usefulness of an institution and another to believe that it is rational and justifiable in itself.

And then Durkheim will readily admit that a good many legal rules or customs can sometimes outlive their usefulness or the ideas which suggested them: in his view, social survivals can indeed occur. It is evidently these which will be the object of rationalist criticism and it is with respect to them that a need for logical coherence will be imperatively felt. Only in the period when the feudal system was no longer inevitably imposed by circumstances was it possible to take full account of how arbitrary or unjust were the irregularities it established. A bold spirit might perhaps have been able to realize this even before such a time – and such minds existed throughout the entire Middle Ages. While recognizing that the feudal system was temporarily inevitable, it was possible to imagine, even if only in a utopian fashion, the reform or disappearance of the conditions which were themselves irrational or unjust and which only provided indirect justification for it (constant wars, general insecurity, etc.). Later, and in favourable social conditions, the utopia may be transmuted into a positive ideal and result in practical demands.

As for discovering where a totally abstract classification would derive its socially active force, this is precisely what I have tried to explain, for good or ill, and it seems to me that it is possible to get a rough idea of it, once one admits, as Durkheim does, in spite of everything, that a certain need for logical coherence does exist in the individual. How, indeed, could the fact of recognizing one particular abstract order as more legitimate than another help but be translated into a certain corresponding practical attitude? All the more as I have said before, because this need clearly always applies to given factual conditions, which simply have to be defined more accurately and rendered more coherent, to sentiments which have to be justified in moral terms and since he could not go so far as to suggest a new order of things out of nothing.

DURKHEIM: Parodi asks how these two conceptions of equality are contradictory. According to the one, salaries and wages remain different according to the relative importance of the tasks and services rendered. It implies a hierarchy. The other conception, on the contrary, implies a complete levelling down. Yet again, these contradictory tendencies are reconciled in practice; but I do not see in this composite practice the manifestation of a logical need for it to remain in harmony with itself.

Furthermore, when I said that non-egalitarian institutions could be justified with respect to given social conditions, I meant to refer to well-founded justifications which derive their authority from the nature of things and not from blind tradition. Also, traditional justifications often have more value than people believe. They are symbolic and figurative and need to be interpreted, but when one learns to discern the reality which the symbol conveys and which lies beneath it, one sees that the justifications are often very close to the facts and determine rational justification.

Parodi concludes by pointing out that an institution may be irrational in itself as well as being founded in the social system. I cannot understand how an institution can be rational *in itself*. The rationality of a fact is relative, as is the fact. If an institution has its fundamental justification in a given social system, which itself has its *raison d'être* in the entire series of historical conditions on which it depends, which consequently cannot be other than it is at the moment under consideration, how can such an institution be irrational?[5] If direct taxation was really founded in the nature of our societies, one would be obliged to admit that it was rational. But when one merely says that it is wise to retain it provisonally because it would be better to replace it prudently and gradually, this does not mean that one is recognizing that an irrational institution can be necessary and founded in the nature of things. On the contrary, there was a moment in history when the feudal system was implied in the organization of medieval societies, which were all they could and should have been in the particular period. At that time the feudal system was rational, just as it was to lose that rationality later. Between these two stages lies an intermediary period when it was wise to retain it *provisionally*, while at the same time preparing for its evolution.

Notes

1 [Parodi (see n.2 below) introduced the discussion. He observed that the notion of social equality was abstract and also that in self-critical and reforming societies, as in western Europe, the notion appeared as a justifiable method to unearth natural superiorities and inferiorities. The ideal of equality appeared in fact in socialist societies. Equality was not a physical fact (for example physical differences) but members in a society were held to be equal. After considerable discussion, Durkheim made the following contribution. – W.S.F.P.]

2 [Dominique Parodi (1870–1955), a philosopher by training and a rationalist, was a member of Durkheim's Année Sociologique group. He was one of the early contributors to the journal, *L'Année sociologique*, and helped to review sections entitled Sociologie générale and Sociologie juridique. In 1910 he wrote *La Problème moral et la pensée contemporaine* in which he defended rationality in all moral activity and wrote that moral action demands a sincere examination of motive powers, which however is not possible without action being seen as eminently rational and capable of abstraction. He was a professor at various lycées and then became Inspecteur général de l'instruction publique in 1919. – W.S.F.P.]

3 [Paul Janet (1823–99) was a philosopher and a psychologist, whose eclecticism was based on the teaching of Victor Cousin. He held that access to metaphysical realities came through reflection on self and by introspection. He was on the jury which examined Durkheim's thesis and on the whole was strongly opposed to the emerging sociology. – W.S.F.P.]

4 [See 1908a(2), translated here, for a further discussion on rationality. – W.S.F.P.]

5 [See n.4 above. – W.S.F.P.]

7 'Introduction to ethics'

1920a

First published in French as 'Introduction à la morale'
in *Revue philosophique*, LXXXIX, pp. 79–97.

Introductory note by Marcel Mauss

The following pages which we have edited are the last thing Durkheim wrote. They date from some time during the period March to September 1917, when his doctors permitted him to work.

This is, in fact, a final copy, and the handwriting is neater than ever, though it is shaky and the ends of words are missing here and there. It is plainly apparent from certain points of style that the author was ailing, yet with the exception of several paragraphs in section II, which he was still revising, he had completed his work on it.

It is our view that there is sufficient material here, albeit fragmentary and incomplete, to provide an indication, in terms of style and general tendency, of how Durkheim would have written his *Morale* (Ethics). These pages were the introduction to it. He had in fact already begun it in a final burst of energy and as a last response to the call of duty, though aware he would not be able to see it through.

We shall probably be able to publish them in the lectures on Physique des moeurs which was the last time but one that he delivered these pages, together with his lectures on Morale domestique.[1] These lecture courses are in fact written out in full.

However the book is one thing, the text of lectures delivered is clearly another.

For this reason it will no doubt be interesting to read the first two sections of the Introduction à la morale, which was to have constituted the first volume of *La Morale*.[2]

Furthermore, they include Durkheim's plan for the first volume. So it will one day be possible to compare this Introduction as it might have been with the corresponding section of the lectures on Physique des moeurs.

A final word of clarification on how the first volume of this great work would have developed.

The manuscript was found on Durkheim's desk in a file which also contained a number of lecture summaries he evidently intended to use, only one or two of which concern matters unrelated to this subject. The majority date from a course of lectures on ethics (*morale*) Durkheim gave at the Sorbonne before the War. It was this material that was to serve as the basis for the following chapters, along lines that had already been tried and tested.

The titles, which speak for themselves, are as follows:

'Aim of course.' Traditional conception of morality. (This corresponds to the pages we have published here.)

'Critique of traditional ethics.'

'Critique of the wholly subjective view of morality.'

'Critique of the theory of Tarde.'

'The problem of the Kantian solution.'

'Critique of Kantian ethics.'

All these lectures relate to the Introduction to the first volume.

Book I [of the first volume – W.S.F.P.] was in all probability to be based on lectures with the following titles:

'Value judgment and ideal' (sociological idealism).

'The individual moral *conscience* and objective morality' (morality and moral *conscience*).

'Objective and subjective viewpoint' (sentiment of justice; notion of justice).

'Relation between public and individual morality' (autonomy and the Kantian solution).

'Collective and average type.'

'Unity of the two elements' (ideal and duty).

'How can we attach ourselves to society?'

In addition, there are also some lecture summaries from completely different parts of the course. Durkheim probably intended to draw on them for the purpose of his *Introduction*:

'Introductory lecture to the course on domestic morals.'
'Divorce.'
'The three zones of kinship.'
These are taken from his course on Morale domestique. There are also four others from the course on Morale, namely:
Two lectures on 'Property. The Kantian theory'.
Two lectures on 'The consensual contract' and 'Sanctions'.

I

The word *morale* is normally construed in two different ways.

It is used to mean all judgments, be they individual or collective, which men pass with respect to their own actions or the actions of others, so as to single them out by ascribing a special value to them, which is regarded as quite separate and distinct from all other human values. This is moral value. Technical skill, however accomplished, has never superseded virtue. Nor has it ever seemed that a dishonest act could be redeemed by a lucky invention, a brilliant painting or a scientific discovery. What constitutes and typifies such a value cannot be stated at this early stage of the enquiry: it is a question we shall endeavour to answer as we go along. But even at this point, the unique and distinctive quality of moral values enables us to establish that moral judgments occupy a special place within the totality of human judgments, and this is all we need to know.

These judgments are imprinted on the *conscience* of the normal adult. We find them ready-made within us, and in most cases without our being aware of having actually formed them in a conscious, let alone scientific or methodical way. Man's reaction, when confronted with a moral or immoral act, is spontaneous, even unconscious, apparently stemming from the very depths of his nature. It is a type of instinct which causes us to praise or blame, without there being any other possible alternative. This is why moral *conscience* is so often envisaged as a kind of voice which is heard within us, even though we are for the most part unable to say what it is or whence it derives its authority.

But *morale* is also used to mean all systematic, methodical speculation on moral data (*les choses de la morale*). What this speculation is exactly, what its object and method are, is something that philosophers are a long way from having determined with any precision.

Admittedly, such speculation has to some extent the same object as the spontaneous judgments of moral *conscience*. Both are concerned with evaluating how we act; how we praise or blame, and apportion positive or negative moral values; and with ascertaining forms of conduct man should follow and others he should reject. Yet the method of evaluation differs on two essential points.

1 Judgments made by philosophers are based on certain principles: they are co-ordinated and systematized. The moralist knows or thinks he knows why he praises or blames. He refuses to obey blind instinct. He gives reasons. In a general way these reasons are deduced from a particular view of man. He is envisaged as a rational or sentient being, as an individual; or, on the other hand, as essentially sociable, as seeking general, impersonal ends or else pursuing quite particular goals, etc. And it is this view which serves as a basis for advocating that he should follow one precept for action rather than another.

The moralist works out the reasons, whatever they may be, as methodically as he is able. Thus all these speculations either are, or else aspire to be, scientific. This differentiates them from the spontaneous judgments of the collective *conscience* (*conscience commune*).

2 The rules of ordinary morality are applied to human actions which they judge and either approve or blame. The doctrines of moralists are applied to the rules themselves, which they judge, accept or reject, depending on whether they do or do not conform to the original principle. In no way does the moralist consider himself bound to follow the general opinion; on the contrary, he arrogates the right to criticize, reinterpret, or if need be, to reform it. At all events, only after a methodical enquiry does he embrace it himself. He is not held back by any of the norms others abide by, no matter how sacred they are believed to be. He may declare that certain practices are criminal, though unanimously respected, or that ways of acting are obligatory though totally devoid of respect. Kant was not in agreement with all his contemporaries. And the theorists of socialism are sharply critical of the ideas upon which

current notions on the right of property are founded.

Every morality, no matter what it is, has its ideal. Therefore, the morality to which men subscribe at each moment of history has its ideal which is embodied in the institutions, traditions and precepts which generally govern behaviour. But above and beyond this ideal, there are always others in the process of being formed. For the moral ideal is not immutable: despite the respect with which it is vested, it is alive, constantly changing and evolving. The future will have a different ideal from that which obtains now. New ideas and aspirations appear which modify or even revolutionize existing morality. It is the moralist's role to prepare the ground for these necessary transformations. And since he is not held back by the established morality, he claims the right to sweep it completely aside should his principles so demand. He is at liberty to create something original and break new ground. Through him all the many currents, which run through society and over which minds are divided, attain awareness and are given conscious expression. It is, in fact, as a direct response to these currents that moral doctrines are engendered. Only those periods which are divided over morality are morally inventive. And when traditional morality goes unchallenged, when there is no apparent need to renew it, moral thought falls into decline.

Moral speculation, which we first thought was scientific in nature, has thus practical aims too. It is the product of thought and reflection; but it is also an element of life, which is why it is said to be both an art and a science. It tends to direct the actions not just of individuals but equally of societies. It claims that its directives are based on more or less positive data. Yet this mixed form of speculation is not confined to morality. It continues to be a feature of educational theory[3] and politics, as it was formerly of medicine and alchemy. It may well be that this ambiguity is not in keeping with the demands of strict logic. The methods employed by science and art differ; there is in fact a fundamental antithesis between them.[4] The domain of science is the past and the present, which it attempts to interpret as accurately as possible. Art is turned towards the future which it seeks to anticipate and construct in advance. But whenever thought is applied to a new order of facts, it does so in response to certain vital and more or less urgent needs. When it performs an active function in this way, it borrows the methods of action, employing them in conjunction with its own. This is how such combinations arise, of which morality, as it is commonly understood, offers us another example.

II

It is incontestably difficult to conceive of moral speculation without some practical feature. The chief object of the rules of morality is to direct action. So speculation as to the rules of morality cannot be dissociated from action. There is no science worthy of the name which does not ultimately become an art, otherwise it would be no more than a game, an intellectual pastime, erudition pure and simple. This is all the more applicable, then, to speculation whose object and subject alike is action itself. Consideration of the practical side of morality merely for the sake of amusement seems somewhat unnatural. The moralist, who went no further than studying morality as a theorist, without seeking to anticipate the ideal form it is destined to realize, would therefore be fulfilling only part of his task.

So how is this practical problem to be tackled?

Moralists of all schools have hitherto proceeded as follows. They postulate that the complete system of moral rules is subsumed within one cardinal notion, of which it is merely the development. They strive to discover this notion and, once they believe they have been successful, all they need do is to deduce the particular precepts it implies and they will have attained the ideal, perfect morality. It is of scant importance whether this morality coincides with or contradicts the one men actually practise. Its task is to dictate morals, to lay down rules for them, without having to follow them. It has no concern with ethics (*l'éthique*) as it is, but only with ethics as it should be.

But how is this fundamental notion to be attained? According to a school which has played a considerable role in the history of thought, but which has only a small number of followers today, the moral idea is part and parcel of our natural make-up. It is something we find ready-made within us, engraved upon our *conscience*.[5] To discover it we have only to look deep within ourselves, to subject ourselves to scrupulous examination and analysis. But even supposing the notion of morality originated in this way, we cannot distinguish it from the other ideas in our minds, unless we already possess a *représentation* of what is moral and what is not – in other words, unless we are already in possession of the very notion we are seeking to discover. The problem is merely transposed, not resolved.

Generally, it is to psychology that the moralist turns for this initial idea.It is accepted as self-evident that as morality is the supreme rule of conduct, it must naturally be contained within our idea of human nature and must be deduced from it. If we know what man is, then *ipso facto*, we know how he should behave in the principal areas of life. And is this not precisely what morality is? Morality would therefore appear to be the simple application of laws that psychology claims to have established.

But to begin with, this concept of morality as applied psychology fails to take proper account of one of the distinctive features of morality. Applied physics or chemistry, hygiene or therapy, deduce from the propositions established by the respective sciences the instruments of action which the applied sciences place at man's disposal for the achievement of the aims he is pursuing. The engineer, for instance, derives the means to build bridges from mechanics and the doctor turns to the laws of normal or pathological biology in his search for cures. Yet none of these techniques legislates on the ends themselves which they take as given. The supposition is that men attach value to them and are concerned solely with the most efficient and practical ways of attaining them. It is a different matter with morality. Morality consists above all in positing ends. It lays down aims man is bound to pursue and is thereby distinguished from the applied sciences as such.

First draft[6]

Moreover, how might moral ends be deduced from psychology? Psychology studies man in all ages, in all countries – man always and everywhere identical to himself. Like the laws of the physical world, psychological laws do not vary. The moral ideal, on the other hand, varies according to time and place. The Roman ideal was no more that of the Greeks than the ideal of the Middle Ages is ours.

83

And this diversity does not stem from a sort of deep-seated aberration which blinds man to his true destiny; it is rooted in the nature of things. The morality which a nation subscribes to expresses its temperament, its mentality and the conditions in which it lives. It is a product of its history and an integral element of all civilizations. Yet, whereas all civilizations have a common basis, they resemble one another only in their most general features. Each has its own particular character and therefore depends only in part upon human faculties in general. The same may be said of morality.

The decisive objection raised by this method is as follows. If we suppose that morality does really express man's nature, it cannot in any case correspond to more than a very particular, specific aspect of his nature, which is to say, the moral aspect. The development of our speculative, aesthetic faculties, of all the various technical aptitudes, of physical strength, etc., is undeniably of the greatest human interest, but morality has no part in it. It is not the task of morality to stipulate how intelligence should be cultivated, the body rendered more supple, tastes refined, human skills increased. Nor should it be concerned with directing all forms of action, or all practical faculties, but only moral ones. It has sometimes been said that morality is the rule of conduct; but this is too general, for it is only certain modes of conduct that morality governs, namely, those with moral ends. But which are they? However important the moral element in man may be, it is not everything. Yet, if that is so, what distinguishes this element from others? How can it be recognized? What properties make it stand out? By what signs is it manifest? Psychology ignores these questions, which it is the function of morality itself to resolve.

As a rule discussion of these matters proceeds as if the question simply resolved itself – as if the solution were the same for everyone. Are not all decent people in agreement as to the nature of good and evil, and consequently about the distinctive characteristics of what is moral? 'Is there any need,' asks Fouillée,[7] 'for lengthy studies in history, comparative jurisprudence or religion' simply in order to find out 'why we should not kill, steal, rape, etc.', or what is the origin of 'brotherly love, respect for children . . . the keeping of promises'? These are self-evident truths, immediately perceptible to the *conscience* at the level of intuition. It is, of course, well known that philosophers disagree over the way morality should be formulated and conceptualized, hence the debates which have gone on since philosophy first applied itself to moral matters. Yet despite these disagreements, it is generally felt that morality can be sub-sumed in a very simple view, that it is founded on an elementary notion which does not presuppose a laborious, methodical or scientific investigation, which could not lead to any true discoveries. Is it not generally said that morality is a matter for everyone, that it is given to all *consciences* and that the question of discovering it simply does not arise?

Yet what justification is there for ascribing to morality such a privileged place in the context of reality as a whole? In science there is no such thing as an immediately self-evident reality. Nor is there a reality which does not first have to be treated as an unknown quantity, whose inner nature is only revealed progressively. Scientists start by noting the outermost signs which point to its existence. These are then replaced by other signs and termed[8] . . . their nature, and psychology cannot answer all these questions by itself.

Second draft[9]

It will be said that the aim of these practices is to arrive at an under-standing of human nature and that, seen in this light, they are no more than practical corollaries and applications of psychology. But to start with, the imperative way they impose themselves, their obligatory nature which, as we shall see, is an inherent and in-dispensable part of them, would be inexplicable if this were truly how they originated. If they merely expressed human nature and were no more than a development of it, then they would not be imposed upon it. And if they are imposed upon it, it is because they convey something other than man, because they convey another order of reality, because they are in some sense more than human. Also, it is because they are related to another world which calls for another type of science.

In addition, when it is said that morality expresses man – man's ends – what is meant is that man has a specific and immutable nature which is always and everywhere identical. It is this per-manent being who belongs to no specific country or epoch that psychology studies. Yet in fact, man, the living creature, could never be contained within the narrow confines of any set and rigid formula. All life is richly endowed with seeds which are infinite in number and variety. Some of these have already sprung into being as a specific response to the demands and present requirements of the environment. Yet many are dormant, potential and unused for the present, though perhaps soon with the advent of new circumstances, they will spring into existence. All life is change and is alien to that which is static. A living creature is not intended for one end only but may be directed towards very different ends and may adapt to any number of situations. It is always premature to say that a living creature is intended for one single type of existence and to lay down in advance a set type of existence from which it cannot diverge. Such fixedness is the negation of life. And it can never definitively be said that this is what the living creature is and that it can never be anything else.

This is all the more true then of human nature. Not only is history the natural context of human life, but man is a product of history. If, disregarding his historical context, we attempt to see him as fixed, static, and outside time, we only denature him. And a man who is static is no longer a man at all. It is not just secondary aspects or characteristics of his nature that he reveals in the course of time, but deep-seated, essential qualities, ways of acting, and basic patterns of thought. The primitive does not conceive of time, space, strength, cause, etc., in the same way as modern man. The notions which are basic to man's mentality have undergone changes at various points in history. The sense of personality which lies at the root of our present morality is a latecomer to the scene and was not found even among the Romans, except in a veiled, obscure form. The way man situates himself in the world, the way he conceives of his relations with other beings and with his fellow men varies according to conditions of time and place. Yet the moral ideal is always closely dependent on man's conception of himself and his place in the universe. It cannot therefore be deduced from the abstract laws of psychology which are invariable. Moreover, is it not one of history's truths that morality is among the essential elements of civilization, and is it not well known that civilization is an essentially changing phenomenon which, though dependent in its most general attributes on the generic constitution of man, none the less exists in the most diverse forms and modes? It must therefore be dependent on some cause which is itself essentially variable, and which consequently cannot be connected solely and directly with the human faculties in general.[10]

Finally, if we suppose that morality does express man's nature, it cannot correspond to more than a very particular aspect of that nature, which is to say, moral nature. The development of the speculative and aesthetic faculties, of all the various technical aptitudes, of physical strength, etc., is undeniably of the greatest human interest, but it has nothing to do with morality. It is not the task of morality to stipulate how intelligence should be cultivated, the body rendered more supple, tastes refined, and human skills increased; nor should it be concerned with directing all the forces of action and all the practical faculties, but only the moral ones. But which are they? That is what we must find out. However important the moral element in man may be, it is not everything. Yet, if that is so, what distinguishes this element from the others? How can it be recognized? What properties make it stand out? By what signs is it manifest? Even if human nature did subsume this ideal entirely, morality cannot be deduced from it until these questions have been answered. For it is not known what constitutes the moral nature of man and what makes him a moral being.

As a general rule, discussion of these matters proceeds as if the question were not a question at all and simply resolved itself; as if the solution were a foregone conclusion, the same for everyone. Are not all decent people in agreement as to the nature of good and evil and consequently as regards the distinctive characteristics of what is moral? (Quotation from Fouillée.)[11] It is, of course, well known that philosophers disagree over the way morality should be formulated, conceptualized and characterized, hence the debates which have gone on since philosophy first applied itself to moral matters. And yet, despite these disagreements which are nevertheless telling and clearly testify to the fact that the reality at issue here is not manifest in itself, philosophers are unanimous in believing that morality may be entirely summed up in a very simple view. The view is founded upon an elementary self-evident notion which cannot, in any circumstances be discovered by methodical, laborious and, strictly speaking, scientific research. It is simply seen as a self-evident truth. It may well be that man's perception of what constitutes it differs; yet though it poses problems, it is not of itself the cause or the result of problems. What is important is to isolate this truth without confusing it with any other and to

87

formulate it as circumstances require. But everyone recognizes that this truth can at least be stated.

In fact, what kind of self-evident truth can this be if no one can agree what it actually is and if men bicker over how it should be expressed? And in a general sense, with what justification is it claimed that a truth or moral reality simply reveals itself to the observer? For the scientist there is no such thing as self-evident reality; there is no reality but that which at the outset of the inquiry is not and should not be treated as an 'x', as a complete unknown. In order to discover it, external signs are first used which most clearly reveal it. Then, as the investigation proceeds, these outward tangible signs are replaced by others. Only when one has gone beyond the level of tangible appearances does it become possible to discover the innermost characteristics of the thing, which pertain to its very essence, insofar as this word can be used in scientific language. All that scientists know about light and electricity when they begin to study them, is what they derive through their senses. They see before them an object to be studied. It is only when they proceed to a deeper analysis that they are able to reach a different conception. Why should it be otherwise with moral reality? We are told that it pertains to man's nature. But man's nature is complex. What does it express? The individual or the collective being? And if it is either of these, what aspect does it convey? If we wish to adopt the mental approach required by the scientific method then we must freely admit that, at this stage in the investigation, we know nothing about it, nor could we know anything. We are in complete ignorance of what makes man a moral being and what has given rise to the various attitudes, ideas, and feelings which go to make up morality. Why is it that man exhibits such an integration, such a highly particular attitude of mind and will, which is not known in animals, except in an indirect and purely analogous form? To what do these states and attitudes correspond in reality? And what is there in the human environment which determines and accounts for them?[12]

Clearly in practice, men take and must take moral truths for granted, regarding them as unquestionable truisms. So deeply rooted are they in the *conscience* of every normal person that they are beyond doubt. Yet they serve as a basis for action, even though no one pauses to consider them or thinks them worthy of consideration. And if they are to act as effective guides to behaviour, they must be accepted as axiomatic truths. Historically speaking, in a situation when the ideas and principles upon which a particular morality is based no longer enjoy sufficient credit to command with authority, and when their legitimacy begins to be questioned, and their reasons challenged, it is because this morality is on the point of collapse. It is because it is no longer sure of itself which it cannot be without losing some of its sovereignty. Yet it is practical truths of this kind that we live by, even if they are truths in name alone and respond only to certain needs for action. So that we can cope satisfactorily with the things of the tangible world, we evolve certain *représentations*. In our minds we portray (*nous nous représentons*) the wind as a breath, the sun as a flat disc a few centimetres wide, and light as a tenuous, intangible body which passes through the air like an arrow, and so on. The scientist divests himself of this so-called truth and replaces these false but useful notions with others, arrived at by quite different methods. There is every reason to believe that the same must be true of moral matters. The *représentation* that the common man has of them cannot correspond to the reality. It may well meet the needs of everyday practice, but it does not convey the essence of things and consequently cannot give rise to new practices.

In conclusion, if it is true to say that the ultimate aim of every morality is to formulate an ideal – a morality superior to that by which men actually live – such a construction presupposes at least one notion which cannot be postulated, which is not found ready-made within us and can only result from a whole body of research, from a complete science. This is the idea of what is moral. What constitutes this science?

The notion of what life is can only come from the science of life, whose advances it takes over and digests. The idea of morality, if it is to be other than a matter of mere common sense, can only be arrived at by the scientific study of moral facts (*faits*). Whatever one's conception of the moral ideal is, morality exists as an observable reality. And even though, at this stage, we do not yet know what makes up moral facts, it can be taken as certain that the word morality, which occurs in various forms in all languages, connotes phenomena which are distinguished from all other human phenomena by clearly defined and uniform characteristics.[13]

To what order of reality do they belong? We cannot say at this point. Whether they are emanations of the individual *conscience* or products of the collective mentality will have to be determined at a subsequent stage in this study. Yet everything allows us to suppose that they are – that they constitute – a category of natural things. So they may, and one can even say in advance that they must, be the subject matter of a science, no matter what our concept of this science is. There must be a way of analysing, classifying and arranging them according to type, of determining their place in the totality of other phenomena, and the causes on which they depend, etc. And it is from such descriptions, analyses, classifications and explanations that the notion of morality must come, a notion which moralists suppose and assume in their doctrines but do not justify. In a word, only the study of moral life can reveal these distinctive properties and can reveal the essence of the moral fact from which it seems possible to deduce the moral ideal in every detail. Even if, as has so often been the case, we suppose that the moral idea does exist wholly and entirely within us and that we are endowed with it as part of our natural make-up, we can only discover it if we begin with an analysis of moral facts. For it is in and through them that the idea becomes a reality, and through them that it can be discovered. To distinguish it from all the other ideas which in varying degrees of importance co-exist with it in our *conscience*, we must use as our starting point these facts – these precepts and practices which express it and convey it more or less adequately. Thereafter we must work back step by step to the fundamental conception from which they stem. If it is true that this inner source of moral life really exists within us, it is at all events through this means alone that we can succeed in discovering it.

Thus, the art of morality and the construction of the moral ideal presuppose an entire science which is positive and inductive and encompasses all the details of moral facts.

This science is much more extensive and complex than even the outline above might suggest. If we accept what has just been said, such a science may be reduced to one single problem: its sole task is to determine the distinctive features of what is moral. Once this notion has been discovered, the art of morality would attempt to outline the moral ideal. Yet, in reality, no science can ever be contained completely in one single problem. The questions it asks are always as many and varied as the facts it studies. And indeed, the problem posed by morality as a whole is repeated in various forms and conditions for each area of moral life in turn. If the moralist needs to know what morality is in a general way, he cannot discuss domestic morality, for instance, unless he first determines the numerous precepts comprising this part of morality, and also their causes and the ends to which they respond. Only later does it become possible to investigate how these precepts must be modified, rectified, and idealized. Is one is to say how family morality is likely to evolve, one must first know how the family is constituted, how it came to assume its present form and what its function is in society as a whole; then how the various domestic duties relate to this function, and so on. Similarly, professional, civic and international morality must also be investigated; in a word, each of the categories of duty.

Moreover, it is easy to see that the generic notion of the moral can be no more than a summary or synthesis of these particular notions themselves: the first is only as valid as the rest. And if one is to gain some idea of what is essential in moral facts, a schematic, more or less summary view is inadequate. Of course at the outset of our investigation, if we are to ascertain what it is we are to study and determine its scope, we may base our definition of these facts upon their visible, external features. As we shall see, this may even be necessary. Yet although these initial, provisional definitions cannot be dispensed with, if we are to obtain a clear idea of where to find and how to recognize the data this science should study, they nevertheless tell us nothing about the fundamental nature of these data. This is only gradually revealed as we come to grips with the reality, as it is (described [*sic*]) analysed in all its various aspects and as the examination of the individual facts proceeds. One cannot speculate on the nature of the moral ideal by means of summary generalities. Rather, what is required is the exploration of a whole area.

The method generally employed by moralists therefore requires drastic revision.

They generally take as their starting point a formula of morality which, as we have seen, has been established by ill-defined procedures and which in actual fact merely expresses their own feelings. From this they then deduce – or so they believe – the moral practices they propose man should adopt. But this formula, for what it is worth, can only be the conclusion of an entire science devoted to the study of moral rules in detail; a conclusion which, furthermore, can only be provisional and subject to constant revision, moving step by step with advances in the science from which it is derived. But this science is still in its infancy. So far, only a mere handful of sociologists have been involved in it. Yet there scarcely exists a more urgent task, for the predictions of moral art neither have, nor could have, any other basis than this science of moral facts, which have been assembled and collated.

The name we now give to this science is the 'science or natural philosophy of social norms' (*science ou physique des moeurs*).[14] The word *moeurs* denotes in our view that morality (*morale*) which men actually observe throughout history and which is vested with the authority of tradition, as contrasted with what the moralist conceives as the morality of the future. But this term is not without a certain ambiguity and has in fact led to a number of misunderstandings. It seems clear that the morality (*morale*) obtaining in a particular epoch is embodied in social norms (*moeurs*) though in a degraded form and reduced to the level of human mediocrity. What social norms convey is the average man's way of applying the rules of morality (*morale*), and he never applies them without compromise or reservation. The motives on which he acts are mixed: some are noble and pure, others vulgar and base. The science we are outlining, on the other hand, aims to discover moral precepts in all their purity and impersonality. Its subject matter is morality (*morale*) itself, ideal morality which is situated in a region above the realm of human actions. It is not concerned with the deformations that its embodiment in everyday practice impose upon it and which can only express it imperfectly.[15] How this can be achieved will have to be discussed. But if this is in fact its subject matter, it would be best to give it an appropriate name. We shall therefore call it the 'science of morality (*morale*)' or the 'science of moral facts (*faits moraux*)' meaning by this that it deals with moral phenomena, with moral reality, as it appears to observation, whether in the present or in the past, just as physics or physiology deal with the facts they study. As for speculations about the future, they are only applied science.

The work of which we now offer the first volume is intended to provide a complete survey of the current state of this science, to describe therefore and to explain to the best of our knowledge the principal facts of moral life, and to draw from these theoretical studies the practical conclusions implicit in them.

But before we begin to discuss the data in detail, there are a number of interim questions to be examined, which will be the object of this introductory volume, and which are as follows:

1 Moral facts cannot be studied unless we know where to look for them, in other words, unless we know which order of reality they belong to. It is quite clear that they are phenomena which relate to *conscience*. But do they relate to the individual or collective *conscience*? And, if they do fall within the province of these two, what proportion does each of them occupy and what role do they play? (Book I)

2 If, as we propose to establish, they are essentially social, and if it is primarily their social aspect that scientific research should concentrate on, what features distinguish them from other social data? (Book II)

3 What is their place in the collective life as a whole? (Book III)

4 Finally, once they have been sited, located and distinguished, and their relation with the phenomena to which they are most closely akin has been established, we shall be in a position to investigate what scientific method should be adopted to deal with them, and also how practical conclusions may be deduced from these theoretical, scientific studies.

Notes

1 [The course of lectures by Durkheim, which Mauss calls 'Physique des moeurs' and in other places 'Physiologie des moeurs', were not in fact published by Mauss but by a Turkish professor of law, H. N. Kubali, in 1950. They appeared under the title *Leçons de sociologie: physique des moeurs et du droit*. In 1957 there was an English translation, *Professional Ethics and Civic Morals*, made by C. Brookfield. Kubali translated six of the lectures into Turkish in 1947 from manuscripts Mauss had apparently given him in 1934. With the help of Mme Halphen, Durkheim's daughter, Kubali was later able to obtain a complete set of lectures in manuscript form which were published in conjunction with the University of Istanbul in, as has been said, 1950. Earlier, Mauss did publish three of the lectures with the title 'Morale professionelle' in 1937, together with introductory notes in the *Revue de métaphysique et de morale*, vol. XLIX.

   The courses Durkheim gave on ethics were many and varied – one course often being a reworking of another. Many of the manuscripts have been lost and the titles of the courses as they have been recorded are confusing and the sources sometimes contradictory.

Mauss refers to such courses in his introductory note of 1937 and in his 'In memoriam, l'oeuvre inédite de Durkheim et de ses collaborateurs' (*L'Année sociologique*, n.s. 1, pp. 7–29). Mauss himself seems to be inconsistent in enumerating and explaining the contents of the courses on ethics, and when they were given. Lukes in trying to unravel the situation observes: '[Mauss] cannot necessarily be relied on for strict accuracy in information of this kind' (Lukes 1972:617 note). We too would underline this observation. (Should the reader wish to pursue this subject he is referred to the articles by Mauss and to Lukes's observations, e.g. 1972:255–7, 263, 617–20, etc.) It might be briefly noted that Durkheim gave courses of lectures with the title 'Physiologie (ou Physique) du droit et des moeurs' from 1890 to just before he died. The set of lectures with the published title *Leçons de sociologie* were according to Mauss based upon those given between 1898 and 1900 in Bordeaux and represented part of the second year – the year itself was loosely referred to as 'La Morale pratique'. In that year there were also lectures entitled 'La Morale domestique'. The lectures as such which are said to have survived Durkheim have been lost. As Lukes notes, it was a pity that his wish that they should not be published after he died was carried out. – W.S.F.P.]

2 [The references of Mauss to Durkheim's *La Morale* are not immediately clear and should be read in conjunction with Durkheim's own comments at the end of the 'Introduction à la morale' (p. 92; all page numbers in the notes refer to pages in the translated text). From our own reconstruction, it would appear that Durkheim planned a magnum opus of at least two published volumes with the general title *La Morale*. The first volume would have had the title *Introduction à la morale*. This volume would have consisted of an introductory section together with at least three books (p. 93) in the format of his previous *Elementary Forms of the Religious Life* (1912a). The introductory section of the *Introduction* was planned to have some introductory pages, and these are reproduced here in translated form (1920a), with the title, according to Mauss, of 'Aim of course'. They were to be followed by the chapters 'Critique of traditional ethics' and 'Critique of Kantian ethics', as on p. 78. Book I would have contained chapters on 'Value judgment and ideal' and 'How can we attach ourselves to society?' also as on p. 78 Mauss noted that Durkheim might have included the contents of other lectures in the volume. Apart from what Durkheim wrote (p. 93), we know nothing about the possible contents of Books II and III. Nor is anything known about what he intended to include in the second or subsequent volumes.

As indicated here by Mauss, *La Morale* was to have been based on various lecture courses and lectures Durkheim gave on the subject. But the problem immediately arises, what courses? What lectures? According to Lukes, working from official records, Durkheim gave the following courses in Paris with the general title 'La Morale': 'La Morale' (including 'Morale civique et professionnelle'), 1904/5; 'La Morale', 1908/9; 'La Morale' (suite), 1909/10; 'La Morale' (suite);

'Droit et propriété – Morale contractuelle – Morale individuelle', 1910/11; 'La Morale' (including 'La Morale civique et professionnelle'), 1914/15. One would have imagined that in the final work Durkheim would have included something on 'La Morale domestique', 'La Morale individuelle', 'La Morale civique et professionnelle' (as in *Leçons de sociologie*, see n.1 above). All this would have roughly corresponded to La Morale pratique, corresponding to the second year of Durkheim's 1898–1900 course. To the first year Mauss gives the title 'La Morale théorique' or 'La Morale de la société' and the *Introduction à la morale* would in all probability have corresponded to this. There is one other source of evidence about the lecture course on 'La Morale'. It comes from the notes of former students Georges Davy and A. Cuvillier taken during the course, probably that of 1908/9. (The notes are to be found in the doctoral dissertation of Lukes, 1968, vol. 2:248–60 and 261–97. We have given them the dating-enumeration 1968c and 1968d.) Attention also ought to be drawn to various lectures Durkheim gave on moral education while he was professor at the Sorbonne (for example, 1925a; 1968a. See Lukes 1972:619–20). – W.S.F.P.]

3 [See 1909a(2), translated here. – W.S.F.P.]

4 [On the problem of the relation of art and science, see Durkheim *Les Formes élémentaires de la vie religieuse* (1912a:544ff./t.1915d:381ff.) and *L'Éducation morale* (1925a:306ff./t.1961a:267ff.). – W.S.F.P.]

5 [This is a reference to Kant and his school. – W.S.F.P.]

6 (This is the only problem in Durkheim's manuscript. From here on, all paragraphs are repeated in almost exactly the same order at the beginning of the part we have termed second draft. But the manuscript is continuous as far as p. 85 (English translation) where, as the reader will see, it stops and then resumes, becoming continuous once again as of the second draft. The reader is given the opportunity of seeing both texts. But it is clear that it was the second draft that was to be the definitive one. Nevertheless, when one considers Durkheim's painstaking attitude to his manuscripts, the note 'Quotation from Fouillée' (p. 87, referring to p. 84) is an unequivocal indication that he intended to get down to the process of editing, necessitated by his change of plan. The easiest approach to this chapter is to skip all paragraphs under the heading first draft, beginning again at 'It will be said . . .' (p. 85). – Marcel Mauss.)

7 [Alfred Jules Émile Fouillée (1838–1912) wrote extensively on philosophical and allied matters, including sociology. He attempted a systematic synthesis of contemporary knowledge in the vein of Herbert Spencer, and tried in particular to relate the work of Leibniz to present-day thought. He was essentially eclectic and at the same time dialectic in trying to reconcile such opposites as idealism and positivism, intuitionism and intellectualism, and above all, philosophy and (positive) science. He was also influenced by Plato, Descartes, Kant and Schopenhauer. He was a rationalist who favoured evolutionism but was opposed to any mechanical form of it. Durkheim reviewed several of his books (1885b, 1901a(iii)(45), 1907a(3)); and although *Les Éléments*

sociologiques de la morale (1905) was dedicated to Durkheim, he accused Fouillée of misunderstanding him. Durkheim said he did not attempt to be descriptive in method but to search for explanation, function and basic social needs. He repeatedly criticized Fouillée for being *simpliste* and utopian in his concept of society and its reform. — W.S.F.P.]

8 (At this point there is a gap, the sentence is left unfinished at the bottom of the page. But filed away with the rest of the manuscript was another unfinished page which clearly carries on from this sentence. One has only to omit the two final words 'and termed' along with the first three words of the correction 'progressively' and the text then reads 'replacing them with others as one goes along' etc. The text is as follows:

Progressively the investigation proceeds. Only when one has gone beyond the level of tangible appearances does it become possible to discover the innermost characteristics of the thing, which pertain to its very essence, in so far as this word can be (used) in scientific language. All the scientist knows about light and electricity when he begins to study them he has through his senses. All he sees is an object to be studied and about which he knows nothing. It is only when he proceeds to a deeper analysis that he is able to come to a different conclusion. Why should it be any different with moral reality?

This paragraph reoccurs in the second draft. — Marcel Mauss.)

9 (This second draft begins with a gap which cannot be a very large one and must have continued at roughly the point we have indicated Durkheim had resumed his redrafting (p. 83). – Marcel Mauss.)

10 (Durkheim has added in the margin) There is such a thing as man in general. But this is not man in his entirety. Man is always alike, always identical, yet always different.

11 [Compare the reference to Fouillée in the first draft. See n.7 above. – W.S.F.P.]

12 [Traugott (1978:267 n.3) suggests that the second draft ended here – W.S.F.P.]

13 (In the margin, the words) These are precepts of a certain kind whose singular properties are clearly perceived by everyone.

14 In teaching, the term we used was the natural philosophy or science of morals and law. Explanation of the two words.

15 (In the margin, the words) Opposition between *moeurs* and *morale*.

Part II **Education**

Introduction
by W. S. F. Pickering

It is becoming increasingly recognized that Durkheim was not just one of the founding fathers of sociology but the founder of the sociology of education. As a pioneer of the subject, he was firmly convinced — and an example of this is in a review which follows (1904a(40) and (41)) — that educational theory must not only be informed by psychology but by sociology as well. When he was writing at the end of the nineteenth century, educational theory was dominated by psychological analysis. Durkheim always admitted the validity of psychology but held that a psychological explanation had to be given within a certain social context. Education is predominantly a social matter which is governed by social needs and social ideals. He therefore stood opposed not only to those who gave pride of place to psychology (see, for example, 1905f(2)) but also to those who stressed the primacy of the individual in education, such as H. Spencer, J. S. Mill, and even Immanuel Kant whom he appeared to admire in so many other ways. For them the object of education was above all else the fullest realization of the distinctive attributes of the individual (1922a:4/t.1956a:30). If one adopts a purely individualistic ideal then clearly psychology has a supreme place to play within the theory of education. But Durkheim's point is that the amount of education that is given, to whom it is given, what is taught, the milieu in which it is taught, are all matters controlled by society and therefore in the past and in the future have been and will be determined by socio-historical factors. Education, in short, is a function of the social organization of society.

Since education is so eminently a social matter — the young are taught by adults to be adults — it is hardly surprising that Durkheim saw that it stood firmly within the province of sociology, the discipline he was attempting to establish in France, a discipline which was so dear to his heart and which he felt would have positively good results for the country as a whole. Further, he alone amongst sociologists made his sociology of education part of his general theory of society. Not only was Durkheim unique in giving such prominence to education compared with most other European sociologists, his enthusiasm was not even apparent amongst his own followers. Many of the Année Sociologique group which Durkheim gathered around him, preferred directing their energies to law, crime, general sociology (theory), method, and so on. Only Paul Fauconnet followed in these particular footsteps of the master but apart from editing posthumous lectures of Durkheim, he published nothing original in education. He was given Durkheim's chair in sociology but he died prematurely after World War I having taught educational theory for a time. Another member of the *équipe*, Paul Lapie, who lectured in philosophy in Bordeaux and was rector of Toulouse University, became involved in primary education in 1914 as a government administrator (Director), not as an academic who lectured and wrote on the subject. And in the journal, *L'Année sociologique*, books and articles on education were thinly reviewed and were not given a section to themselves. Perhaps there was not enough of them to warrant anything more than a few pages at the end of the last section of reviews (section VII, Divers). Even those Durkheimians who did show some interest in educational theory tended to reduce it to its relations to morality and law.

Generally speaking, the sociologist of education found it difficult being accepted even in France, where the importance of education was from time to time perceived by university authorities. However, Durkheim lamented that there was an old French prejudice that looked with contempt on the whole business of educational theory (1938a:10/t.1977a:4). And what Durkheim said about France might also be said to be true of sociology until very recently, namely, that whereas political systems are held to be of supreme importance, 'educational systems inspire indifference . . . or even a kind of instinctive aversion' (ibid.).

In England there appeared to be an even stronger dislike of education than in France. The major universities, particularly Oxford and Cambridge, projected an air of strong indifference or even disapproval of preparing teachers systematically for their vocation. Teaching was something that was caught not taught. Or, if it was seen as a technical subject, it was beyond the dignity and concern of those who controlled the older, traditional English universities. Certainly it was not an academic subject but was generally

seen as something that came automatically to the amateur gentle-
man. England during the nineteenth century never had an equivalent of *agrégation* of the French universities, which was a minimum
qualification necessary to teach in a university or lycée.

Durkheim was compelled to come to terms with the subject of
educational theory in practice because his first appointment in the
University of Bordeaux in 1887 was chargé d'un cours de science
sociale et de pédagogie. It was only under the umbrella of education that sociology was first introduced into a French university.
But from the beginning it was apparent that Durkheim did not take
his duties of lecturing in education as a chore to be discarded as
quickly as possible, but rather as an integral part of his task of
establishing sociology and integrating within it the role of education. Whilst he was in Bordeaux he gave weekly lectures on
educational theory to primary school teachers, as well as lectures
in sociology. When he was appointed to Paris in 1902, he took
over the work of Ferdinand Buisson, professor of education,
and his title was chargé d'un cours de science de l'éducation. In
1906 he was made professor. Neither of the titles of appointment
carried any reference to sociology. It was not until 1913, and at his
own request, that his chair was renamed Science de l'éducation
et de la sociologie. Fauconnet, who edited the collection of items
which appeared as *Éducation et sociologie* (1922a/t.1956a),
reckoned that between one-third and two-thirds of Durkheim's
lecturing time was given to educational subjects. In some respects it
is true to say that Durkheim was primarily an educationalist!
Those who would see him essentially as a sociological theorist
should not forget this fact.

Most of what we know about Durkheim's sociology of education
comes from books which were published posthumously. In the
main they are the contents of lecture courses he gave which were
formulated around the turn of the century. None the less they stem
from Durkheim's most creative period, roughly from 1895 to 1906.
L'Éducation morale (1925a/t.1961a) was his most systematic treatment of teaching in schools and was given in various editions from
1889 to 1912 in Bordeaux and Paris. His great lecture course on
university education, *L'Évolution pédagogique en France* (1938a/
t.1977a) was also begun at this time in Paris and continued over
many years. The opening lecture was published in 1906 (1906c)
and was included in a set of four essays, *Éducation et sociologie*,

published in 1922 (1922a/t.1956a). Two of the essays were reprints of articles which were originally to be found in Ferdinand Buisson's *Nouveau dictionnaire de pédagogie* (1911). (For full details of 1922a, see Bibliography.) A third article which Durkheim contributed to the dictionary was written in conjunction with Buisson and is translated here (1911c(2)). From 1888 onwards, Durkheim lectured on the classics of educational theory. The only remnants of these lectures that have come down to us are the notes he himself wrote on Rousseau's *Émile*, which again were published posthumously, in 1919, and which are also translated here. Considering the amount of lecturing that Durkheim devoted to education, it is most regrettable that very little has been handed down to posterity. The manuscripts of most of his lectures have been lost and the position is only partially remedied by the fact that certain students have kept notes of the lectures they heard. In 1903–4 Durkheim gave a course of lectures entitled 'De l'Enseignement de la morale à l'école primaire' and notes of these were made by Raymond Lenoir (1968a, reproduced in Lukes 1968 vol. 2:147–241). However, there are some scholars who would maintain that the authenticity of the notes is not absolutely certain (*RFS*, XVII, 1976:196). (For full details of the titles of all Durkheim's courses on education, see Lukes 1972:617–20.) A few items were published during Durkheim's lifetime on the subject of education, in addition to those which have been mentioned so far. Some of them are translated here and full details can be found in the Bibliography.

It was not only the demands of his university appointment and his conviction of the rightful place of educational theory within social theory that forced Durkheim to see the importance of education in society. His own experience carried an inner conviction. Born in Lorraine he was particularly aware of the swift and humiliating defeat France suffered in 1870 at the hands of the Germans, which was followed by the disastrous Commune. Part of the blame was thought to lie in France's educational system, which had changed but little since the time of Napoleon, and which, unlike the German system, gave relatively little place to the sciences. It was commonly said that the war had been won by German schoolmasters. Honoured by the French government while he was a lycée teacher, Durkheim was sent to Germany in 1885–6 to visit German universities. He was able to see at first hand how such institutions had developed the natural sciences and also how they applied the method to areas other than those of natural phenomena, for example, human behaviour. He also saw that the German educational system as a whole was able to inculcate scientific knowledge in a large section of the population. He was convinced, as were many other middle-class intellectuals, that the revitalization of France had to proceed from a new and invigorated teaching system. He believed that his particular contribution was in offering a scientific basis to the emerging secular morality and also the means of extending it by the training of qualified teachers. They would go forth into the world, grounded in sociology and also the techniques of communicating it to school children. The parish priest had no place in the secular thinking of the Third Republic. Its avowedly lay or secular outlook could only be propagated in the parishes through the schoolmaster or schoolmistress – the lay priest and priestess – who would offer an alternative system of values and morality to that centred on the parish church and the curé. In such thinking and strategy Durkheim, in the company of others who held similar ideas, such as Buisson, Pécaut and Jacob, could well be called a leading idéologue of the Third Republic, especially during the two decades which preceded the First World War. The foundation of secular education stems from the earlier thinker, Edgar Quinet (1803–75). Ideas based on 'la morale laïque' were incorporated into the reforms in primary education carried out by Jules Ferry in the early 1880s.

The educational processes supported by Durkheim and others were thus intended to inculcate the ideal of modern secular man. Durkheim openly admitted in 1905 success in this direction and that his influence over teachers seemed to be for the good (see 1905b on p. 36; also implicit in 1916c, on p. 158). In 1906 his course on education (1938a) was declared compulsory for all *agrégation* students working in sciences and letters. By this means his influence on secondary school teaching was assured. After his death the alleged dominance of Durkheimian thought in teachers' training colleges became an issue that provoked considerable national opposition and political disturbance (see, for example, Bouglé 1938; Richard 1923 and 1928; Pickering 1979). Paul Lapie, a disciple of Durkheim who has already been mentioned, introduced, as director of primary education, sociology within the course of civil ethics and political economy. Doubtless taken by surprise at the suddenness and strength of the opposition, in which Jean

Izoulet (professor of sociology at the Collège de France) was provoked to make outrageous statements, Lapie found it wise to return to administration in the academic world (see Izoulet 1928). The whole episode has yet to be carefully assessed. However, there can be no doubt that Durkheim thought it right that education, its institutions and its curricula should be used for what we might call ideological purposes. In Durkheim's eyes, education is nothing if it is not ideological, since its object is to create adults out of children who reflect the ideals of their society. It is not to fulfil the innate needs of a child, though certain societies may claim that this is their overt aim. Even if it is, then that claim issues from society itself.

This brief introduction cannot consider the content of Durkheim's sociology of education as a whole. It is beyond its scope to show Durkheim's extraordinarily wide coverage of the subject and how he raised many issues that are still being dealt with by sociologists today. Nor is it possible to raise in detail and consider the validity of criticisms levelled against his work, such as the confusion he made between co-operation and restraint, his failure to deal with the issues of power, élitism and class divisions in education, and the inevitable weakness of the term society, which is crucial to his theory (see, for example, Loureau 1969). Nor again can there be a consideration of the proposition that his analysis was essentially related to the French situation and has little to relevance outside it. For such exposition and assessment the reader's attention is drawn to analyses that have already been published (see de Gaudemar 1969; Lukes 1972:ch.6; Wallwork 1972:ch.5). Not without significance is the fact that until only recently there was very little indeed by way of a critical commentary on Durkheim's sociology of education. All that this introduction attempts to do is to refer briefly to the items translated in the pages that follow, which have not been available before in English, and to show their place within Durkheim's approach to education.

Definitions

Some difficulty in understanding Durkheim's sociology of education has always arisen from his use of particular words, which appear to be similar or synonymous, but which in his thought need to be differentiated. The words are *éducation*, *enseignement*, *pédagogie*. Peter Collins in his translation of Durkheim's *L'Évolution pédagogique* rightly suggests that pedagogy and its cognates is not an appropriate word in English and so he translates *pédagogie* as educational theory (Collins 1977a:xviii–xix; also Ottaway 1955:215). This practice has been followed here. The phrase theory of education is also employed (see the translations, p. viii). Lukes, basing his observations on the opening pages of *L'Éducation morale,* states that Durkheim distinguished the scientific study of education from the art of education, and the two are combined in the word *pédagogie* – practical theory – which is 'an intermediate between art and science' (Durkheim 1925a:2/t.1961a:2. See Lukes 1972:111 n.9). Durkheim wanted to differentiate the good teacher (*maître*) from the good educational theorist. The art of education is associated with 'habit, practice, and organized skill' (ibid.) – it is *savoir faire* derived from the practical experience of the teacher. Lukes finds the distinctions 'very valuable': Collins has no enthusiasm for them.

The problem is clearly restated in the discussion on the effectiveness of moral doctrines (1909a(2), translated here). Durkheim says that *éducation* has as its object, action and application: it is directed towards the will. *Enseignement* (teaching) has for its goal, comprehension and explanation: it is to make facts intelligible. *Enseignement* is not a normative discipline, for the given facts are already before it. As chemistry does not create substances, but studies them – and here Durkheim seems somewhat naïve in his knowledge of chemistry – so *enseignement* does not create the data it examines. It is therefore not the task of teaching to bring into existence values or rules. These are given by society. The teacher's task is to communicate an explanation of them to the pupils. All this tends to confirm what Durkheim wrote in *L'Éducation morale* and by extension to see that *pédagogie* (educational theory) equals *éducation* (art of teaching) plus *enseignement* (the science of what is taught). *Pédagogie* means practical theory (1911c(3)/r.1922a:59/ t.1956a:91; see also 1910c(2)). Durkheim rightly suggests that the contrasts he makes allows one to show that educational theory, say that of Pestalozzi, was at variance with the education of his day. Thus, through educational theories, changes can be brought about. He wrote: 'Their objective is not to describe or to explain what is or has been but to determine what ought to be. They are directed not towards the present or the past, but towards the future' (1922a: 67/t.1956a:99). And let it not be overlooked that Durkheim was ardent in his support of educational reform. But *enseignement* does not allow for the possibility of social change. The starting point is always that society dictates what shall be taught, because that which is taught reflects its own ideological position. Durkheim's unwavering assumption is that the educational processes have a marked effect on the strengthening of society itself. The *teacher* is inevitably the instrument of some 'higher' social authority.

Durkheim's distinction between the art and science of education is in keeping with his general distinction between art and science (see Introduction to Part I, Morals). In his important but much overlooked chapter, 'Teaching aesthetics and history', in *Moral Education*, he relates art to the will and the senses, whereas science, based on reason and logic, is grounded in a particular method which is universally accepted by scientists. Here and also in *The Elementary Forms of the Religious Life*, Durkheim in the last analysis holds science to be in some fashion superior to art. Art has about it something that is not real, it is like a game, it is open to flights of fancy, and makes us forget life as it is. Not so science. It is based on the immovable rock of things, of reality. Art is connected with the lighter side of life: science by contrast with *'la vie sérieuse'*. After all, not all life is play, as Durkheim remarked (1925a:183/t.1961a:160). (See 1920a, translated in Part I, Morals, especially n.4, for the contrast between science and art.) Art is essentially practical: its goal is not the formulation of theory. Durkheim uses the word art in two different senses which are not clearly differentiated – art as a practical skill emanating from intuitive apperception, covering a wide range of activities; and art as creative activity, exemplified in the poet, painter, or musician.

Durkheim does not want to belittle the work of the practical teacher, indeed it is of great importance, nevertheless, according to his conceptualization, he sees the educational theorist as combining both science and art and this makes him a somewhat superior kind of being. It is through the agency of the educational theorist that changes can be brought about. Such is his unique task.

The purpose of education

It is necessary at this point to see how Durkheim defines education in general. In a well-known passage in *Education and Sociology* (1922a:41/t.1956a:71) he says education is:

> the influence exercised by adult generations on those that are not yet ready for social life. Its object is to arouse and develop in the child a certain number of physical, intellectual and moral states, which are demanded of him by both political society as a whole and the social milieu for which he is specifically destined.

Durkheim was convinced that education viewed in the widest sense had existed ever since society had existed. Indeed, education is necessary for the very being of society. The reason is simple enough (ibid:40/70):

> Society can survive only if there exists among its members a sufficient degree of homogeneity; education perpetuates and reinforces this homogeneity by fixing in the child, from the beginning, the essential similarities that collective life demands.

Man's prime vocation, the serious side of his life, is his place – and it might be added his useful place – in society. To this end, education is the necessary means. Although Durkheim called himself a humanist, and for him education is anthropocentric, his concept of man, as is well known, is not of an isolated creature, but of one whose creatureliness is found only within and is derived from society. Therefore the prime purpose of education is to make man, or rather the child, see his place within the environment and to realize its influence upon him, both as a fact and as an ideal. In this respect, as we shall see, he was a strong supporter of much of Rousseau's educational theory. But he went further. Education is the point of mediation between the individual and society, and it is therefore not only anthropocentric, it is sociocentric.

Firmly committed to liberal democracy, Durkheim was strongly opposed to the ideals of both a marxist type of society as well as one hierarchical in form and governed by royalty. However, his conception of education was not as thoroughly liberal as some might have imagined or would now think correct. It must be stressed that he never wanted education to be given for its own sake and in this sense alone he was utilitarian. He was much opposed to the humanism of the sixteenth century in so far as it exalted the search for knowledge, unchecked by discipline emanating from an external source (see, for example, 1938a:ch.16). He objected to the ideals

107

of Erasmus and Rabelais who may be said to be amongst the first in the modern period to write systematically about education. The purpose of education, Durkheim argued, should not be for aesthetic pursuits or to bolster the ego by accumulating knowledge (ibid./ t.1977a:230). By contrast, it is for 'the needs of real life'. It should be a means of gaining an occupation, of furthering a vocation, but above all, a preparation for moral life, for the acceptance of that morality which is the foundation of a given society.

Durkheim admits that education – the influence of adults over children – covers physical, intellectual and moral states in accordance with the political society and for 'the special milieu for which he (the child) is specifically destined' (1911c(1)/r.1922a:41/ t.1956a:71). All societies have a certain number of ideas, sentiments and practices which it is the purpose of education to inculcate. Within each society there is admittedly diversity, but above differences of caste, class, even religion, there is, argues Durkheim, a common morality, common ideals, even a common religion (ibid.:39/t.69). It is these which have to be imparted and accepted by the younger members of society. By education society guarantees its own survival. By it, it is able to recreate itself by insuring in its future generations an ideal image of what they ought to become. Education creates in man a new being. Such is the grandeur of the work facing the teacher and educator.

All this implies a seriousness in education. It is not fun and games – not kids' stuff. It is an adult business, by adults and for adulthood. The school is an adult institution and society is mirrored in it. Thus, education is very much part of *'la vie sérieuse'*. At its base must be authority, closely coupled with an established moral system. In more practical terms, Durkheim does not demand rigidity and rejects a military type of structure. But he sees the necessity of firmness in the light of the vulnerability of the unsocialized child and the demands of society.

With an emphasis on educational theory and moral education, there is little in his lectures which have been handed down to us which directly relates to the physical or intellectual development of the child (but see below). His primary concern was with moral teaching and character formation in an ethical rather than a psychological dimension (Wallwork 1972:123). Little wonder, then, that his most thorough work on education, which we have, apart from the historical *L'Évolution pédagogique*, should be called *L'Éduca-*

tion morale, which covered not only morality as it should be taught to children but such topics as the sociology of the classroom and discipline.

Infant education

Perhaps one of the reasons why Durkheim gave relatively little space to aspects of the child's education in its early years was that he thought that the study of the child during such years was more within the province of psychology than sociology (1904a(40) and (41), translated here). It is therefore of some general interest that included in the translations here is his article entitled 'Enfance' (1911c(2)). This was written in collaboration with Ferdinand Buisson (see n.1 on page 154) for the *Nouveau Dictionnaire de péda-gogie et d'instruction primaire*. There is much in the article which appeared in the dictionary that is difficult to associate with Durkheim, for example, the sentence about the young child: 'He is the puniest of beings, a small body that the merest blow can break, that the slightest illness imperils, a collection of muscles, nerves and organs which are, so to speak, made of milk. . . .' How much of the article is Durkheim? How much Buisson? We shall never know largely because there are no authentic lectures extant given by Durkheim on the early years of the child. Interestingly enough, the article is signed by Buisson and Durkheim, not by Durkheim and Buisson. One thing is clear however: the authors demonstrate their indebtedness to Rousseau's educational theory. They want the child to grow freely, and weak though he may be, he should not be physically hampered (see below). Education must be adapted to the capabilities of the child. And the influence of Rousseau can also be seen as they observe that 'neither good nor evil is very deep-rooted in his (the child's) nature'. The responsibility of the teacher is great, not least on account of the mental and physical fragility of the child.

However, Durkheim and Buisson suggest that although it is easy to make the child acquire habits, he also should be encouraged to adopt them. Here critics will readily alight on a change in argument, for the authors switch from the norm of freedom to be accorded to the young child to that of control, first by habit and

109

later by moral education. How and when does the change come about – the change which Durkheim speaks of as 'a veritable metamorphosis'? One answer is in the mental growth of the child, which Durkheim and Buisson see as a natural process. But there is another possibility. Despite the tendencies to anarchy that exist within the child at a very early age, there is also a traditionalist component and it would seem that in the passage of time, through growth, the traditionalist component wins and the anarchist element is filtered out. The reasons for the change are not clearly stated but merely that 'nature does in fact place in our hands the means necessary for transcending it'.

Influence of Rousseau

Another glance at Durkheim's consideration of the education of the child in its youngest years comes from his notes on Rousseau's *Émile*, which are also to be found in the translation below. Steven Lukes asserts that Durkheim was greatly influenced by Jean-Jacques Rousseau (1712–78) in formulating his conception of human nature (1972:125–8). In addition to an exposition of Rousseau's *Du Contrat social* published in 1918, Durkheim also lectured on *Émile*, the radical treatise on educational theory which Rousseau published in 1762, the same year as the *Contrat*. This book was said to have had such a powerful influence on Immanuel Kant that in reading it he missed his regular walk. But it was also a book which gave great offence, on the one hand to Christian believers, both Catholic and Protestant, and on the other, to the Encyclopedists. Probably no book has had a greater effect on education than Rousseau's *Émile ou de l'Éducation*, and its ideas are still being discussed today. Its thorough approach, covering the span of birth to manhood, challenged even the treatment of babies. As in all aspects of education, the main theme was the encouragement, not repression or straitjacketing, of innate desires and potentialities, physical as well as emotional and mental, that are latent in the child. Rousseau's ideas, in this as well as in other matters, were a movement towards Romanticism brought about as a reaction against the outcome of the Enlightenment, which was to a large extent based on a mechanistic world-view derived from the work of Newton. The Enlightenment not only attacked traditional Protestantism and Catholicism, it tended to abolish the holy and the sacred in terms of God and of man's relation to man seen in spiritual or personal terms. What Rousseau stood for was a full acknowledgment of nature as a force to be understood and accepted in its own right.

It is impossible and indeed undesirable to try to deal with the many themes of *Émile* or the widespread controversies that have arisen in interpreting the book. (See Morrish 1967:ch.4.) All that can be done here is to refer briefly to those ideas which emerge in Durkheim's treatment of *Émile*.

From the late 1880s until he died, Durkheim lectured at frequent intervals on the history of educational theory, in which he covered a large number of thinkers. Only his notes on *Émile* have been preserved, and it is these which are translated here (1919a. See Lukes 1972:124 n.67). How the notes came to be published is described in the introductory note written by Xavier Léon to whom they were entrusted by Durkheim towards the end of his life, when he thought death was not far away. That he should have taken this action, along with presenting his work on Rousseau's *Du Contrat social*, indicates the importance Durkheim attached to these items. It seems that he wanted it to be widely known that he interpreted Rousseau not as someone proposing a doctrine of extreme individualism, as Rousseau was popularly interpreted, but as someone who admitted the virtue of restraint and the influence of the social. Durkheim desired recognition that Rousseau's thought had influenced his own, and that there was much in his educational theory that was highly commendable. Lukes holds that Durkheim embraced much of Rousseau's concept of freedom. The point that we would emphasize is the influence of Rousseau in the matter of the ideals and techniques of teaching, which have running through them the notion of freedom, which for the first time was enunciated in *Émile* as a basic principle of education.

Rousseau may be seen as the architect of the adolescent, and his prime interests appear to have been in the education of the child around the age of puberty, which he saw as a second birth (Musgrove 1964:33). But the notes that Durkheim handed on to posterity deal only with about the first 250 pages of the French edition (Book I and half of Book II), that is up to the age of twelve years. Is this particular apportioning significant? Did Durkheim give only four lectures on Rousseau (based on the notes that were published) and feel that the most important part of the book was its beginning? Or did he give other lectures on Rousseau covering the entire book but which he did not see fit to pass on to Léon? The lack of any general conclusion at the end of the fourth lecture encourages one to think that other lectures on Rousseau followed, but one cannot be certain. Leaving such speculation aside, one thing is sure – the importance of Rousseau in Durkheim's concept of education.

There are two terms which frequently appear in the notes and which to English ears require a certain amount of explanation. They are 'to denature' and 'things'. Indeed, much of what is meant by these terms goes a considerable way to summarizing the contents of Durkheim's four lectures. However, it must be admitted that he uses both terms ambiguously.

To denature means: to change the nature of something; or, to render something unnatural. These meanings are different. The former speaks of a factual process; the latter, using normative criteria, refers to what is pathological. For Rousseau, to denature means to transform nature. In the process of education, man has to come into contact with nature, he is part of nature, but at the same time, because the child needs to be strengthened, he has in some way to use nature to his own end, so he can mould nature through education. Thus Rousseau could maintain that education transforms nature, it denatures it. The point is that nature, powerful though it is, is not perfect in every respect and therefore needs to be bent. It is assumed that man is born as part of the universe and exists within a specific milieu. This milieu has to be taken fully into consideration in the process of education. But on the other hand, to denature a child is to abstract him from the milieu, which means to truncate him, to deny him his natural environment. This occurs when he reaches a point of self-sufficiency, for nature now makes no demands on him, and in this way he transcends nature, he renders himself unnatural.

It would appear that Durkheim is not critical of Rousseau's ambivalent use of this word. In addition to his references to denaturing in the lecture notes, he also refers to the subject in an essay in Part I of this book, where he writes: 'If, disregarding his historical context, we attempt to see him (man) as fixed, static, and outside time, we only denature him' (1920a).

Both thinkers support the antithesis that man is subservient to

112

nature and yet has to transform it and even transcend it. Nature is both good and imperfect. Man is free and yet endeavours to become free. As Rousseau was to write, 'Good social institutions are those best fitted to make a man unnatural, to exchange his independence for dependence, to merge the unit in the group, so that he no longer regards himself as one, but as a part of the whole, and is only conscious of the common life' (*Émile*, t.1911:7).

The word 'things' is a way of emphasizing the reality of the environment in which man is placed. It is the givenness of life, interior and exterior to the individual – the necessities of life – to which the individual has to become adjusted, to accept and to mould as best he may. Things produce a feeling of necessity. Since things are subject to laws, they project laws of necessity onto the individual. Thus, things possess a power over the individual and make him see that he is subject to external forces governed by laws. Education fastens its attention on things, in the main physical objects, to demonstrate to the child the force of the environment, the fact that the child has to take account of such forces and to accept them. Thus, he is to have his basic education in things as over against books, words, concepts.

If therefore the child is to be taught by things, by nature, the teacher offers no verbal lessons, nor commands, nor does he exert power over the child. Things, or the experience of them, are his only teacher. The human tutor is virtually passive. He certainly takes no direct action or intervention, neither does he administer any punishment. Where he does speak to the pupil, it is really the things which speak through him. Of course, the ever-present tutor may direct and manipulate things, certainly according to Durkheim's reading of Rousseau, for he has a certain power over them the pupil has not. But at least, it can be said that the authority in the learning process is no longer the state, the church, or abstract reason. Rather it is nature with its visible and immediate representative, the tutor. In this respect the role of the tutor in Rousseau's system is strikingly similar to that proposed by Durkheim.

Durkheim stressed the importance of things as a way of opposing philosophical idealism, such as that of Hegel and his successors. The issue here is more than educational theory. Durkheim observed that Leibniz and seventeenth-century German thought generally emphasized things and showed a predilection for the real world (1938a:330/t.1977a:288). Humanists as a whole have a philosophical weakness because they envisage man in the abstract instead of seeing real men in a world of things (ibid:333/291). For Durkheim things form the path to correct thinking. They are instructive because they stimulate the grasping of reality and tend to resist abstraction. Durkheim wrote that 'the mind is made for thinking about things, and it is by making it think about things that one fashions it' (ibid:365/318), and 'right thinking is a matter of thinking about right things' (ibid). It was Diderot, Durkheim said, who wanted education to be based on things, not on words, which was the education planned for priests, monks and poets (ibid:332/291).

Durkheim echoed the thought of Rousseau in that he wanted education to be based on things which for him implied the reality of the environment. One might suggest that this is essentially a scientific approach. Its basis is in finding out and observing what is external to the individual, and this is at the heart of the natural sciences.

But Durkheim is no naïve materialist! Thinking about things leads to thought in other dimensions. Instruments of culture can be said to be things and it is these instruments of culture which are the basis of moral action. Thinking in terms of things therefore leads to the recognition of some form of authority and moral force, which takes one to society itself, the ultimate reality. Such a recognition is necessary both for realization of the true nature of freedom, but perhaps more importantly, to the realization of the concept of the moral.

At a more practical level Durkheim strongly supported Rousseau in so far as in his day he was convinced that young children were not sufficiently in contact with natural phenomena to which they were required to respond spontaneously. Freedom in relation to natural phenomena is the key to very early education (ibid:23/16). The strengthening of the child that is required is achieved specifically by coming into contact with nature and by the child learning to use his reason in the face of nature. But it is more. This early stage lays the foundation for later moral awareness. To the young child, things – the heavy yoke of necessity – constitute the basis of discipline, which is 'the discipline of natural consequences'. Discipline is learnt this way and means essentially self-restraint which is at the heart of freedom, coupled as it is to liberty, but which is not to be seen as equivalent to licence or unlimited power.

Durkheim offered an interesting example of the combination of the terms denature and things in his analysis of the Jesuits (ibid: 302–3/264). The Jesuit disciplinary system was admirable in principle to the extent that it was grounded in the nature of things, 'that is to say the condition of society in the sixteenth century'. But the spirit of discipline was over-applied since the tutor was kept too close to the child. In such stifling procedure, which was coupled with excessive competition, the Jesuits denatured the principle of discipline and hence denatured the child. Here Durkheim uses the term denature in a normative sense, indicating that it is wrong to attempt to disregard the force of nature. In this way man ceases to be natural.

Durkheim saw that Rousseau in the early part of *Émile* was primarily concerned with the natural or physical education of the child, not his moral education. That was to be considered later. As we have had occasion to note in connection with his article 'Enfance' (1911c(2)), Durkheim was perhaps less interested in the first stage of education than in the later stages. It is therefore logical to assume that he relied uncritically on Rousseau. Further, as we have suggested, he wanted to show that he was developing his sociology of education which was in some respects cradled in the thought of Rousseau. Strongly opposed to individualistic utilitarianism, as he most assuredly was, he attempted to show that Rousseau was not the founder of individualism and anarchy and thus his own thought was not as removed from that of Rousseau as some might imagine. Durkheim was of the opinion that since the second half of the eighteenth century, that is from the time of Rousseau, education had gone through a crisis which had not been resolved. The old had given rise to the new, but the new was still not sure of itself (see, for example, 1922a:108/t.1956a:141; admittedly Durkheim is referring here to secondary education, but the sentiments surely express his attitude to education as a whole?). In the attempt to crystallize the new, which Durkheim saw as something of a vocation, he was convinced that he had a valuable contribution to make.

In another respect Durkheim applauds the position of Rousseau. For Rousseau education is man-centred, more accurately child-centred, not god-centred. Rousseau strongly opposed a clerical form of education, especially that epitomized by the Jesuits who were expelled from France in 1762, the year of the publication of

Émile. In keeping with the ideals of the Third Republic, education was organized so as to be essentially lay in spirit and controlled by lay teachers. It was neither focused on leading men to God nor was it to be in the hands of the clergy and religious orders. Lay or secular education is but the logical extension of the notion that reason alone determines what is good and evil.[1]

Problems of relativism and authority

We have already observed that Durkheim was an unrepentant relativist when it came to moral systems (see Introduction on Morals and 1905b in this volume). The content of morality changes with the passing of time: each society has its own particular system which is never the same as that of another society. Nor is it possible to prove which set of morals is superior, for each seems to work well for the particular society in which it is found. The same can be said of educational systems. But perhaps unrepentant is too strong a word, because although Durkheim identified himself with a secular ethic, he was also aware of the difficulties of the position, especially the practical difficulties raised by teaching a secular morality. His fears, and those of others like him, are amply demonstrated in a discussion of the subject held in 1909 amongst members of the Société Française de Philosophie (see 1909a(2), translated here).

According to Durkheim, the issue is one of teaching, not educating. Stemming from the definitions which have been given earlier, the problem rests with the teacher for it is his task to explain and expound to the pupils the moral system in which they find themselves, and to do it in such a way that they will appropriate the system. By contrast, education is concerned with the will and the art of communication.

The weakness of a secular moral system is not its inherent relativism but, as Durkheim admits, its lack of a central idea, a lack of unity, and in the last analysis an absence of a convincing authority. Up until modern times, moral systems in most societies nestled in the bosom of the religion of the society or were supported by religious symbols, which were themselves identified with ultimate reality. It is the old question which keeps on repeating itself in one

116

form or another: if you reject the moral or theological base, is all sense of authority supporting the concrete moral structure destroyed? If so, who will accept and embrace such a system? A moral system, it is generally assumed, is necessary for the well-being of a society. As Durkheim argued, how, for example, can the child understand the way morality arises and that there is a general sense of duty, when at the same time morality is seen to be eternally changing? And to be more concrete, how can someone be persuaded to abide by monogamy when polygamy and other forms of marriage are practised by numerous societies?

Parodi, who was a member of Durkheim's Année Sociologique group and who was present at this meeting of the Société, indirectly supported his master about the inevitable failure of trying to teach something held to be false. The effectiveness of a moral doctrine has to be seen in terms of its truth and rationality. He also saw the weakness of a secular morality but in the terms of the fact that it did not have a constitution. Each person, whether teacher or not, sees it through his own eyes. The question was, and it might be said it still is, how is a sense of unity to be achieved, given the particularly non-authoritarian nature and lack of cohesive content of secular morality?

If these criticisms are accepted, two logical positions follow. One is to acknowledge the consequences of an ethical system lacking authority and to hope that people will appropriate it in an adequate, though not necessarily firm way. Such a system would be supported by law and other sanctions, and indeed in this case morality in concrete form tends to come close to law. The path may be somewhat hazardous since the moral system exists without the foundation of an authority which possesses metaphysical or near-metaphysical status. Some would agree that western Europe in the mid-twentieth century has such a moral system, which, for better or worse, appears to work. The alternative is to search for a surrogate authority replacing religion. Delvolvé, a philosopher who introduced the discussion in which Durkheim took part, in fact found himself in company with the grand master of sociology in focusing on the weaknesses of secular morality, and also in a search for an alternative to the buttress traditional religion had become. Delvolvé held that the alternative could be found in the concept of nature and a somewhat vague notion of God as the intuition of the universal – what he called a tendency. For Durkheim, and for

117

others present at the discussion, all this was too vague and inadequate to act as a reinforcement for moral action. Instead, as
every student of Durkheim would know, he sought authority in the
sui generis nature of society which he held was endowed with the
sacred. In locating authority in society Durkheim felt that with a
single stroke of the pen he had achieved a 'sacred' base which,
on the one hand, could not be misconstrued with traditional religion, and on the other, was thoroughly realistic, in so far as
society was empirically ascertainable and at the same time man-
made. To be fair to Durkheim, he supported the notion that
honesty is the best policy — best because it is more effective. A
doctrine which is false cannot be propagated and assimilated for
long, even by the most skilful of artificers. Therefore one cannot
pretend to offer reasons for upholding an ethical system which
one believes is wrong. It is necessary for the teacher to be thoroughly
convinced that what he is teaching is true and that what is taught
is firmly based on a sense of reality. And what could be more real
than society itself! Sociology thus solves the dilemma thrown up by
the teaching of secular morality!

The point is that morality, if it is to be effective in restraining
man's egoism and giving him self-discipline, must be undergirded
by some form of authority. Morality is by its nature fragile and is
readily shattered without the support of an authoritative base. It
must therefore possess some transcendental element evident at its
source. As Durkheim wrote: 'the teaching of morality must give
the child the sensation of reality — the source of life — from which
he derives comfort and support' (1909a(2)). The question is whether
his solution meets the requisites he lays down. Does society itself
contain for the child, as well as for the adult, the necessary transcendental element? Is it seen as a reality which at the same time
possesses a component which is, or is equivalent to the sacred?
Some would want to reply to such questions by turning to recent
history and suggesting that modern western society has voiced a
vigorous denial of holding to anything which might be seen in terms
of the sacred.

Boarding schools

The family and the school are today the main institutions of education. To these is to be added the university; important though it is

118

within education, it concerns but a minority of the population. All these institutions, and perhaps the school in particular, are reflections or miniatures of the major institutions of society. The school and the university are mirrors of adult society. Despite his admiration for the family as an institution, Durkheim held it to be unsuitable for educating children beyond early years. The child required a more rigorous discipline than that which the family could supply (see 1925a:165–9/t.1961a:144–8). But unlike many sociologists, he saw the school as an 'adult' institution – something that was only just removed from the life of the adult. It constituted the prelude to being an adult and was something that had to be taken very seriously. For this reason he appears to have been unique not only in respecting the institutions of education but attempting to trace their evolution. This he did, especially with regard to universities where he demonstrated his historical talent, in his lectures, *L'Évolution pédagogique en France* (1938a).

In the items presented here there is little reference to educational institutions as such. Articles on the university have been excluded (see Preface). The reader is referred to his *L'Éducation morale* (1925a) in which can be found Durkheim's fullest treatment of the school itself. Here however there is an interesting allusion to boarding schools and 'New Schools' (1912b).

France was and is still, compared with England, Holland, or Belgium, a rural country. Sparsely populated regions and large numbers of small villages create practical problems for the schooling of children. One way of overcoming them is to bring in the children from the countryside and educate them in schools in towns and cities. Boarding facilities then have to be found. This was the policy that was adopted in France, and to meet the need for accommodation lycées created their own *internats*. Durkheim himself lived in the *internat* of the Lycée Louis-le-Grand in Paris, situated near the Sorbonne. In England, with a much higher density of population and with numerous towns, there was no need to provide government boarding schools as happened in France.

Durkheim observed in the discussion that the Jesuits – and this may seem strange from a limited knowledge of the Jesuits – did not want to have boarding facilities. It was the parents and municipalities which demanded them and the Order agreed. The Central schools of the Revolution failed, according to Durkheim, because boarding facilities were not provided.

Sex education

It is apparent that sex education was thought to be a subject worthy of academic discussion amongst France's leading intellectuals in the years that immediately preceded the First World War. In the deliberations of the Société Française de Philosophie, the question was not whether sex education should be carried out in school, but rather, what kind of sex education should be inculcated. Doléris, a prominent doctor and hygienist, proposed that the education should primarily have a rational basis and concentrate on the physical aspects of sex (1911a, translated here). Durkheim, who replied to the introductory paper by Doléris, opposed such an approach on the grounds that the sexual relation between human beings is more than a biological relationship, which as such is seen to be on a par with digestion and the circulatory system. Sex has, he said, a strong moral component and above all, is characterized by being a sacred relationship. All societies have acknowledged the need for some kind of sex education, and they have also placed sex within the framework of the sacred. Durkheim was bold enough to claim that he knew 'the exact moment' when, from anthropological data, he derived the generalization about the awe-inspiring nature of sex. In the past, religious systems have always supported this approach to sex; and in societies where religious dogma is now rejected there is a corresponding rejection of the mystical concept of sex. Secularization can thus be said to be instrumental in desacralizing the intimate relations between man and woman. In one sense Durkheim stands precisely here, by the demythologizing of sex, in so far as he is on the side of science which replaces the mysteriousness of the act with a rational or scientific understanding. On the other hand, he deplores the results of the intervention of science. He is strongly opposed to the notion that the sexual act is a 'common' or ordinary event. Sex is unique – *sui generis*. Consequently, he follows traditional thinking in maintaining that continence, except in marriage, is a duty. And it is interesting to note that the whole tenor of the discussion is aimed at the young man rather than the young woman. Modesty, which is to be seen *par excellence* in sex, is also to be upheld. Indeed, the sacredness of sex is to be found in the modesty that surrounds it and such modesty demands remoteness and reserve, together with a concealment of the body from prying eyes. To touch the sacred object, even to see it, is to profane it. Only in marriage, in a permanent union, are the negative effects circumnavigated and the taboo safely eliminated.

Since Durkheim held that the sentiment was universal, he believed it pointed to a basic underlying reality. He accepted the reality, whilst rejecting the religious symbolism with which it is associated. He put forward three reasons for upholding what is little more than Jewish-Christian morality regarding sex. Some would call it typical middle-class liberal morality of the nineteenth century. The first reason is that sexual activity outside marriage breaks up the stability of married life. (Durkheim's great concern for marriage and the family as social institutions cannot be considered here.) The second, derived from Kant, is that sex outside marriage is immoral since it uses the other person for pleasure. And the third, which is basically a metaphysical reason, near to that of traditional Roman Catholicism as well as certain sections of Protestantism, is that in sexual intercourse there is a communion of a most intimate kind, in which the two people through sustained contact become one and so a new personality is born which embraces both of them.

The importance of these views for education is that, as has been mentioned, the teacher has to impart what exists in society. His task is not to produce a new morality or his own interpretation of contemporary morality but to explain it in such a way that it will be understood and appropriated.

The debate showed, however, that it was not the case that every member of the Société Française de Philosophie present agreed with Durkheim about the sacredness of sex. But in another direction Durkheim's own case is somewhat weakened by his attempt to posit conclusive reasons for upholding the sacred, reasons divorced from their religious imperative. Durkheim wants to demythologize sex and at the same time maintain its sacredness, which he sees as being necessary for social health. Here as elsewhere he seems to have forgotten his many references to the fact that the entry of scientific enquiry and investigation into religion, and therefore the sacred, undermines both the strength of religion as well as the sacred (see references to science, the sacred, etc., in Pickering 1975). As always, he wants the best of both worlds – he wishes to stand on the side of science and to claim that scientific knowledge is the most reliable and surest of all knowledge, and yet at the same time desires to retain what in fact science undermines. But quite apart from the dilemma in which Durkheim finds himself, is it not true that over recent years the scientific approach to sex has in fact demystified it and eliminated the component of sacredness which it formerly possessed?

Nationalist overtones

One of the vulnerable points of Durkheim's doctrine of the primacy of society over the individual and with it the necessity that the state be highly involved in education is that, in the last analysis, as critics have frequently observed, it gives rise to nationalism, even if that nationalism or patriotism is 'spiritually conceived' (Mitchell 1931:104; and Durkheim 1904a(40) and (41), translated here). If society is the ultimate authority, then that authority in a given situation either is or readily becomes the nation; certainly so in modern Europe. *La Nation*, France, was of overriding concern to Durkheim. It was to be seen in a great deal that he wrote: it was in part the *raison d'être* of his scientific approach to society – his sociology. If there were any doubts about his nationalism before the outbreak of the First World War, his fervent identification with France during the four years of the holocaust immediately dispelled them. But who is not a nationalist in wartime? Amongst several articles of a propagandist kind Durkheim published during this period, one was a short article on morality and the school system, which has only been recently unearthed (1916c, translated here; see *RFS*, XVII, 1976:193–5). The article is interesting because not only does it show Durkheim's nationalist outlook which is certainly pardonable if not laudable, but he attributes France's moral greatness seen in the heroism of her troops and the patience of her civilians to the educational system – the system developed under the Third Republic. Therefore it can be argued that the strength exhibited by France during the war justifies the method of teaching which he helped to build up, if not create, and which was centred on the state schools (see 1905b, translated in Part I, Morals). His call therefore was that there should be no abandonment of what had been established in the educational system. All that was required was an improvement of what had been shown to be so successful. For France there was the need for some form of ambitious outlook which would match the inherent strengths of the nation, and for high ideals that would transcend selfish sloth and egoism. But above all, the call was for meaningful discipline in schools and in society, a discipline which should be seen as something sacred. Frenchmen needed to have their moral greatness tempered by self-control. How often Durkheim wrote about the subject of discipline, and nowhere was it hammered home more than in his lectures on *Moral Education* (1925a; see especially chs 2, 4, 9-13). In the article here and elsewhere Durkheim stood against the excessive discipline of the past. He was also opposed to corporal punishment. Instead, he emphasized moderation and meaningfulness within discipline so that through the school the child would become in adult life self-controlled and would willingly accept such discipline as society deemed necessary. Durkheim set his face strongly against what might now be called permissiveness. For him it implied the erosion of the moral fibre of society and savoured of social anarchy. Society could exist and grow strong only through the acceptance of external controls, rationally conceived as being generally beneficial, but which were at the same time endued with the aura of sacredness.

Conclusion

Debesse in his brief introduction to the second edition of Durkheim's *Éducation et sociologie* (1966:7) suggests that a great deal of progress has been made in the human sciences since the time Durkheim first propounded his sociological approach to education. No longer is there conflict between the claims of psychology and sociology. Durkheim's aim was mainly concerned in dislodging the primacy of psychology in education. True though this may be, all is not sweetness and light between the two disciplines, especially with regard to present and future needs in education. In many respects it seems that some of the more important issues before educationalists are those of a philosophical, ideological and indeed sociological kind - questions relating to curriculum, to moral instruction, and discipline in which psychology plays some but not a dominant part. Faced as teachers and educational theorists are by the state of society at the present time, by violence, by vandalism, by a lack of respect for authority, much that Durkheim has to say in emphasizing the social element of education is highly relevant to many of the educational problems today. Durkheim's educational sociology is not just a chapter in the history of ideas and which has little value except for historians. The issues and the way in which he poses the issues seem particularly appropriate now. Above all, Durkheim helps us more than any other great sociological mind to see the relation between, on the one hand, the teaching process and the institutions associated with it, and on the other, their place within society and their reflection of society. It is here that he has something to offer both in analysing and perhaps solving some of the crucial issues that are to be found in contemporary educational theory.

Note

1 This issue of secular education was facing thinkers in the late nineteenth century not only in France and in other countries in Europe, but in the United States as well. It is to be seen in the writings of the sociologist E. A. Ross, the philosopher John Dewey, and others. The interest in what was going on in France is reflected in the fact that in 1919 an American publisher thought it worthwhile producing an anthology on contemporary French education written by French scholars and administrators, where the emphasis was on moral teaching not based on religion (Buisson and Farrington 1919). The question was of considerable concern to certain English educationalists. They organized The First International Moral Education Conference, held in London University in 1909 (Spiller, ed., 1909).

References

(Nearly all the references relate to items to be found in the Bibliography. Those not specifically concerned with Durkheim's sociology of education are listed below.)

124

IZOULET, J. 1928 *La Métamorphose de l'église ou la sociologie fille du décalogue au Collège de France*, Michel, Paris.

PICKERING, W. S. F. (ed.) 1975 *Durkheim on Religion*, Routledge & Kegan Paul, London and Boston.

PICKERING, W. S. F. 1979 'Gaston Richard: collaborateur et adversaire', *RFS*, XX. pp. 163–82.

RICHARD, G. 1923 'L'Athéisme dogmatique en sociologie religieuse', *RHPR*, 1923, pp. 125–37, 229–61. (Translated in Pickering 1975.)

RICHARD, G. 1928 'L'Enseignement de la sociologie à l'école normale primaire', *L'Éducateur protestant*, 7, pp. 198–208; 233–43; 295–307.

SPILLER, G. (ed.) 1909 *Papers on Moral Education communicated to the First International Moral Education Conference*, Nutt, London.

8

1904a(40) and (41)

Review 'Durkheim, "Pédagogie et sociologie"[1] and Paul Barth, "Die Geschichte der Erziehung in soziologischer Beleuchtung"'

First published in French in *L'Année sociologique*, VII, pp. 683–6.

In the first of these articles, we have been concerned to establish in a general way that educational theory needs at least as much support from sociology as it does from psychology. Education is indeed an eminently social matter. It is social in its aim, and far from seeking to establish the individual nature of man in general, it varies from one society to another. For one thing, once societies have attained a certain level of differentiation, educational theory is itself observed to become differentiated according to classes and professions. This specialization is dictated by social needs (*besoins*); for it responds to the way the social task is divided up and organized in each historical period. It is true that all the special types of education only diverge at a certain point, prior to which they intermingle. Yet even this education which is common to them is a function of the social state, for each society seeks, through education, to inculcate its own particular ideal. Even the most advanced European societies cannot escape from this law. We do of course say that we wish to make men of our children, and not merely citizens in the narrow sense of the word. But this is because only a truly human culture can provide the European nations with the citizens they need. In societies as vast as ours in Europe, individuals are so different from one another that they have virtually nothing in common, apart from the property of being men in general. It must also be added that to some extent every nation envisages man in a personal way, because this view reflects the needs, the particular mentality and the historical past, and so on, of that nation.

126

To sum up, the aim of education, far from being simply to develop man as he is fashioned by nature, is to graft onto him an entirely new man. It creates within him a being previously present only in vague, embryonic form, and this is the social being. It is education which teaches us to control and resist ourselves; it is also education which determines the level and nature of the knowledge which, according to its needs, the child shall receive. And just as it is through education that the knowledge acquired by previous generations is conserved, so it is also education which passes it on to generations to come. It is education, therefore, which creates within us all that lies outside the realm of pure sensations; our will and our understanding are fashioned in its image.

But the influence of social action extends even to the nature of the means employed to achieve this goal. Naturally the means will vary according to our notion of the *conscience* of children, and as a result according to the data of psychology and child psychology in particular. But first, if the ends of education are social, the means must also necessarily be so. And in fact, educational institutions are often an abbreviated form of social institutions proper, for instance, school discipline has the same essential features as civic (*de la cité*) discipline. Furthermore, the nature of the end predetermines the means. Certain procedures are proscribed or pursued inasmuch as they do or do not conform to society's conception of the ideal to be achieved. The origin of the Pestalozzian method, for example, was its author's feeling about the moral aspirations of his time, far more than psychological knowledge.

The same ideas underpin the work of Barth, who undertakes to show in historical terms how the form and content of education has in fact varied with societies.

His main findings are first that he discerns no link between the organization of the family and the nature of education; and it is indeed our belief that education is much more directly dependent upon the overall organization of society. An important factor in this would appear to be the type of industry involved. He maintains that there is a general lack of educational discipline as a whole among hunting and fishing peoples. The child is left to his own devices, under no compulsion to contain or resist himself. This is because the occupations of such people are irregular and subject to whim, and as a consequence, there is felt to be no need to subject the children to a very strict set of rules. Conformity to rules is much

127

greater among pastoral and agricultural peoples whose societies moreover are much more inclined to be warlike. They attack and are themselves attacked because for them the land holds a value which it did not previously have. So education trains the child to resist his passions. It teaches him patience, forgetfulness of self and subordination. This reinforcement of discipline increases among more highly skilled agricultural peoples, such as the early Greeks or the Germans of Tacitus. As culture and the art of war grew more complex, the military and agricultural techniques in which children were instructed became equally complex. At the same time, greater strictness was required in domestic *moeurs*. Last, where education is organized into classes, education too becomes a specialized function. On the other hand, it becomes diversified according to the environment and varies from one class to another. And it becomes more complex by virtue of the greater complexity of social life.

Naturally, such a rapid review of a multitude of different peoples did not permit the author to make use of original material and for the same reason the conclusions he has reached are rather general. Yet this attempt to link education directly with the social conditions on which it depends nevertheless deserves to be noted.

Note

1 [Opening lecture of Durkheim's course on L'Éducation morale, 1902–3, given in Paris and reproduced in *Éducation et sociologie* (1922a/t.1956a). – W.S.F.P.]

9

1909a(2)

A discussion on the effectiveness of moral doctrines

First published in French under the title 'L'Éfficacité des doctrines morales', séance du 20 mai 1909, in *Bulletin de la Société Française de Philosophie*, IX, pp. 219–31.[1]

DURKHEIM: I readily concur with Delvolvé[2] that the secular teaching of morality does in fact quite often, perhaps even quite generally, merit his criticism. It is insufficiently linked to a central notion. Particular attention is attached to explaining the detail of duties more or less adequately, but insufficient thought is given to the task of making the child understand how it arises that there are in a general sense duties, why it is that man has obligations and what the underlying reason is for this *sui generis* discipline which constitutes morality. But although this defect is a genuine and grave one, I am far from believing that it is inevitable. Indeed, the chief aim of my own course on educational theory is to show to students how they can give their teaching this essential unity. On the other hand, I doubt whether the method advocated by Delvolvé would enable him to remedy the fault he points out and to achieve his declared aim.

But a distinction must be made at the outset if I am to make myself clear on this point.

In his paper Delvolvé quite often, it seems to me, confused *moral education* with the *teaching of morality*. He spoke of habits to be formed, sentiments and motivational *représentations* to be awakened, etc. All of this is part and parcel of education (*éducation*), for its immediate object is action and application. Teaching (*enseignement*) has quite a different aim. It is not a preparation for action; it is essentially bringing about comprehension, and as far as it is possible, explanation. It is an attempt to render intelligible

129

a given order of facts. The teacher (*maître*) does not address himself directly to the will, but to the understanding. So the truly original feature of our scholastic enterprise is that for the first time we have endeavoured − I will not say to teach morality in a secular way − but quite simply to teach it from primary school onwards. Previously, it was not taught at all. It was inculcated by the catechism for example. Children were drilled in it and it was not presented to them in a rational form. And if we have assumed this task, we have not done so from some wild passing fancy, but because circumstances forced us to do so. Regret it as we may, we cannot prevent the spirit of free inquiry from raising questions of morality as well. We must therefore respond to it. The child who leaves our schools must have some idea of the underlying reasons for the moral discipline he is asked to practise. He must know not just what his duties are but, at least to a certain extent and varying according to age and level of culture, the *wherefore* of these duties. For a day will surely dawn when, partly of himself and partly under pressure from the environment, he will wonder by what right they should be observed. If so, the complexity of the problems is such that his thought on the matter will most likely go astray if they are not appropriately oriented in advance and provided with key ideas. The reasons for moral maxims are not so apparent that a simple question will show what they are. As a result the child will be liable to regard them as mere optical illusions, and the result of superstition, which is often the case. He will believe that it is governments and the ruling classes who have invented morality in order to bring the people to heel more effectively. At all events, we shall abandon him defenceless to the innuendoes of vulgar polemics and journalistic arguments. We must therefore arm his intelligence with solid reasons which will stand up to the inevitable doubts and discussions.

Yet if God were accepted, would we be any better able to solve the problem? Of course, this procedure would make it relatively easy for us to represent the transcendent aspect of all moral ideals and the authority and majesty with which they are vested in relation to individual *consciences*. But there are other aspects of moral life which are no less essential and which we cannot explain in this way.

It can no longer be maintained nowadays that there is one, single morality which is valid for all men at all times and in all places.

We know full well that morality has varied. It has varied not only because men have lost sight of their true destiny, but also because it is in the nature of things that morality should vary. The moral system of the Romans and Hebrews was not our own, nor could it have been so. For if the Romans had practised our morality with its characteristic individualism, the city of Rome would never have been, and nor consequently would the Roman civilization, which was the necessary antecedent and condition of our present civilization. The purpose of the morality practised by a people is to enable it to live: hence morality changes with societies. There is not just one morality but several and as many as there are social types. And as our societies change, so will our morality. It will in the future no longer be what it is today. Such and such a rule that horrifies us at the moment may well be practised tomorrow. It is not that one is truer than the other, merely that the needs of the time will have changed.

If children are to be given an idea of what moral life is, they must therefore be made to feel that it is normally subject to variations, yet without these variations discrediting it in their eyes. They must be made to understand that the morality of the future will probably not be that of today. At the same time the morality of today will still appear worthy of their respect. It should be possible to explain that there are indeed different moralities but that children must be bound, in the main at least, to the morality of their own time and country. This complex conception is indispensable, for morality does indeed possess this double aspect. If man does not see why morality is entitled to respect throughout history, he will not respect it, or will only respect it outwardly when he is obliged to do so. If he does not see why it must change, he will resist the necessary changes on the pretext that it is immutable.

But how can this variability be explained if morality is founded on God, if it expresses the nature of God, no matter how one chooses to represent him? God is eternally the same. He exists and what emanates from him must also partake of this same immutability. Even if he is merely another name given to the reality which, according to Delvolvé, we experience in some obscure way − and supposing this reality evolves − it is quite clear that the evolution is without bearing on the ceaseless changes which take place in moral life and are bound to do so. A morality based on religion is thus of necessity opposed to new ideas and there is no

131

doubt that it has always been so. Consequently any teaching of morality conceived in this spirit cannot fulfil the second of the two conditions I referred to a few moments ago. Of course, morality can only be taught or, in other words, explained, if it is related to a reality which the child can be made to feel to be a reality. But this reality, whilst being relatively stable, must perpetually be in the process of becoming and this becoming must be of such a kind as to be perceptible to the child.

But in fact I do not think there has ever existed a genuine teaching of morality without a theological support for a foundation. Religions may well have been able to claim the guarantee of divine authority for morality as a whole, but never to my knowledge has any attempt been made to derive the detail of moral rules from the nature of God. Earlier on, Belot quite rightly showed how such a derivation was impossible. It is true that Delvolvé attempted to demonstrate how the value of monogamy could be explained from his point of view. I must confess that his demonstration seemed singularly vague and awkward. The widespread practice of sexual union is the maximum that the so-called tendency of life to spread can justify. But how could this fundamental tendency enable us to understand that this or that form of marriage was suitable in Rome and another kind in Christian societies, etc.? And what would happen if we broached such questions as the right of personal or landed property, or professional morality?

DELVOLVÉ: I thank M. Durkheim for his criticisms. They bring out perfectly an initial misunderstanding which needs to be cleared up if our exchange of views is to be fruitful. You appear to believe that I wish to found morality upon the notion of God, in other words, that I wish to derive *a priori* from the notion of God the specific content of the individual duties. Or am I mistaken?

DURKHEIM: If, according to Delvolvé, the notion of God is not employed as the basis of duties, then I confess I have not understood him.

DELVOLVÉ: (*Summary*. The notion that God should be the basis of duty was to be rejected. Secular moralists in fact deduced moral rules from a general principle. For Delvolvé the divine was not a concept but an intuitive experience distinct from scientific experience. It was an intuitive knowledge of nature and of man's vital relation to it. Morals could not be deduced from it: they came from the mind of individuals who saw them in conformity with universal tendencies. Educationally the child must be made to see the universal nature of the tendencies in an intuitive way and also duties in a psychological way that are linked with the will. Monogamy was not to be justified scientifically. The tendency for man to spread beyond himself was a dynamic basis for family duties and was best fulfilled by the moral aim of two people.)

DURKHEIM: But what will have to be explained to the child is that which requires and obliges him to desire monogamy at the present time, whereas if he were an ancient Hebrew or an Australian aboriginal, he would have to desire another form of matrimony. The rule must therefore be related to conditions of time and place. How will you achieve this?

How can even this need you mention convey any impression of the idea of duty? These two notions are poles apart. Whatever tendency you choose to start with, how will you get your pupil to understand that he *must* do a particular thing – that he is bound to do it?

DELVOLVÉ: I consider that duty and the universal tendency, which is the true source of the sentiment of obligation, are of precisely the same character.

DURKHEIM: But it is a fact that duty exists. And it is not for you to lay down arbitrarily that it is this or that. A duty is something quite different from a tendency.

DELVOLVÉ: In philosophy there are several non-mutually exclusive meanings of the word duty. I am fully aware of the objective existence of duty, such as you envisage it, as a moral rule which exists in a given society. But I take a different view. I do not consider duty from the outside as a social rule, but from inside, as the intellectual reinforcement of the sentiment of obligation in the soul of the individual. And I ask myself how through teaching one can implant this reinforcement securely in the child's mind. I say that the rule of conduct must be linked to a whole group of tendencies which have already been determined in a general way.

DURKHEIM: I have no need to remind you that the demands and the necessities to which I have alluded have nothing to do with the vague tendencies you have mentioned. To know the former and make them understood, there is no need whatever to have recourse to an intuitive knowledge of this *nescio quid* you have

133

outlined. These are demands and necessities of a social order, which consequently one can actually point out to the child.

DELVOLVÉ: I do not agree at all that from where I stand on the inside, moral obligation is a necessity of a social order.

DURKHEIM: But I come back to the question I asked you. How do you explain that monogamy is the only matrimonial system which is suitable today, whereas in days gone by, polygamy was perfectly acceptable?

DELVOLVÉ: I do not have to explain it. This is for you to do, since you have chosen to view it from the angle of an historical explanation. As for me, I need only make the child aware of the conventional relationship between the rule and our practical nature observed in the present, in other words, of the inner needs which are his own.

DURKHEIM: But you cannot escape the fact that one day or another the child will be confronted with new practical problems. If he does not know that even the most hallowed moral rules can change, or what variable causes occasion these changes, how will he be able to decide what the moral rules shall be? As he is not prepared by a suitable education (*culture*) to resolve these questions, he will be the victim of the press and indiscriminate reading.

DELVOLVÉ: Before the child is taught that things change, he must be given a sense of the present. Showing him that his country changes is no way to endear him to it in its present form.

DURKHEIM: So you recognize that the notion of one's country is part of a reality which varies. But if you make it dependent on an invariable reality, you will sooner or later be caught out, as this notion will change.

DELVOLVÉ: I fail to see why nature should not be invariable. When the notion has changed, nature will have prepared for the adaptation of the tendencies to new rules by a parallel evolution.

DURKHEIM: You well know how far the morality of the Romans differed from our own. Yet nature – the world around us – has not varied: it is still the same universe. At the very least, the changes which may have occurred are nothing compared with the quite considerable variations which moral ideas have undergone. Therefore it is not immutable nature which can form the basis of the constantly changing morality. Again, if you agree that nature has undergone a proportionate parallel evolution, it is because you are re-introducing society into what you term nature.

DELVOLVÉ: How could I consider excluding society from what I term universal nature? We agree then, but you have changed your point of view.

PARODI:[3] (*Summary*. Delvolvé's case was ambiguous. The effectiveness of moral doctrine could not be seen apart from the question of its truth or rationality. His criticisms of positive religion as being idealistic applied to his own concept of religion. The effectiveness of a moral doctrine was that it should be held to be true and universally accepted. There was not really a properly constituted secular morality, which was the object of profound and unanimous conviction. Each educationalist saw it in his own way. The question was basically one of how public education was to obtain moral duty. To a short comment by Delvolvé, he repeated his charge of ambiguity. As was evident in William James, what was necessary for the person to act was a belief in the truth of what he was doing. What did Durkheim think of the problem?)

DURKHEIM: I do not believe either that a false doctrine can be practically effective. Yet from the point of view of teaching, the question of effectiveness can be stated differently. One can say in fact that if one does not succeed in linking moral ideas as a whole with a reality which it is possible to point out to the child, then moral teaching is ineffective.

LE ROY:[4] One would therefore have to look elsewhere for an alternative to what is provided by religious morality. But I do not think that our present secular morality provides this alternative.

DURKHEIM: It is quite certain, and on this point I am in agreement with Le Roy, that the teaching of morality must give the child the sensation of a reality – the source of life – from which he derives comfort and support. But a concrete, living reality is needed for this, and an abstract, artificial, logically constructed conception could not fulfil this role, even if it were built with the most rigorous logic.

DELVOLVÉ: I am seeking its equivalent in secular terms and what I want to do precisely is to link the particular determinations of the will to a reality which is felt intuitively – to the intuition of the universal, which I call God.

DURKHEIM: Very well then! But before imagining such a reality, I would ask that we explore a reality which lies extremely close to us, a reality which envelops us and permeates us on all sides,

135

that is to say, society. For there are forces at play in society that the vulgar observer is unable to perceive, but which are none the less real, and which perpetually support, nourish and strengthen us. I would ask that people be aware of all we may demand of them before they resign themselves to the leap into the unknowable which we are all invited to make.

LE ROY: For the believer God is a reality of an experiential order. That is not to be questioned.

BELOT: It should be a universal experience.

LE ROY: That is a matter for discussion. An experience may be genuine and true and yet require that certain conditions be met in order that the individual participate in it.

DURKHEIM: The question is whether all that is essential in religious matters cannot be expressed in secular terms.

BELOT: Delvolvé has not replied to the essential question. What is his reason for believing that the social fact is not effective enough to serve as the basis for duty? Why would his idea of nature be more effective?

DELVOLVÉ: The question has not been put to me. I have examined it in my articles.[5] I can only give a brief outline of it here. I do not believe that the analysis of the conditions of society is sufficient to link will and social duty. Such an analysis has no hold over the will: far from strengthening it, it paralyses it. It does not reinforce social bonds: it weakens them.

DURKHEIM: We have no need to create these bonds. They already exist. I think you are losing sight of the fact that it is a question of *teaching*, not educating. It is not the task of teaching to reinforce the bonds in question, but to explain them and convey the sentiment of their reality.

DELVOLVÉ: We are in complete disagreement here. I regard moral teaching not as a scientific discipline, but as an integral part of the technique of education. I have already had occasion to explain myself on this point.

DURKHEIM: To repeat myself, it is not the task of teaching to create moral rules, but to show what they are and to make them understood. The chemist who explains air does not have to create the nitrogen or oxygen in it.

DELVOLVÉ: It is not a question of creating links *ex nihilo*, but of strengthening them.

DURKHEIM: But the bonds concerned are themselves forces, for they result from certain *représentations* and these *représentations* are active forces.

BOUGLÉ:[6] (*Summary.* Both Delvolvé and Durkheim saw the need to appeal to some kind of reality which underlay morality: for the former it was nature or the divine; for the latter, society. But how could the transformation or link be made from the reality to the morality? People were critical and were not inclined to be conformist. How could society, which was the basis of duty, be shown to be sacred? Would not sentiment rather than science have to be appealed to?)

DURKHEIM: I wonder if this question was really necessary? I cannot allow that a false idea could be practically effective, thanks to some skilful artifice. I can think of nothing more distasteful to my mind. If society does not in fact already possess the character I attribute to it, then my efforts to see that this is attributed to it will either *fail* or else will not produce good results. If it is proved to me that I can only foster this sentiment in men on condition that I deceive them, it will be because I shall have deceived myself.

BOUGLÉ: It would seem the fact nevertheless remains that you must appeal to sentiment if you are to forge a link between men and the social reality our science teaches them.

DURKHEIM: It is quite clear that one cannot educate without having recourse to sentiment. Even in teaching, there may be occasion to resort to it in certain conditions and in a certain way. But do you believe that as soon as one appeals to sentiment one is thereby practising some sort of *obscurantism*? Normally, sentiment is only a confused expression of the real. It is founded in reality; it can be expressed in intelligible terms. Sentiment can therefore be put to quite a different use other than confusing people's reason and so concealing from them the true nature of things.

BOUGLÉ: Need I observe that in my opinion it is perfectly permissible to appeal to sentiment, without being taxed with 'obscurantism'?

DURKHEIM: It is agreed, then, that I can appeal to sentiment without contravening the principles which inspire me. Are you now asking how I could convey to an anarchist the sentiment of society understood in this way? This is just as impossible for me as to communicate the sense of colours to a man blind from birth.[7] But will you be any more successful than I am? Is there a method which can succeed, and succeed for certain in a case like this? I do not see how the difficulty you draw my attention to would be peculiar to me.

BOUGLÉ: Delvolvé has dealt more than adequately with social morality. He merely wishes to give it a wider background.

DURKHEIM: I myself reject the idea that there is any similarity. There is as wide a gulf between the views of Delvolvé and my own as there is between agnosticism and rationalism. Perhaps he and I do have a common feeling, yet we convey it in two singularly different ways. But let me come back to your objection. I was saying, in fact, that I recognized that it was hard for me to convey a notion of what society and morality are to the person whose mind is afflicted with social and moral blindness, so long as he remains in that state. In the first place, such a state is exceptional. For normal, average subjects, there is no reason why I could not make them feel things as they are and society as it is, namely, a moral power superior to the individual, enjoying a sort of transcendence analogous to that which religions ascribe to divinity. If one supposes that society does indeed possess these characteristics, which is a supposition which is not under discussion for the moment, why would I require some kind of ruse to make the child see them?

Furthermore, even in the case of the anarchist I mentioned a moment ago, I am not always, necessarily, powerless. Admittedly, so long as he is afflicted with the blindness I have just referred to, there is nothing one can do; but I can look for the source of the blindness. It is, from my point of view, a phenomenon which is undeniably abnormal but perfectly natural and depends on natural causes. By knowing what these are, I can modify and attenuate their effect, namely that disposition of the mind which prevents certain individuals from seeing social things as they are. There are curable anarchists. It is even an eminently soluble question of moral education to find out what makes up the spirit of anarchy, anti-social attitudes and impatience with rules. For it is on this condition alone that it is possible to predict or rectify this vicious attitude of character and intelligence where it exists.

In a word, if, as I suppose, there does exist something empirically demonstrable outside the individual and which transcends him, then what special difficulty can there be in conveying such a sentiment to him?

Notes

1 [The subject was of considerable concern to certain philosophers of the day. The long discussion was opened by Delvolvé (see n.2 below) who had recently written two articles on the subject in *Revue de métaphysique et de morale*, 1908 and 1909. He focused, in introducing the discussion, on certain ideas he had raised in the articles, namely, the practical problem of teaching positive morality to young people. The effectiveness of a moral system was in some measure a criticism of its doctrines. Religious moral systems had advantages in that they were supported by an authority, which in the end was God. In them rational reasoning was of secondary importance. Further, the religious systems offered a more organic type of coherence with regard to practical morality. In the discussion, Delvolvé's concessions to religious morality and his emphasis on the weaknesses of positive morality were strongly opposed by Belot. The debate closed with the speech of Durkheim which comes at the end of this extract.—W.S.F.P.]

2 [Jean Delvolvé, born in 1872, was a positivist philosopher and moralist but there are indications here and elsewhere that he went beyond such a position and moved towards idealism. In 1906 he published *Essai sur Pierre Bayle, religion, critique et philosophie positive.* – W.S.F.P.]

3 [See 1910b, n.2, on p. 76.–W.S.F.P.]

4 [E. Le Roy, philosopher and lay Roman Catholic with modernist sympathies. – W.S.F.P.]

5 [See n.1, above. – W.S.F.P.]

6 [Célestin Bouglé (1870–1940) was associated with Durkheim's Année Sociologique group. In 1899 he wrote a doctorat ès lettres on egalitarianism. He was primarily a philosopher and taught in the University of Toulouse and then in 1906 was appointed professor at the Sorbonne until 1935. From 1935 to 1940 he was Directeur of the École Normale Supérieure. His interests were mainly in educational administration in which he assumed the role of Inspecteur général de l'instruction publique. Academically his most creative period was up to the First World War. His most scholarly book was probably *Essais sur le régime des castes* (1908). – W.S.F.P.]

7 [For a similar reference, see Durkheim, contribution to F. Abauzit, *et al.*, *Le Sentiment religieux à l'heure actuelle*, 1919, p. 101, See W. S. F. Pickering, *Durkheim on Religion*, Routledge & Kegan Paul, London, 1975, p. 184 – W.S.F.P.]

10 A discussion on sex education

1911a

First published in French under the title 'L'Éducation sexuelle', séance du 28 février 1911 in *Bulletin de la Société Française de Philosophie,* XI, pp. 33–8, 44–7.[1]

DURKHEIM: It is pointless, I think, to transfer the discussion to the actual principle of sex education. No one disputes the need for this type of education. And in fact no society has ever existed which has been totally without it. Yet each civilization interprets it in its own way.

Similarly, there can be no debate on the matter of sexual hygiene and all the various precautions that should properly be recommended to the young man and to the adult in general.

But Dr Doléris[2] passes from sexual hygiene to morality and it is much more difficult for me to follow him here. He appears, in fact, to agree that it is possible to legislate on morality in the name of hygiene, whereas he would consider it strange that one could claim to legislate on hygiene in the name of morality. Indeed, these are two quite distinct social functions which should be studied separately, unless one were to take into account their mutual reactions, should the need for this arise.

From the moral point of view, the real question lies in discovering why continence is a duty and how the reasons for this duty can be expounded to the young man. Yet I find only one reference to this problem in the whole of Doléris's report; nor is it treated as a separate, independent matter. Doléris merely shows that by entering into a free union, one is laying oneself open to physical risks and even moral difficulties (illegitimate children, the resulting domestic upheavals and their repercussions). And given the fact that the institution of marriage exists in present-day society, it is

140

perhaps only too clear that any extra-marital sexual union will necessarily give rise to all kinds of social problems and might even be a danger to health. But this is not the question. What we must find out is whether, and if so in what way, the young man can be made to understand that the state of marriage is justified in law and that extra-marital sexual intercourse is immoral. And this question requires independent treatment all the more so because the solution generally offered is such that it will affect the teaching of sexual hygiene, which is the concern of Doléris. For if the young man is to be made aware of the moral aspect of sexual intercourse, scientific knowledge should only be employed with the sort of reserve and discretion that the doctor might not fully appreciate, if he were left to his own devices.

In fact Doléris begins with the axiom that the mysterious character, which is attributed to the sexual act by public opinion and religious beliefs, is no more than a simple prejudice which has no true basis in reality. Yet if this is a relic, it is a relic from a singularly remote past and from inordinately tenacious customs. Admittedly this way of envisaging the sexual act seems to go hand-in-hand in every epoch with a whole set of religious beliefs, for example, Christian dogma. The rejection of these beliefs and dogmas consequently seems to imply the rejection of the apparently mystical conception of the sexual act. But when a collective sentiment has persistently asserted itself throughout history, one may rest assured that it has a factual basis, whereas the religious slogans which have justified it in the past are not rationally defensible. However, the most recent and sophisticated religions are not alone in attributing this singular character to the sexual act; the crudest and most primitive religions are unanimous in regarding it as a grave, solemn and religious act.

Such widespread ideas could not result from a simple aberration or deception under which men have laboured for centuries. It may be that the religious symbol conveys the corresponding moral reality imperfectly; but this does not mean that it is devoid of all reality. On the contrary, it can be taken as virtually certain that it must correspond to something in reality, in other words, to some sentiment which men of all times have truly felt. And in that case the problem at issue is to investigate what the sentiment is, how it is made up, how it originates, in other words, what aspect of human life it expresses.

I cannot of course embark upon an analysis of such a complex sentiment here; I must limit myself to a few pointers. When it is said that there is something mysterious about the sexual act, what is meant is that it cannot be grouped together with the acts of day-to-day life, that it is exceptional, that it is disconcerting and disturbing in some ways and that it awakens contradictory feelings in us. What this means is that it shocks, repels and offends us and at the same time attracts us. Now it can scarcely be that this sentiment is the product of a pure illusion. If there is such a thing as modesty, the sexual act is the immodest act *par excellence*. It negates and offends against modesty and since modesty is a virtue, the sexual act is immoral by reason of this alone. But on the other hand, there is no act which creates such strong bonds between human beings. It has an associative, and consequently moral power without compare. Is it surprising that, faced with such a complex and ambiguous relationship, moral *conscience* remains hesitant, perplexed, confused and divided against itself? It cannot advocate such an act, nor condemn it, nor can it praise, stigmatize or above all declare it unimportant. For although it moves the moral *conscience* in contrary directions, in no way does moral *conscience* remain indifferent to it. This is why moral *conscience* accepts the sexual act while at the same time requiring that it be veiled in darkness and mystery.

However summary this analysis may be, it is perhaps sufficient to convey the fact that the sexual act is not just any act but, on the contrary, that it is unique, that by virtue of its strangeness it occupies a place apart in moral life. But if this is so, sex education would clearly be falling short of its aim were it not understood in such a way as to convey to the young man the original, *sui generis* character of this singular act. For what matters above all is that it should give him as adequate an idea as possible; that it should make him comprehend the sexual act as it really is. Yet I fear that sex education, as the doctor is inclined to construe it, does not take sufficient account of this primordial necessity, of the reserve and discretion it implies. If, as Doléris appears to demand, we speak of the sexual act as one of the ordinary acts of physical life, in reality we denature it. We deprive it of what, for man, is its essential element. For man, it implies a great deal more than the material acts Doléris suggests. The contradictory, mysterious and exceptional character which the public *conscience* recognizes it to have, is an integral part of its nature. How could it possibly retain its character if it were discussed quite openly and without any kind of precaution? And what would be the moral result of encouraging young men to regard sexual intercourse as no more than the manifestation of a biological function, on a par with the digestion and the circulation?

Far be it from me to question the usefulness of the sort of scientific education which would inform the two sexes about the physical nature of this act. But when I hear Doléris referring to the conceptions which make the sexual act an act apart, obscure and confusing and in a sense mysterious, and calling them superstitions, I wonder if he is not neglecting a whole facet of the problem. Is he sufficiently aware, after all, how delicate and difficult it is to give this instruction? In a word, I am afraid that he is simplifying the question somewhat. It is not a matter of giving in to bourgeois prudery, but rather of inculcating in our children a sentiment without which sex education would be fundamentally unsound. Everyone knows what methods religions have used to inculcate this sentiment. We must employ other methods, but it is a mistake to believe that religions have totally misunderstood the nature of the aim to be pursued.

DOLÉRIS: (*Summary.* He said that in his particular field, biology, the sexual act was fundamentally a biological act, though men had refused to recognize it as such. The sociologist should try to discover why it had been shrouded in mystery. He said that most matrimonial prejudices must have originally had social or economic causes. He wanted to consider the sexual act in all its simplicity and he had confronted the child being educated with the facts of sex. He believed that this would improve the current state of sexual relations in general. With Durkheim he agreed that decency, prudence and simplicity were necessary, especially where girls were concerned. However, knowledge of sex did not imply immorality; for example, it did not exist amongst girls who work in medicine. These facts had led him to believe in the need for perfectly frank and open sex education.)

DURKHEIM: I shall restrict myself to two points of my argument, not wishing to repeat the basic essentials of the discussion.

When I spoke of the necessarily mysterious nature of the sexual act, I was not doing so as a man, but on the contrary exclusively as a sociologist. I am quite aware that it is not to education that I

143

owe the sentiment I endeavoured to analyse briefly. The dark, mysterious and awe-inspiring nature of the sexual act was revealed to me through historical and ethnographic research, and I even know the exact moment I was struck by the extremely general nature of the fact and how wide its implications were.

Furthermore, when I speak of mystery and obscurity, it is by no means my intention simply to inspire in the child some impression of fear, as well as of superstitious, irrational respect, and leave it at that. Far be it from me to wish to exclude reason from the field of sexual relations. On the contrary, it is my belief that it should be applied to them ceaselessly, but not only to the external gestures by which they are manifest, and which the psychologist studies, but also to the sentiments, ideas and institutions which give these relations their specifically human form. It is in this way that one could and indeed should show the child how the dual aspect of the sexual act, to which I was referring earlier, is closely bound up with our current moral and social ideas. And it is the needs of this moral education which I believe demand a great deal of discretion in the teaching of sexual hygiene.

BUREAU:[3] I had thought that Durkheim would answer the question which, on his own admission, is the one and only question raised by this discussion, namely, why does sexual morality exist and what valid reasons can one give to those who are asked to adhere to it, *which will make an impression on the 'conscience'*? In other words, what is the reason for continence?

DOLÉRIS: As for the education of the will which Parodi so earnestly advocates, I am the first to affirm its essential importance and I have quite explicitly indicated this in my submission. But I also feel it necessary to bring in utilitarian considerations which can act as a most effective brake. Otherwise, if one restricts oneself to the theoretical maxims, it will be impossible to leave the realm of the abstract and actually reach the adolescent mind. And in fact, as I said earlier, it is utilitarian considerations which are the basis of religious or philosophical ideas in sexual matters, but they are always vague and shrouded in darkness, rather than being clear and out in the open. The reason for the mysterious character of the sexual act lies here and nowhere else: societies reacted against the abuses which, in most of the peoples of antiquity, disturbed sexual relations. This is the probable origin of the awkward and exaggerated rules of abstinence which have been proclaimed at all times by religions and philosophies for the purpose of social protection.

DURKHEIM: I shall reply to the questions put to me by Bureau and Parodi together.

Bureau, taking up an openly religious standpoint, has indicated to us how he would justify continence in the eyes of the young man. Yet I am struck by the prodigious gap between this justification, the principles on which it is based, and the particular fact or the specific precept of which it claims to take account. These principles, to give an example, are such affirmations as, 'a glorious destiny unfolds before us' or 'human life is of incomparable value at all times.' We could all of us agree on such principles without much difficulty. It is quite certain that in the world man is something entirely apart, that we ascribe a value to him that cannot be compared with that of other creatures. Only, what results from this general idea is that all the acts accomplished by man have, for this reason, a quite special significance that the same acts, considered in the animal, could not have. The way Bureau presents the sexual act to us has therefore nothing about it which relates to the act in particular. Instead of considering it in itself and explaining what is specific to it, he merely classes it among human acts in general. But what is it that singles out the sexual act? Bureau does not tell us. But he himself recognizes that this act displays characteristics which are peculiar to it alone, in that he distinguishes it from all other everyday acts such as eating and drinking. And he, too, finds something particularly disturbing about it. If this act, as I have indicated, derives its mysterious, disturbing character from the fact that it necessarily seems immoral in one of its aspects, and in another, profoundly moral, then to resolve or at least broach the problem of sexual morality, these two contradictory aspects will have to be explained and their mutual opposition and correlation will have to be accounted for. But once this has been achieved, Bureau's religious explanation will no longer suffice, for owing to its extremely general nature, it avoids what is essential to the fact in question. I now come to this problem.

I would point out to begin with that it is not a problem which can be resolved by a short discussion and by means of a few fine phrases. The sexual act needs to be studied in conjunction with all its social concomitants and its domestic and other repercussions. When one realizes the complexity of the social facts, it becomes evident that this question supposes a whole body of research. Yet,

145

so as not to remain purely negative, I shall endeavour to indicate what procedure might be adopted in order to justify this rule of contemporary morality, without resorting to any confessional postulate.

In the first place, one would have to explain the fundamental reasons for marriage and show how they are bound up with our domestic morality as a whole; how, as a result, extra-marital sexual relations have a disruptive influence on our family organization which is one way of establishing their immorality. But it only appears so in an indirect and mediate way. I therefore believe that the best way to make an impression on a young man's mind is to make him understand the reasons for the singular, disturbing character of the sexual act which I was referring to earlier; for it is only on these terms that he will not indulge in it lightly.

Even Kant felt that there was something about sexual relations which offended against the moral sentiment.[4] This, he says, is because in sexual relations one individual serves as an instrument of pleasure to another, which is contrary to the dignity of the human being. But I believe the reason for the moral anxiety this act causes us is deeper and more general. The sentiment that lies at the root of our morality is the respect that man generates in his fellows. As a consequence of such respect, we keep our distance from our fellows and they keep their distance from us; we flee intimacy and do not permit it; we conceal our body as well as our inner life from prying eyes; we hide and isolate ourselves from others, and this isolation is at once the token and the consequence of the sacred character which has been vested in us. If we touch a sacred object without observing the respectful precautions laid down by ritual, we profane it and commit sacrilege. It is also a kind of desecration to fail to respect the boundaries separating men, to overstep these limits, and to intrude without due cause on other people. This is what engenders the sentiment and the duty of modesty, whether physical or moral. So there is no need to show that in the sexual act this profanation reaches an exceptionally high level, since each of the two personalities in contact is engulfed by the other. On no occasion is the abandoning of that reserve – which is merely another aspect of our dignity – so complete. This is what comprises the seed of basic immorality which is contained within this curiously complex act.

But at the same time it also contains within it the wherewithal to eradicate and redeem its constitutional immorality. For in fact this desecration also produces a communion, and a communion of the most intimate kind possible between two conscious beings. Through this communion, the two persons united become one; the limits which originally circumscribed each of them are first displaced and later transferred. A new personality is born, enveloping and embracing the other two. Should this fusion become critical and the new unity thus constituted become lasting, then from that moment onwards the desecration ceases to exist, since there are no longer two distinct, separate people, but one. Yet this result is achieved only on such terms. On the other hand, should the two individuals separate again after having become one, should each reclaim his independence after first giving himself to the other, then the desecration remains complete and irredeemable. This is why morality cries out against free union, quite apart from the repercussions that it can have on domestic harmony. The public *conscience* is well aware that in itself the sexual act forms a bond, that this binding force is inherent in it and that, to break these natural bonds, to fail to respect them, only aggravates the morally shocking aspect that the act already possesses. Here is the origin of the moral embarrassment we feel when the two partners of a divorce find themselves face to face again. We are aware that there is something abnormal in two individuals treating each other like strangers whereas, in fact, neither holds any mystery for the other. This is not, of course, to deny that divorce is an indispensable necessity. But there is no altering the fact that there is something disconcerting in certain of its effects that one should be able to recognize.

These indications will perhaps suffice to give an outline of how one can rationally explain that the sexual act is grave and solemn and that it binds together the persons it brings into contact, even if it is embarked upon without fulfilling the obligations which would legally sanction it.[5]

Notes

1 [The debate was introduced by Dr Doléris (see n.2 below), who circulated a paper beforehand and then spoke on it. Doléris held that the family was an inadequate agent in the matter of sexual instruction, at

least in the majority of cases. Therefore such education had to be carried out in schools where it could be based on scientific knowledge. He admitted that moral education in this matter was necessary but first had to come scientific education, based on biology. He advocated participation in sports, as a means of checking the sexual instinct. – W.S.F.P.]

2 [Jacques-Amédée Doléris (1852–1938) achieved considerable success in undertaking research in medicine. He was president of the Academy of Medicine. Just before this meeting of the Société Française de Philosophie, he had given a paper in August 1910 to the Third International Congress of School Hygiene on sex education with reference to family, science, morality and health. – W.S.F.P.]

3 [Paul Bureau (1865–1923) was a sociologist of the Le Play school. He wrote a controversial book, *Crise morale des temps nouveaux*, which was a pragmatic appeal for the establishment of a personal discipline, which in the end should be based on religion. For some time he was professor of law in Paris. – W.S.F.P.]

4 [Compare what Durkheim says about the way Kant deduced constitutive rules of marriage from the universal notion of charity. In the Introduction to *De la Division du travail social* in the first edition (1893), which was subsequently changed in the second edition of 1902 (t.1933b:413), he wrote:

> According to him [Kant], that act of sacrifice by which one mate consents to be an instrument of pleasure for the other is in itself immoral, and cannot lose that quality unless it is compensated for by a similar and reciprocal sacrifice on the part of the other. It is this barter of personalities which puts things in their places and which establishes the moral equilibrium again!

To Durkheim such a deduction was 'nothing more than pathetic' (ibid.). – W.S.F.P.]

5 [Lutoslawski, following Durkheim's comments, offered practical advice in terms of medical techniques and Catholic piety in dealing with male incontinence. – W.S.F.P.]

11 'Childhood'

1911c(2)

First published in French as 'Enfance' with F. Buisson
in *Nouveau Dictionnaire de pédagogie et d'instruction
primaire* publié sous la direction de F. Buisson,
Hachette, Paris, pp. 552–3.

Childhood, in the strict etymological sense, is the age when the man to be cannot yet speak (from the Latin *in-fans*, not speaking). But common practice has increasingly been inclined to extend the period to which this word is applied; it should, says Littré, extend 'from birth to approximately the age of seven'; but he adds that in popular usage it extends 'a little further than that, to the age of thirteen or fourteen'. The *Dictionnaire de l'Académie* has 'to the age of twelve or thereabouts'.

From the point of view which concerns us, it is useful to make a clear distinction between these two interpretations, for they correspond to two quite different periods of education. On the one hand, 'early childhood', including only the first three or four years, to which, in recent times, 'child psychology' or the study of the early phenomena of the small child's physical, intellectual, and moral life has turned its attention; and on the other hand, the 'second period of childhood' or childhood in the more usual and general sense of the word, which interpretation leaves aside the very special questions of the physiology and psychology of early childhood and refers to the normal period of education and instruction.

In this article, we shall deal only with the second of these subjects, in other words, we shall just discuss childhood in the usual sense of the word.

First, we have to ask ourselves what the characteristics of childhood and the natural laws of that period of life are, and

149

consequently, the quite general conditions that the science of education must satisfy.

All the distinctive features of childhood, and in particular those which education must take account of, derive from the definition of childhood itself. The essential function of this age, the role and purpose assigned to it by nature, may be summed up in a single word: it is the period of *growth*, that is to say, the period in which the individual, in both the physical and moral sense, does not yet exist, the period in which he is made, develops and is formed. What is needed then for growth to take place? What does this phenomenon necessarily suppose in the person where it occurs? Two conditions are assumed, which are always the same in all domains and in the most diverse forms: on the one hand weakness and on the other, mobility. These are, one might say, two aspects of the same situation: the person who grows finds himself in a sort of unstable and constantly changing equilibrium; he grows because he is incomplete, because he is weak, because there is still something he lacks. And he grows because deep in his nature there is a force for change, for transformation or rather formation and rapid assimilation which permits him to undergo constant modification until he attains full development.

In everything the child is characterized by the very instability of his nature, which is the law of growth. The educationalist is presented not with a person wholly formed – not a complete work or a finished product – but with a *becoming*, an incipient being, a person in the process of formation. Everything in child psychology and in educational theory derives from the essential characteristic of this age, which is sometimes manifest in the negative form – as the weakness and imperfection of the young person – and at other times in the positive form as strength and need for movement.

What is the child from the physical point of view? He is the puniest of beings, a small body that the merest blow can break, that the slightest illness imperils, a collection of muscles, nerves and organs which are, so to speak, made of milk and which only form, develop and increase in strength by their being placed in a wonderful environment of careful attention, of consideration, of favourable circumstances and protective influences. Physical childhood is essentially weakness itself from birth to well beyond the age of twelve mentioned by the *Dictionnaire de l'Académie*. The child cannot fend for itself and begins and continues to grow only

150

through the ceaseless intervention of the parents or their substitutes. Yet on the other hand, what rapidity of growth, what marvels there are in the development of this weak little body which unfolds its limbs, takes shape, hardens and grows though no man can say how, which changes before one's very eyes and is constantly in process of renewal! There is in all of this a power of movement, of growth and development whose ceaseless progress, intensity and inexhaustible exuberance baffle the imagination.

And if we turn to the mental aspect, the same two characteristics are apparent. Whichever stage in the period of childhood is chosen for consideration, one is always confronted with an intelligence which is at one and the same time so weak and fragile, so newly-formed and delicately constituted, endowed with such limited faculties and acting, as it were, in such a miraculous way, that one cannot help trembling with fear, when one gives the matter thought, for the safety of this delightful but fragile mechanism. And at the same time, the mechanism is never still; from one day to the next it generates, so to speak, new parts; it never stops. Do not ask it to come to rest; rather than remain idle it runs to no purpose at all; it is capable of everything except rest and inertia. It is fickle, changeable, capricious, full of disappointments and pleasant surprises.

Lastly, the moral aspect evinces the same weakness and mobility. The child's expressions of will are the faintest of impressions and are scarcely traces. As a rule, neither good nor evil is very deep-rooted in his nature; he is incapable of great and sustained effort; good resolutions are no sooner made than forgotten. But, at the same time, what eagerness greets every novelty! This diminutive *conscience* is a veritable kaleidoscope. The most varied mental states, the most contradictory passions and attitudes follow one another in succession: laughter gives way to tears, playful submissiveness to stubborn resistance, outbursts of tenderness to explosions of anger. These passions and enthusiasms wane just as quickly as they are aroused. Nothing is ever definitive. Everything is continually made and unmade.

It is the duty of the educationalist to bear in mind this dual character of the child whom he undertakes to train in every aspect of that process. Whether it is the senses, the intelligence or the will which is concerned, he knows that the most fragile of organisms has been placed in his hands, an organism which is scarcely formed

151

and which is so tender and soft that he must always beware of exhausting its strength and of interfering with its growth by wishing to hasten it. And, as it is important throughout this period to discover what the precise needs are that correspond to it, what powers lie at the child's disposal, and the exact level and true extent of his faculties, the first law of teaching is to adapt the education the child receives as closely as possible to the level of his capabilities. In the most rigorously ideal conditions, the tutor should ask himself, as he embarks on each exercise, each moral or intellectual lesson: has my pupil really reached this stage? might I not be over or underestimating his present capabilities? Without taking this concern too far, one may say that nothing is of more benefit to the tutor than frequently to call to mind the weakness of childhood, the allowances he should make for it and the progress which, taking everything into consideration, the very child who seems to be making the least progress, has already achieved, though this may not be apparent. So much for the first of the two points of view we have distinguished.

The second is no less important, though the attitude it implies is somewhat more complex and tricky.

On the one hand, it is plainly evident that one must take into account the child's acutely felt need for movement which, to varying degrees, subsists until adolescence. Any attempt at brutal repression of this tendency would incur the risk of extinguishing the flame which must be kindled. It would choke the keen and joyous impulses of a young life, of a strength which is as yet ill-balanced though powerful, in its weakness, by virtue of its very mobility. One must, for the sake of the child, beware of the fatigue which nullifies all efforts, its own as well as its tutor's. And fatigue does not occur only when too much is demanded of the child's faculties, but also when their free development is inhibited. This is not all, for one can get the child to work harder and apply himself more by learning how to yield to this highly imperious natural need of his, by making frequent changes of subject, by ending the lesson at the precise moment attention wanes and by allowing the pupil some degree of initiative, freedom and movement. He should set about his work with the same wholeheartedness he puts into play, with all his being, with that plenitude of activity, that passion and vigour which never tire him so long as they are expended freely, spontaneously and naturally. One can only hope to obtain this result from the sort of educational system which makes special allowances for all the child's pleasures, such as varied activity, free movement and unhindered development.

But on the other hand, one should not lose sight of the fact that this lack of continuity and equilibrium is a state which cannot last: it has to be outgrown. The child must learn to regulate and co-ordinate his actions; he must not remain the victim of circum-stances, dependent on the sudden shifts of his mood and the incidents of life outside him; let him learn to control himself, to contain and master himself and formulate his own principles; let him acquire the taste for discipline and order in his conduct. As we have shown in 'Éducation',[2] self-control, the power to contain, regulate and overcome oneself is one of the essential characteristics of the individual. In this respect a veritable metamorphosis is required. The state that has to be created appears to be at the opposite pole from the one which we set out with.

Happily, nature is of such richness that it provides us with the very instruments of action this transformation requires; we need only learn to apply them. We obtain the remedy from the same source as the trouble.

Whilst the child is a sort of anarchist, ignorant of all rules, re-straints and consequences, he is also a little traditionalist, even a stick-in-the-mud. If he is made to repeat a movement several times over, he will repeat it *ad infinitum*. The stories he knows best and which he has heard the most often are those he clamours for most enthusiastically; he does not tire of hearing them again. He refuses to eat with a different knife and fork from those he is accustomed to and to sleep in any other bed than his own. He would sooner go without food or sleep. Though, in some ways, he seems enamoured of novelties and changes, he would also appear to have a true horror of all change and novelty. These two sentiments, however contradictory, are each effects of one and the same cause: his instability. It is precisely because he never ceases changing that every state, movement or idea which happens to be repeated a certain number of times assumes, by virtue of this repetition, a power – a force of action which cannot be resisted because it has nothing to counterbalance it. Other states have no hold over him, just because they are fleeting and superficial. Hence any state which succeeds in acquiring some fixity, however tenuous it may be, tends of itself to be repeated, and becomes a need which can easily be tyrannical unless care is taken. *For this reason, it is very*

153

easy to make the child acquire habits.

The power which habit has over him as a result of the instability of his psychic life allows such instability to be corrected and contained. The taste for regular habits is already an early form of the taste for order and continuity. It is like an initiation into moral life and can begin very early; for almost as soon as he is born it is advisable to make him acquire set habits in all that concerns the principal circumstances of his existence. If this first seed is nurtured with prudence and wisdom, the child's life will gradually and progressively cease to present the contradictory spectacle of extreme mobility which alternates with an almost manic routine. Its fleeting and mobile aspects will become fixed; it will become regularized and thoroughly ordered. Admittedly, this somewhat mechanical order does not in itself possess any great moral value, but it paves the way for a superior quality of order. The taste for regularity is not yet respect for rule and duty, but it is on the way to becoming so. And, moreover, we have seen in the article entitled 'Éducation',[3] how it is possible and relatively easy to impart to the child the sentiment of moral authority and discipline, which constitutes the second stage in the formation of character and will. So nature does in fact place in our hands the means necessary for transcending it.

Passing on now from these general principles to their application, we have given an outline, under the heading *Organisation pédagogique*, of the rules which to our way of thinking seem to derive from it. (See also the headings *Éducation*[4] and *Pédagogie*.[5])

Notes

1 [Ferdinand Edouard Buisson (1841–1932) was largely responsible with Jules Ferry (1832–93) for the organization of primary education. He was director of primary education from 1879 to 1896, then professor of the science of education at the Sorbonne, from 1896 for ten years. In 1902 he was made a member of the Chamber of Deputies and one result was that Durkheim was appointed to the Sorbonne to take over much of his lecturing. Buisson's academic interests were more in psychology than in sociology. – W.S.F.P.]
2 [1911c(1); reproduced in *Éducation et sociologie* (1922a/t.1956a). – W.S.F.P.]
3 [ibid.]
4 [ibid.]
5 [1911c(3); reproduced in *Éducation et sociologie* (1922a/t.1956a) – W.S.F.P.]

A discussion on the boarding school and the New School

First published in French in contributions to a discussion of: 'Sur la culture générale et la réforme de l'enseignement' in *Libres entretiens,* 8th series, pp. 319–20, 322, 332.[1] [Desjardins' contribution, immediately below, starts on p. 318. The few words by Durkheim on p. 332 have been omitted. – W.S.F.P.]

DESJARDINS:[2] The advantage to the child itself is at once plainly apparent, but where does the general interest of society lie? Will you concede the principle that the work of education must, as the interest of society demands, be as far removed as possible from what is ruinous to education, that is in this case, from the hectic bustle of towns? Will you concede the principle that the educationalist must deliberately seek support outside unstable social reality, so as to be capable of resisting its influence? My mind is made up on this point, and I know how I shall proceed. But certain practical questions arise.

If the system of sending boarders to the country, rather than letting them remain as day-boys in towns, becomes more widespread, which type of organization will be the better and the more natural? In the New Schools[3] we have two groupings: family and school. The head of the household is distinct from the teacher of a class. Is this duality a good thing? Is it detrimental? . . . Is it not possible to imagine two groups of boarding schools, one family and the other scholastic? Might there be anything detrimental in that kind of organization?

DURKHEIM: My friend Desjardins' question seems to me to be little more than theoretical. It would indeed appear that in France we are unable to do without boarding schools. The Jesuits wished to do without them. They were forced to yield to the entreaties

155

of families and municipalities. The Central Schools of the Revolution had no boarding section; this was one of the causes of their failure.

The whole question is how to organize the boarding school. It is suggested that it be moved to the country. But it is well known what boarding schools in the country cost. They are accessible only to a minority of well-to-do children. This cannot be a general solution, which seems to me to largely undermine its appeal.

DESJARDINS: Should the boarding school approximate to family life?

DURKHEIM: There can be no question of that. An organization such as the one that has just been described is much too costly. But on the other hand, our great boarding schools are unnatural. A compromise solution should be found, but perhaps this is impossible.

DESJARDINS: . . . But one of the causes which make the creation of New Schools necessary is the fact that the modern French family is unfitted to the task of bringing up its children.

DURKHEIM: Is it not an exaggeration to speak of the modern French family in such terms? I admit, and am the first to deplore it, that the notion of authority has become more lax in the family and at school. But it should not be forgotten that in the older generation discipline was excessively harsh. Our immediate predecessors strove to soften it: they went too far, I agree, but one should not forget their achievement and the debt we owe them. To sum up, there is no proof that the family is appreciably inferior to what it was formerly. It is merely different.

Notes

1 [The discussion held amongst the members of the Union pour la Vérité centred on the principles of organizing boarding schools. There were references to English boarding schools, such as Abbotsholme and Bedales, and even to cricket! Much of the debate centred on the *internat* (boarding facilities in lycées) and various attempts to board children out in homes of their teachers as well as in other households. Some of the members present were in charge of experimental boarding schools. – W.S.F.P.]

2 [Paul Desjardins was a writer concerned with philosophical and moral

issues of his day. To discuss such issues he organized from time to time conferences at the abbey of Pontigny, where he died in 1940 at the age of eighty-one. Although he was an agnostic he was interested in religious questions and his book, *Catholicisme et critique: réflexions d'un profane sur l'affaire Loisy* (1905), caused a great stir. He helped to found the Union pour l'Action Morale in 1892, which became the Union pour la Vérité in 1906 and published its findings in *Libres entretiens* of which Desjardins was secretary. – W.S.F.P.]

3 [New Schools constituted an attempt to create boarding schools in the country for urban children. The influence of Rousseau is evident in this movement. – W.S.F.P.]

13

1916c

'The moral greatness of France and the school of the future'

First published in French as a contribution to: 'La Grandeur morale de la France: l'école de demain', *Manuel général de l'instruction primaire. Journal hebdomadaire des instituteurs et des institutrices,* 83 (17), 8 January 1916, pp. 217–18.

Dear Sir and respected colleague,

I hasten to answer your question which I am honoured to have been asked, namely, what will the school of the future be and what ought it to be?

But before we attempt to foretell the future, let us for a moment consider the past. For it is only by reference to the past that the future may be surmised.

Perhaps the only undisputed fact, if such there be, is that since the war France has created in the eyes of the world a moral climate entirely without parallel. All nations, even Germany herself, pay homage to the virtues she has displayed, to the heroism of her troops, and the calm, solemn patience with which she endures the appalling calamities of a war without historical precedent. Surely this can only mean that our educational methods have produced the main effect that was expected of them? The schools have made men of the children entrusted to their care. It is, of course, the state school which is largely responsible for this, since its pupils represent the majority of the school population. One can therefore quite safely conclude that it has carried out its task creditably. And there can be no question whatever of abandoning the principles upon which its teaching is based: the war has proved their worth. This is a fact which cannot be disputed and it should put an end to certain controversies.[1]

But it is clear that there are some lessons arising from the war of which we must take note. And whilst we may be satisfied with what has been achieved, we nevertheless need to press on with our work and improve it. The terrible experience we have undergone for almost seventeen months now shows us which points should be the principal target of our endeavours.

On the eve of the war, France was burdened with a chaotic and mediocre public life: she nevertheless experienced the upsurge of heroism the world admires. This is clearly because she carried within herself unsuspected strengths which from the lack of a precise aim to which they could be applied, lay dormant. It was natural that as soon as the country was in danger, a communal goal should emerge as a focus for the will of every individual. Instead of coming into conflict with one another and so causing mutual paralysis, they converged and through the convergence of their action accomplished great things. The miraculous rebirth of which people have spoken, is essentially a psychological phenomenon of the simplest kind which nevertheless redounds greatly to our honour and justifies a good many hopes. It testifies to our vitality and indicates what we are capable of, once we have a clear picture of what needs to be done. If, therefore, we wish to avoid the pitfalls of the past, the wills of all individuals need to be directed, not only in time of crisis but in a normal, regular way, towards one single goal, transcending all religious symbols and party slogans. And this goal is not hard to find. *It is the moral greatness of France.* Everything is contained within these few words, our duty as individuals to our country as well as our duty to humanity.

This idea will have to be the focal point of all our teaching. It must be the principal task of the school to awaken the appropriate sentiment, to implant it within all hearts and foster it to the utmost. Admittedly, not a little has already been achieved in this direction. Our moral education is sound, as experience has proved, but it lacks focus. It must be centred upon a single and quite distinct goal. It must receive greater emphasis if it is to act forcefully. The memories left by the terrible ordeal we are undergoing will easily provide the means.

This sentiment, once it has been fixed in the *conscience*, will have the effect of unifying action, but it will all the same be a powerful stimulus to the will. In the spheres of individual and national action we have for some time appeared a trifle nonchalant. We desired nothing more than to live a calm, untroubled existence, fighting shy of long-term undertakings which were demanding and not without risks. Yet a great people should have ambitions to match its inherent moral strengths. It must have the ambition to create a lasting work and to leave its mark upon history. The strong personality cannot assert itself just by acts which are expressive of it. Whilst there may be something morbid in Germany's passion of the colossal, an inordinate taste for mediocrity is not worthy of a great nation. The wills of individuals must therefore be linked to some high ideal which shakes them out of their natural sloth and repeatedly invites them to rise above themselves. Surely the ideal we have just referred to is the most likely to produce this effect?

Yet there is another serious lacuna that the war has brought to light in our moral constitution.

Events have proved that our liveliness and natural good humour did not exclude the spirit of sacrifice and self-denial. For a great cause it has been seen that Frenchmen could be brave and endure the ultimate. But it has also certainly had to be recognized that we did not possess the spirit of discipline in like measure. We are less able than our enemies to regulate our movements so as to conform with those of other people and to act in concert and submit to the general law. We are too much inclined to go our own way. Naturally, there can be no question of subscribing to the blind, mass discipline practised by Germany which supposes, in those who submit to it, a passivity of which we are incapable. It is nevertheless true that *respect for rules* is the condition of all corporate action.

Yet there is no doubt that this feeling has weakened in France. The very idea of moral authority, which is the basis of all sound discipline, has come under strong attack. One of our best educationalists, one of the noblest figures of our times, declared some years ago that the notion of authority, of obligation, of the rule that is respected because it commands, is archaic and contravenes the very principles of democracy.[2] And since, in fact, it is the chief aim of democracy to arouse and foster the sense of personal autonomy, and since autonomy and authority are considered – quite unjustly so – to be mutually exclusive, it seems perfectly natural that democracy should imply and cause a weakening of the sentiment of authority. In this way a relaxation of discipline has occurred both at school and in society.

The school of the future will have to make good this serious error. Respect for legitimate authority, which is to say moral authority, will have to be reawakened and the religion of the rule will have to be inculcated in the child. He will have to be taught the joys of acting in conjunction with others, according to the dictates of an impersonal law, common to everyone. Assuredly the mechanical, punctilious discipline that was practised formerly cannot be too strongly condemned, for it worked contrary to its aim in that, through its unreasonable demands, it kindled the spirit of resistance and rebellion. School discipline, on the contrary, must appear to children as something good and sacred – the condition of their happiness and moral well-being. In this way, when they are men, they will accept spontaneously and consciously that social discipline which cannot be weakened without endangering the community.

As you see, the reforms I earnestly advocate are above all improvements (important ones, to my mind) of what has already been accomplished. Under no circumstances is there any question of a revolution.

Notes

1 [These would appear to relate to the old dispute of secular versus religious education, which persisted in the wake of the policies of the Third Republic in favour of the secularization of education. State education was attacked because of its failure to provide moral instruction worthy of the name. What was happening in the war, Durkheim believed, disproved the charge of inadequacy, since young people educated in state schools were proving their moral stature. – W.S.F.P.]
2 [This probably refers to Henri Marion (1846–96), who was a famous French educationalist and professeur de Science de l'education at the Sorbonne. He emphasized rational discipline and the influence of the master over the student. He believed that morality was to be dictated by the *conscience* and by reason. He attempted to provide an authoritarian form of education for the purposes of strengthening democracy in France. Philosophically he was a Cartesian and near to the thought of Renouvier and Secrétan. – W.S.F.P.]

14 'Rousseau on educational theory'

1919a

First published in French as 'La "Pédagogie" de
Rousseau' in *Revue de métaphysique et de morale*,
XXVI, pp. 153–80.

Introductory Note by Xavier Léon*

When Durkheim thought death was approaching, he put his manuscripts in order and added the following note which will be found at
the beginning of the previous article on Rousseau[1]:

> Rousseau. *Social Contract.* For possible publication. Promised
> to Xavier Léon. I have attached some notes on *Émile* which
> should complete the *Contract.* The two themes are closely linked
> thought this is not generally realised. Might there not be a case for
> publishing these lecture outlines? Let someone else decide.

The executors of Durkheim's posthumous works are of the
opinion that his lecture notes on Rousseau's educational theory
merit publication, even in outline form.

Durkheim gave the course twice in Paris. This was an aspect of
Rousseau's work as an educationalist which he himself noted and
to which he attached great importance. In his view, nothing was
further from the truth than the generally accepted interpretation
of Rousseau's doctrines in which he is seen as the father of individualism and anarchy. This he proved in the previously published
article.

Yet it is also confirmed by Rousseau's educational doctrines

---

* [This appears as a footnote at the beginning of the article. Xavier Léon was
editor of *Revue de métaphysique et de morale* at the time. — W.S.F.P.]

themselves, which prove how far Rousseau was aware of the social nature of man and of the reality of society. In this way, they confirm Durkheim's own views on the work as a whole.

Further, the lecture notes are interesting in themselves as the first attempt to develop a rational theory of education based on the principle that education moulds man as a social animal.

The interest of the notes is thus self-evident. In their present form they contain the proof, and the critical method by which it is obtained, of Durkheim's views on Rousseau's theory of education. They are thought-provoking and easy to read. As lecture notes, they are well thought out and organized. They are quite conclusive and contain all the necessary texts and quotations. This is not partially prepared work: it is complete.

A note on the presentation of the manuscript. It is, as far as possible, a faithful reproduction of the notes in their original form. Durkheim went to infinite trouble to make a complete draft of his lectures. Indeed at the outset of his teaching career, he painstakingly wrote out every sentence in full. Only at the end, when at the height of his powers, did he forgo this time-consuming task and make do with indicating the theme of each sentence, certain thereby that in its every detail he was master of his thought.

Durkheim would proceed to his lectures with only an extremely brief résumé, which generally consists just of headings, and with all the texts meticulously marked and annotated. He would speak without notes, and took great pains to make sure his students knew the original text.

The Rousseau texts published here were read in the order they occurred in the lectures and should be read as they were at the time.

We have been unsuccessful in tracing the edition Durkheim used in his notes which he referred to as 'in-12' [duodecimo – H.L.S.].

All the texts have been collated with the edition of *Émile* published in London in 1781.

There are four lectures. Their titles have not been found and no attempt has been made to deduce them. The first lecture is clearly devoted to the method and principles of Rousseau's pedagogy. The second, to education and nature. The third, to education by things and to the relations which develop between master and pupil. The fourth, to the concept of negative education and the application of this theory to moral education.

The first two lectures are extant in only one form with the exception of the end of the second lecture (see C. *Things*, p. 175) which reappears in the second draft of the third lecture.

The third and fourth lectures were delivered in successive forms. The second is patently the only definitive one, since it is to this that Durkheim's own blue pencil numbers refer. It is this one, therefore, that is published first.

Yet Durkheim kept the manuscript of the first draft which he had given as the formal outline of his lectures, clearly believing that his editor might usefully refer to it and supplement excessively brief indications by borrowing from the original draft.

We also felt bound to publish this first draft, as an appendix to the second, yet without reproducing the texts, which the reader will easily find for himself.

The passages underlined [here shown in italics – H.L.S.], whether in Durkheim's or Rousseau's texts, were underlined by Durkheim himself. It was these that he read out or enlarged upon in his lectures with particular care and attention.

Outlines of lectures

Lecture One

A. The ideal and abstract nature of the method

I The method of the Contract. Rousseau's aim was to draw up a plan for a society which would suit man in general; a plan based accordingly on man's nature. The basic problem therefore was to highlight the essential elements of man.

II The problem of education is posed by Rousseau in the same terms. He does not enquire which form of education is appropriate to a particular country or epoch. These are *chance conditions* which have no bearing on the fundamental nature of things and should be disregarded.

Text 1 The ideal and abstract nature of Rousseau's pedagogy (*Préface*, ix/t.2–3)*:

There are two things to be considered with regard to any scheme. In the first place, 'Is it good in itself?' In the second, 'Can it be easily put into practice?' With regard to the first of these, it is enough that the scheme should be intelligible and feasible in itself, that what is good in it should be adapted to the nature of things, in this case, for example, that the proposed method of education should be suitable to man and adapted to the human heart. The second consideration depends upon certain given conditions in particular cases; these conditions are accidental and therefore variable; they may vary indefinitely. Thus one kind of education would be possible in Switzerland and not in France ... Now all these particular applications are not essential to my subject, and they form no part of my scheme.

Text 1(b) The ideal nature of educational theory (I,17/t.10): (Read the passage on the mobility of human things which follows the quotation.)

We must therefore look at the general rather than the particular, and consider our scholar as man in the abstract, man exposed to all the changes and chances of mortal life.

It is therefore a man who is to be educated.

Text 2 It is a man who is to be educated (I,15 and 16/t.9):

In the natural order men are all equal and their common calling is that of manhood, so that a well-educated man cannot fail to do well in that calling and those related to it. It matters little to me whether my pupil is intended for the army, the church or the law. Before his parents chose a calling for him nature called him to be a man. Life is the trade I would teach him.

When he leaves me, I grant you, he will be neither a magistrate, a soldier nor a priest; he will be a man. All that becomes a man he will learn as quickly as another. In vain will fate change his

---

* [The references so marked relate to Rousseau's *Émile*. The French edition is that of 1781. The English translation, denoted by t., is that by Barbara Foxley, *Émile, or Education*, Dent, London, 1911. *Préface*, ix/t.2–3 means p. ix of the French text and pp. 2–3 of the translated text. Similarly, I,17/t.10, means Book I, p. 17 in the French and the corresponding English translation is found on p. 10 of that by Barbara Foxley. — W.S.F.P.]

station, he will always be in his right place . . .

The real object of our study is man and his environment.

Again and again, the need is to set aside the accidental, the variable and to get at the essential, the rock upon which human reality rests.

B. The optimism of Rousseau's educational theory

I According to certain well-known texts, the child is naturally good. All that issues from man is evil.

Text 3 Innate goodness (I,1/t.5):

God makes all things good; man meddles with them and they become evil. He forces one soil to yield the products of another, one tree to bear another's fruit . . . he destroys and defaces all things; he loves all that is deformed and monstrous; he will have nothing as nature made it, not even man himself.

Does this mean that one should do nothing? (I,1/t.5):

. . . Otherwise (if a man was not educated and his nature not distorted – Durkheim) things would be even worse, and mankind cannot be made by halves. Under existing conditions a man left to himself from birth would be more of a monster than the rest. Prejudice, authority, necessity, example, all the social conditions into which we are plunged, would stifle nature in him and put nothing in her place.

The educational consequences. Laisser faire. The child has an intrinsic morality. Man should therefore maintain a distance between himself and the child, whose judgment is naturally just. Let us not deform it.

From this point of view, the whole discussion will turn upon the question of whether the child is perfect; whether he has not any natural vices, etc. This is the thesis frequently attributed to Rousseau.

II However the following text should make us think more carefully.

Text 4 Education. Its power (I,5/t.6):

We are born weak, we need strength; helpless, we need aid;

foolish, we need reason. All that we lack at birth, all that we need when we come to man's estate, is *the gift of education*.

Nature needs to be bent. *Thus it is not perfect in every respect.*

III If this were the idea attributed to Rousseau, then education should be reduced to the minimum, and development allowed to proceed unimpeded. But no one has a more acute sense of the power of education and the need for it than Rousseau. Education transforms nature, it denatures it.

Text 5 Denaturing (I,10/t.7):

> The natural man lives for himself; he is the unit, the whole, dependent only on himself and on his like. The citizen is but the numerator of a fraction, whose value depends on its denominator; his value depends upon the whole, that is, on the community. Good social institutions are those best fitted to make a man unnatural, to exchange his independence for dependence, to merge the unit in the group, so that he no longer regards himself as one, but as a part of the whole, and is only conscious of the common life.

(See examples.)

Why? (1) Weakness of the child. Harmony between desires and strength. It does not exist in the child.

Necessary weakness (see *Émile*, p. 89).

Text 5(b) Weakness of childhood. Reasons (I,4/t.6):

> If a man were born tall and strong, his size and strength would be of no good to him till he had learnt to use them; they would even harm him by preventing others from coming to his aid; left to himself he would die of want before he knew his needs.

(2) Contradiction between natural and social (*civil*) man. Necessary denaturing.

IV The educator has therefore a positive goal to pursue. To establish harmony between the child and his environment.

Text 6 The ideal (I,127–8/t.44):

> What then is human wisdom? Where is the path of true happiness? The mere limitation of our desires is not enough, for if they were less than our powers, part of our faculties would be

167

idle, and we should not enjoy our whole being; neither is the mere extension of our powers enough, *for if our desires were also increased* we should only be the more miserable. True happiness consists in decreasing the difference between our desires and our powers, in establishing a perfect equilibrium between the power and the will. Then only, when all its forces are employed, will the soul be at rest and man will find himself in his true position.

In this condition, nature, who does everything for the best, has placed him from the first . . . It is only in this primitive condition that we find the equilibrium between desire and power, and then alone man is not unhappy.

Text 7 Denaturing. Producing harmony in us (I,11/t.8):

He who would preserve the supremacy of natural feelings in social life knows not what he asks. Ever at war with himself, hesitating between his wishes and his duties, he will be neither a man nor a citizen. He will be of no use to himself or to others. He will be a man of our day, a Frenchman, an Englishman, one of the great middle class.

Text 8 Not to be taken as a model (I,140/t.48. Incorrectly given as p. 40 in the French text. – H.L.S.):

Parents who live under our ordinary social conditions bring their child into these conditions too soon.

The forming of social man.

C. Why nature should be taken as a guide

I For this, take nature as model and guide.

II Why? The child is man in the *natural state. Prior to society.* But the state of nature is perfection. Not absolute perfection, but of that order. In a sense it is therefore a model. 'Let us lay it down as an incontrovertible rule that the first impulses of nature are always right; there is no original sin in the human heart' (I,165/t.56). Explanation. Imperfections: where do they originate? Desires inappropriate to nature: whence could they come?

But there is no original goodness in the positive sense.

III This is why the child's nature must be respected. Is the child perfect? No, since it needs to be educated. In what way? In keeping with its nature, while this remains in a state of purity.

Is this all? Is this the ideal? No. Rousseau merely says that since it is a child, it should be educated as such, in accordance with its nature, which is that of a child. This is the natural state of man at birth because it is his nature. *'Nature would have them children before they are men'* (153/t.54). *'Mankind has its place in the sequence of things; childhood has its place in the sequence of human life'* (126/t.44). See p. iii of the *Préface*.

Text 9 Look for the child in the child (*Préface*, iv/t.1–2):

The wisest writers . . . are always looking for the man in the child, without considering what he is before he becomes a man . . . Begin thus by making a more careful study of your scholars, for it is clear that you know nothing about them.

IV Yet why this preference? Not the only ideal. Why not the other? Same antithesis. Isn't the question already decided in advance?

Far from it. Conciliation is possible. We have seen how and why. The problem is posed in the same terms for education. Two types of education. Nature and man. Conciliation is necessary.

Text 10 Denaturing. In what it must consist (I,14/t.9):

If the twofold aims could be resolved into one by removing . . . man's self-contradictions, one great obstacle to his happiness would be gone. To judge of this you must see the man full-grown; you must have noted his inclinations, watched his progress, followed his steps; in a word you must really know the natural man. When you have read this work, I think you will have made some progress in this enquiry.

How is this possible? One is stable and constant. The other is variable and determined by us. The first must provide the norm. *'Since all three modes of education must work together, the two that we can control must follow the lead of that which is beyond our control'* (6/t.6). *'Everything should therefore be brought into harmony with these natural tendencies'* (8/t.7).

V The basis of this doctrine. The idea that physical nature is the only [illegible word] thing; all the rest is variable, changing.

Cannot furnish any stable principle of conduct. Education is essential. This is what distinguishes man.

VI Importance of the principle. It has sometimes been said that the novelty of Rousseau's theory of education is its psychological character. True. Study of the child. But character is derived, and derived from a more general, more important principle.

How is pedagogy to become scientific? By basing itself upon a science. *What we mean by science* is the objective study of a given reality. Thus providing a guarantee against subjective impressions. Objective criterion.

Heretofore, educational theory has not met this condition. It has conveyed feelings, aspirations. Montaigne. Rabelais. Reasons masquerading as arguments. *Nothing to study.*

Rousseau. Exaggeration to be avoided. His starting point is passion and the influence of the environment. Yet now the idea is put forward that *to be normal, education must reproduce a given model in reality.* Not a construct, since there is something to find out. Refer to the given fact, placed beyond the realm of fantasy.

Incipient science. Critique of the idea of nature. Strongly *a priori*. Yet, in principle, an objective standard.

VII The psychological repercussion. Abstract, artificial psychology. An understatement. Progress of nature.

Principle of the *Encyclopédie*.

Lecture Two

A. *What does nature teach us about education?*

I To come back to the principle. Two kinds of education. Education by nature and education by man. The former is the prototype. Why? *Is it simply an impossibility?* Another reason. If this kind of education cannot be changed, it is because it is rooted in the nature of things. It is therefore perfect within its order. *Thus we have a model.*

Importance of this principle. The model is not arbitrary. There is something to find out and to observe. It is the stuff of a science on which pedagogy is based. Educational theory consequently becomes a less exclusively subjective and emotional construct.

II What does nature teach us about education? *First Rule.* It teaches us that there are a certain number of basic needs which can be satisfied simply if they are allowed to develop freely. What the free development of activity means when it is not interfered with. *Animal.* Let it be our model. Let it not be interfered with. Hence the rule of freedom which underlies all the teachings of Book I. *No swaddling clothes.* No reins.

Text 1 No restriction of movement (I,72/t.27):

When the child draws its first breath do not confine it in tight wrappings. No cap, no bandages, nor swaddling clothes. . . . As he begins to grow stronger, let him crawl about the room; let him develop and stretch his tiny limbs; you will see him gain strength from day to day.

Spontaneous cures by natural means. No doctor.
Text 2 Spontaneous cures. No doctor (I,57/t.22–3):

As the child does not know how to be cured, he knows how to be ill. The one art takes the place of the other and is often more successful; it is the art of nature. When a beast is ill, it keeps quiet and suffers in silence; but we see fewer sickly animals than sick men. . . . I shall be told that animals, who live according to nature, are less liable to disease than ourselves. Well, that way of living is just what I mean to teach my pupil; he should profit by it in the same way.

III But there is one rule which in some ways is the direct opposite of this. *Remember the Contract.* If the citizen is to be natural, he must feel that he is under the sway of a moral force comparable in strength to a physical force. It is necessary and inescapable, it limits and stops him.

The same feeling should be induced by education. *The yoke of necessity.*

Text 3 The feeling of necessity (I,161/t.55):

Let him (the child) early find upon his proud neck the heavy yoke which nature has imposed upon us, the heavy yoke of necessity, under which every finite being must bow. Let him find this necessity in things, *not in the caprices of man*; let the curb be force, not authority.

171

Text 4 Necessity (I,136/t.47; incorrectly given as p. 36 in the French text – H.L.S.):

Oh, man! . . . Keep to your appointed place in the order of nature and nothing can tear you from it. Do not kick against the stern law of necessity, nor waste in vain resistance the strength bestowed on you by heaven, not to prolong or extend your existence, but to preserve it so far and so long as heaven pleases.

IV Why? The ideal state of all being is adaptation to their environment. Harmony between needs and means, powers and desires. This is the true strength, the true power, the condition of true happiness.

Text 5 The ideal. Powers (I,129/t.45):

What do you mean when you say, 'Man is weak'? The term weak implies a relation, a relation of the creature to whom it is applied. An insect or a worm whose strength exceeds its needs is strong; an elephant, a lion, a conqueror, a hero, a god himself, whose needs exceed his strength is weak. . . . When man is content to be himself he is strong indeed; when he strives to be more than man he is weak indeed.

Text 6 The ideal (I,127/t.44):

A conscious being whose powers were equal to his desires would be perfectly happy.

But what does this harmony presuppose? That a being should not continue to develop endlessly and that he should stop or be stopped. Idea of a limit, of an impassable limit. *'The world of reality has its bounds, the world of imagination is boundless'* (I,129/t.45). This equilibrium is achieved naturally in animals. And everywhere in nature. It is therefore also part of man's destiny. Yet it is harder to achieve. *Man has superfluous, potential powers.*

Text 7 Potential powers (I,130/t.45):

The other animals possess only such powers as are required for self-preservation; man alone has more. Is it not very strange that this superfluity should make him miserable?

Text 8 Potential powers (absence of limit) (I,128/t.44):

(Nature) has stored all the rest (those not currently needed) in his (man's) mind as a sort of reserve, to be drawn upon at need . . . As soon as his potential powers of mind begin to function, imagination, more powerful than all the rest, awakes, and precedes all the rest.

In the natural state they lie dormant, but it takes a mere trifle to awaken them. They are more than strong enough to deal with what confronts them. Anticipation. Not adapting. Whereupon the limit ceases to be felt.
Imagination.
Text 8(b) (I,128/t.44):

It is imagination which enlarges the bounds of possibility for us, whether for good or ill, and therefore stimulates and feeds our desires by the hope of satisfying them. But the object which seemed within our grasp flies quicker than we can follow; when we think we have grasped it, it transforms itself and is again far ahead of us. We no longer perceive the country we have traversed, and we think nothing of it; that which lies before us becomes vaster and stretches still before us. Thus we exhaust our strength, yet never reach our goal, and the nearer we are to pleasure, the further we are from happiness.

V What is the result of this? There is no longer anything which can satisfy us. We can only invent. But then, whatever we do, we are limited. The world does not yield to us. Hence a feeling of pained surprise.
Text 9 Usefulness of the feeling of resistance (I,151/t.52):

They are used to find everything give way to them; what a painful surprise to enter society and meet with opposition on every side, to be crushed beneath the weight of a universe which they expected to move at will!

(But for this, they must be surrounded by things.)

VI Yet limitation and resistance imply suffering. But first and foremost suffering is part of nature.
Text 10 Hardening. Negative education (I,32/t.14):

Fix your eyes on nature, follow the path traced by her. She keeps

173

children at work, she hardens them by all kinds of difficulties, she soon teaches them the meaning of pain and grief . . . Sickness and danger play the chief part in infancy.

Text 12 [sic] The need for grief. An element of man's natural state (I,148/t.51):

Do you think any man can find true happiness elsewhere than in his natural state; and when you try to spare him all suffering, are you not taking him out of his natural state?

Moreover, grief and resistance – where it is seen to be necessary – do not tax man's patience or irritate him. *They are accepted.*

Text 11 [sic] The feeling of necessity. It induces calm (I,162/t.55):

. . . It is in man's nature to bear patiently with the nature of things, but not with the ill-will of another. A child never rebels against, 'There is none left', unless he thinks the reply is false.

The basis of this idea. What is necessary has a reason. That which has a reason cannot be bad. Even the necessity of death. Texts from pages 131 and 133. Obscure and scarcely rational feeling of the rightness of what is necessary.

VII *A little known aspect of Rousseau's doctrine.* The common view of it. A different sentiment. A different principle. How they are reconciled. True freedom: doing what one can. The feeling of the impossible is thus implied.

Yet the fact remains that we are dealing here with a completely different sort of freedom. Freedom which is contained, which is limited. The notion of limitation is essential to it. *Strict discipline.* Misunderstanding of Rousseau.

B. How is this sentiment to be induced? By the agency of man?

I Which powers are to be resisted? Man's will? Commands? Obedience? *But in that case, there will be no necessity. For will is arbitrary.* To command is to demand that something be done just because it is commanded, not because it is necessary. What is desired by one may not be desired by another. Contingency. As soon as the child comes up against will of this kind, he can triumph over it. Means of obtaining submission.

II Moreover, on what grounds does will command? On those of opinion? Yet opinion does not express things as they are. It denatures them. It is an artificial thing. Death. Illness.

Text 13 Opinion (I,129/t.45):

Health, strength and a good conscience excepted, all the good things of life are a matter of opinion; except bodily suffering and remorse, all our woes are imaginary.

Text 14 The origin of moral ills (I,132/t.46):

Our moral ills are the result of prejudice.

Even illness. It is the idea of the illness itself which causes our suffering. All the more so, then, with death (I,132/t.46):

Live according to nature; be patient, get rid of the doctors; you will not escape death, but you will only die once, while the doctors make you die daily through your diseased imagination, etc. . . .

III Yet what of moral precepts? The child can have no notion of them. Why? Morality is discerned by reason, and the child has no reason.

Text 15 Morality and reason (I,94/t.34):

Reason alone teaches us to know good and evil. Therefore conscience, which makes us love the one and hate the other, though it is independent of reason, cannot develop without it. Before the age of reason we do good or ill without knowing it, and there is no morality in our actions, although there is sometimes in our feelings with regard to other people's actions in relation to ourselves.

Putting the cart before the horse.
Text 16 Reason comes last (I,155/t.53):

To make a man reasonable is the coping stone of a good education, and yet you profess to train a child through his reason! You begin at the wrong end, you make the end the means. If children understood the reason they would not need education.

A child is morally neutral. He does not understand the reason for commands. He cannot submit to them of his own free will. Exterior

175

obedience. (Text from page 156.) *False ideas.*

IV No commands in the true sense. No authority to be invoked. Consequently the usual motives are proscribed. Discipline through emulation. All this is artificial.

Text 18 Proscription of the usual motives (emulation, fear) (I,163/t.55):

> It is very strange that ever since people began to think about education they should have hit upon no other way of guiding children than emulation, jealousy, envy, vanity, greediness, base cowardice, all the most dangerous passions . . . ever prepared to corrupt the soul.

C. Things[2]

I Only things can induce the feeling of necessity. For they alone are subject to the laws of necessity. Nothing arbitrary here. They are what they are. (Text)[3]

Here, there is no capricious will. The possible and the impossible. (Text)[4] *The power of things.*

II Things known through feelings. Hence, educate the child in a purely sentient environment. Befitting to the child's nature. He has nothing but feelings. (Text)[5]

III A great innovation. The former principle of education – man educated by man.

The principle in reverse. To educate man by things. *Things hitherto placed outside the moral sphere. Still are in a sense.* Yet they contribute to the education of moral man. An essential, pre-paratory part of his education. *The sentiment of absolute necessity stems from this.* He is to be initiated into the moral world. He does not stem from it.

Why? Because moral man is the father of nature.

Lecture Three: definitive draft

A. Dependence on things

176

I A little known aspect of Rousseau's doctrine. *Liberalism.* Need for discipline, restraint. Not infinite. Limitation. Desires which are restricted. Equilibrium.

II But *restricted by what*? By human will? *This is contingent.* Dependence is contrary to nature. *Why one will against another?*

The example of nature. Everthing that is finite stops. Cannot do otherwise. No choice: inflexible laws.

III Back to the *Social Contract.*[6]

IV *No orders; no obedience.*
   Text 1 No obedience (I,143/t.49):

Let there be no question of obedience for him or tyranny for you.

No verbal lessons.
Text 2 No lessons (I,164/t.56):

Give your scholar no verbal lessons; he should be taught by experience alone.

No actions of the child involving the tutor.
Text 3 Neither obedience nor commands. Necessity (I,159/t.53):

Your child must not get what he asks, but what he needs; he must never act from obedience, but from necessity. The very words *obey* and *command* will be excluded from his vocabulary, still more so those of *duty* and *obligation*; but the words strength, necessity, weakness, and constraint must have a large place in it.

So, no *punishment.*
Text 4 No punishment (I,192/t.65):

Children should never receive punishment merely as such; it should always come as the natural consequence of their fault.

(Application of this to lies.)
In any case, has no morality.
Text 5 (I,164/t.56):

Wholly unmoral in his actions, he can do nothing morally wrong, and he deserves neither punishment nor reproof.

177

V But, in that case, where shall we find the power to stop and restrain him? In things. *They act from necessity; impersonally.* Do not obey any individual will. Thus it is *from them alone that this early education must emanate. The power of things.*

The feeling of what is possible or impossible.

Text 6 The power of things (I,163/t.56):

Do not undertake to bring up a child if you cannot guide him merely by the laws of what can or cannot be.

The natural limits of things. *Feeling of necessity.*

Text 7 Force, not authority (I,161/t.55):

Let him early find upon his proud neck, the heavy yoke which nature has imposed upon us, the heavy yoke of necessity, under which every finite being must bow. *Let him find this necessity in things, not in the caprices of man; let the curb be force, not authority.*

Physical obstacles.

Text 8 Dependence on things: (I,143/t.49):

Keep the child dependent on things only. By this course of education you will have followed the order of nature. Let his unreasonable wishes meet with physical obstacles only, or the punishment which results from his own actions, lessons which will be recalled when the same circumstances occur again. It is enough to prevent him from doing wrong without forbidding him to do wrong. Experience or lack of power should take the place of law.

VI No punishments as such.

Text 9 No chastisement (I,164/t.56):

Never punish him, for he does not know what it is to do wrong; never make him say, 'Forgive me', for he does not know how to do you wrong. Wholly unmoral in his actions, he can do nothing morally wrong, and he deserves neither punishment nor reproof.

What this is. *Curb accepted because it stems from the nature of things.* What could be put in their place? *Physical consequences of this act. Method* of natural consequences.

VII Authority excluded from this early education. *Sui generis* in
178

character, imposing respect and obedience. Acting out of respect for authority. An idea explicitly repudiated by Rousseau.

Excluded from education as a whole? From all social and moral life? No. *From early education only. Authority will come later.* Authority of the law. But it will have to be modelled on the action of things, that is to say on physical necessity. Necessity, the prototype of obligation.

This specific order is necessary for the feeling of authority to be natural.

VIII Compare with Spencer. He rejects all discipline. All restraint. Feeling of the useful and the harmful. *No constraint.* Look to interest.

Rousseau feels discipline indispensable. An active sentiment, everywhere present. Restraint. *Self-control.* A kind of morality.

Debatable whether morality can arise in this way. A feeling of morality. *A feeling of authority.* And *same truly impersonal, general type* of moral authority. The rule. Kant and Rousseau. *But the imperative element is no less necessary.* Impersonal commands.

B. Relations between tutor and pupil

I He must therefore live surrounded by things. *Which are consequently perceptible to the senses.* This, furthermore, is in keeping with his child's nature. Man in the natural state.

Text 10 Sentient milieu (I,155/t.53):

> Act in such a way that while he only notices external objects his ideas are confined to sensations; let him only see the physical world around him. If not, you may be sure that either he will pay no heed to you at all, or he will form fantastic ideas of the moral world of which you prate, ideas which you will never efface as long as he lives.

II *Is there to be no master, then?* No action? A misinterpretation. *No direct action.* But not all action is forbidden. Tutor *is master of things*; *is behind them*; is legitimately master of them.

179

Considerable power. Tutor can impose his will not by means of orders, but by making things act for him.

Text 11 The tutor and things (I,250/t.84):

> Let him (the pupil) always think he is master while you are really master. There is no subjection so complete as that which preserves the forms of freedom; it is thus that the will itself is taken captive. Is not this poor child, without knowledge, strength, or wisdom, entirely at your mercy? Are you not master of his whole environment so far as it affects him? Cannot you make of him what you please? . . . No doubt he ought only to do what he wants, but he ought to want to do nothing but what you want him to do. He should never take a step you have not foreseen, nor utter a word you could not foretell.

Given this, one can do as one pleases.

Text 12 The power of the tutor through the force of things. (What is important is to convey the impression of the force of things.) (I,163/t.56):

> The limits of the possible and the impossible are alike unknown to him, so they can be extended or contracted around him at your will. Without a murmur he is restrained, urged on, held back, by the hands of necessity alone; he is made adaptable and teachable by the mere force of things, without any chance for vice to spring up in him.

III This explains the co-called contradictions. *The illustration of the broken windows.*[7] Not a contradiction in fact. It is no violation of the principle to convey a sense of *the force of things, to present them in whatever way is appropriate so that they will bring about the action* latent within them. It is the things themselves which act. It is their lesson which educates.

IV But where can a suitable environment be found? Difficult.

Text 13 Where early education should take place. (So place him in isolation.) (I,171–2/t.58–9):

> But where shall we find a place for our child so as to bring him up as a senseless being, an automaton? Shall we keep him in the moon, or on a desert island? Shall we remove him from human society?

180

. . . I admit that I am aware of these difficulties; perhaps they are insuperable; but nevertheless it is certain that we do to some extent avoid them by trying to do so. I am showing what we should try to attain, I do not say we can attain it, but I do say that whoever comes nearest to it is nearest to success.

The village. Outside society.
Where education should take place (I, 173/t.59)[8]:

You will not be master of the child if you cannot control everyone about him.

Where education should take place (I, 175/t.59):

In the village a tutor will have much more control over the things he wishes to show the child; his reputation, his words, his example, will have a weight they would never have in the town; he is of use to everyone, so everyone is eager to oblige him, to win his esteem, to appear before the disciple what the master would have him be.

V Yet the principle cannot be inflexible. Child questions tutor. Tutor answers him. Relationship inevitable. What kind of relationship?

VI Same principle. Not the tutor who speaks; but things through him. Not the child who must be listened to; but the nature of things themselves. Tutor should not let him have his way because he desires it; but because that desire is rooted in the nature of things. Things demand compliance. Need.
Text 14 (Thus it is need, which is to say the nature of things, which must govern the way the educator conducts himself.) (I, 143/t.49)[9]:

Give him, not what he wants, but what he needs. Let there be no question of obedience for him or tyranny for you. Let him feel his liberty as much in your actions as in his own.

And since it is things which speak, the tutor must speak as things. *His will must be expressed so as to resemble the manifestations of nature. Necessity.*
Effectiveness of necessity as a means of restraint (I, 163/t.56):

Without a murmur he is restrained, urged on, held back, by the

181

hands of necessity alone; he is made adaptable and teachable by the mere force of things, without any chance for vice to spring up in him.

Irrevocability.
Do not yield to tears, but to need (I,145/t.50):

If his words were prompted by a real need you should recognise it and satisfy it at once; but to yield to his tears is to encourage him to cry, to teach him to doubt your kindness, and to think that you are influenced more by his importunity than your own goodwill.

A wall of brass.
Text 15 Will, a wall of brass (I,161/t.55):

If there is something he should not do, do not forbid him, but prevent him without explanation or reasoning; what you give him, give it at his first word without prayers or entreaties, above all without conditions ... but let your refusal be irrevocable; let no entreaties move you; let your 'No', once uttered, be a wall of brass, against which the child may exhaust his strength some five or six times, but in the end he will try no more to overthrow it.

VII A great innovation. Hitherto, education of man by man. Nature excluded. The material and the spiritual.
  The principle reversed. Things. *Still retain their earlier form, in a sense.* Not themselves the domain of morality. But they lay the foundations of moral education. An essential preparatory part of education. *It is from them that the sentiment of absolute necessity comes* (discipline, moderation). *It will have to be modified*; take on a new form. *But must first exist if it is to be transformed.* Can only be educated by things as his teachers.
  Why? *Social man in the image of natural man.*

C. Negative education

I How is one to term this education? Negative? It has been so described. Rousseau uses this expression. 'Therefore the education of the earliest years should be merely negative.' (t.57; page number of the French edition is omitted in the original text. – H.L.S.)
  Why? [10]

II Broadly speaking because it excludes man from acting. Whence negation of morality.

III But this negative morality also has a positive value.

The first, non-definitive draft of the third lecture

A. Dependence on things

I A reminder of the principle. Man must feel that he is restrained, stopped. He needs to be curbed. *Why?* A condition of that equilibrium which is itself a condition of happiness. But curbed *by what?* Human will? Physical force? Resistance must be felt to be necessary if it is to be accepted. It is legitimate because it is rooted in the nature of things. The force of things conveys their nature.

Human will must be disregarded. *It is contingent.* Either it demands purely and simply what is demanded by things and is useless, or else, superimposed, it has an adverse effect on them. Superimposes on the real world a world of fictions and imagination. Opinion. Morality?

II So we are left with things. They alone can induce the sentiment of necessity. They are subject to the laws of necessity. *Inflexible. Nothing arbitrary: they are what they are.* Their action stems from their nature. (Text)[11]

What stops him is the feeling of the impossible. (Text) *And this restraint is accepted.* It is the source of a spontaneous discipline. (Text)

III No orders. No commands. No obedience. (Text) In general terms, no *verbal lessons. Things speak.* (Text)

Consequently, *no punishment* as such. What punishment is. No place for it. (1) No orders. (2) No morality. Latter replaced by the natural consequences of the act. (Text)

IV It is the idea of authority which is repudiated. Define this idea. *Sui generis* in character, imposing respect and obedience. Acting out of respect for an authority. Authority of the rule and of the individual.

Rousseau is quite clear about this consequence of his doctrine. (Text)

V But it is through sensation alone that things are known. Thus, the child must live in a purely sentient environment. In keeping with his nature. Not mature enough for the moral world. (Text)

B. The role of the tutor and his relations with the pupil

I So is there to be no tutor or witness? No. It is direct action which is proscribed. Not all action. Tutor is master of things. Is behind them. Considerable power. (Text)

This *explains the so-called contradictions.* The illustration of the gardener; and the broken windows.

II And it is this reason in fact which determines where early education should take place. *A difficult problem.* (Text) *In the village.* Why? (Text)

III Yet Rousseau is well aware that the principle cannot be absolute. *Child questions tutor.* Tutor answers him. Direct relationship inevitable. What kind of relationship?

IV Determined by the same principle. Previously, things were the intermediary between pupil and tutor. Now it is the tutor who gives expression to things. Yet it is not the tutor who should speak. But things through him. *Not the child who must be listened to*; but the nature of things themselves. *No giving way or resisting because he demands it or gives satisfaction.* But because things impose compliance. Need. (Texts)

And since it is nature which speaks, the tutor's will must be expressed so as to resemble exactly the manifestations of nature. Necessary. Irrevocable. Wall of brass. (Texts)

Still the same principle. Social Contract.

V A great innovation. Hitherto, sole instrument of education has been man. Man is educated by man. *Expand. No nature.*

Principle reversed. Things. Hitherto placed outside the sphere of morality. Opposition between the spiritual and the material.

Things still are outside it in a sense. No morality. But they lay the foundations for the making of moral man. *An essential preparatory part of education. The sentiment of absolute necessity* stems from it. *Sentiments of discipline, harmony and moral order. Transferred from the natural state to the moral sphere.* How possible? Because moral man is the father of natural man. The latter is the model.

C. The concept of negative education

I Is this education negative? Rousseau uses this expression. (Texts)[12]

II Accurate in a sense. Man and society excluded. Neither opinions. (Text) Nor morality. *A wholly negative morality.*

III But this negative morality also has a positive value. It is the essential part of morality. (Texts) Why? The state of innocence. Negative morality. So must also be the prime virtue. Concept of social life: individuals not doing wrong to each other, nor encroaching. No fusion, no communion.
    Method of voting.

IV In general terms, the action of things has a positive effect. It pre-forms. It constitutes the principal part of education. (Text) Why? Because man in the natural state is the basis of moral and social man and because everything depends on the foundations. The one is modelled on the other. Back to the two kinds of education. Whence great importance of early education and education of the earliest years. (Text)

V The above contains the essence of the doctrine. The rest is much less original and profound. So we shall be more brief.

Lecture Four: definitive draft

A. The concept of negative education

I Summary of above. It is early education we are dealing with. It is things which are the tutor. From them, educative action stems. Self-effacement of the tutor.

185

II *How is this education to be described?* It is positive if sentiments and ideas are transmitted. In this case none. Tutor remains aloof. At a distance. Offers *no information.* Thus negative.

Text 1 Negative education (I,168/t.57):

> Therefore the education of the earliest years should be merely negative. (Why?) It consists, not in teaching virtue or truth, but in preserving the heart from vice and from the spirit of error. If only you could let well alone, and get others to follow your example; if you could bring your scholar to the age of twelve strong and healthy, but unable to tell his right hand from his left, the eyes of his understanding would be open to reason as soon as you began to teach him.

Text 2 Policy of wait and see (I,14/t.9):

> What must be done to train this exceptional man? We can do much, but the chief thing is to prevent anything being done. To sail against the wind we merely follow one tack and another; to keep our position in a strong stormy sea we must cast anchor.

III Term negative accurate in a sense. For something has been eliminated, excluded; man. Society. *No imparting of information. Opinions eliminated.*

Text 3 Negative education (I,3/t.5):

> The important thing is to 'shield this young tree from the crushing force of social conventions'.

Distinctly negative as regards morality.

Text 4 The child must remain in ignorance of the moral world – (This would introduce notion of vice) – must be aware of physical world only (I,154/t.53):

> Before the age of reason it is impossible to form any idea of moral being or social relations; so avoid, as far as may be, the use of words which express these ideas, lest the child at an early age should attach wrong ideas to them, ideas which you cannot or will not destroy when he is older. The first mistaken idea he gets into his head is the germ of error and vice; it is the first step that needs watching. Act in such a way that while he only notices external objects his ideas are confined to sensations; let him only

see the physical world around him. If not, you may be sure that either he will pay no heed to you at all, or he will form fantastic ideas of the moral world of which you prate, ideas which you will never efface as long as he lives.

(Compare with Descartes.)

IV But first, *negative morality has a positive value.* The essential part of morality.
   Text 5 Importance of negative morality (I,203/t.69):

The only moral lesson which is suited for a child . . . is this: 'Never hurt anybody'. The very rule of well-doing, if not subordinated to this rule, is dangerous, false and contradictory. Who is there who does no good? Every one does some good, the wicked as well as the righteous; he makes one happy at the cost of the misery of a hundred. . . . The noblest virtues are negative, they are also the most difficult, for they make little show, and do not even make room for that pleasure so dear to the heart of man, the thought that someone is pleased with us.

Why? Man in the natural state lives in innocence. Because they (*sic*) live as on a desert island.[13] No society: nor evil. Thus absolute morality.
   Apply this point of view to the social sphere: men not doing wrong to each other, or encroaching; respecting limits. Social Contract. No fusion or communion. Wholly negative relations.
   Method of voting.[14]

V This morality is positive in another sense. The action of things. Which is positive. *It pre-forms. Imprints upon the mind* certain specific attitudes which will crop up again and again, which are the basis of everything. The essential part of *all education. Basis of all moral and intellectual make-up.*
   Text 6 Importance of spontaneous education (I,79/t.29):

Man's education begins at birth; before he can speak or understand he is learning. Experience precedes instruction; when he recognizes his nurse he has learnt much. The knowledge of the most ignorant man would surprise us if we had followed his course from birth to the present time. If all human knowledge were divided into two parts, one common to all, the other peculiar to the learned, the latter would seem very small compared with the former.

This is because social man is based upon natural man and because everything depends on the foundations. *The one modelled on the other.* This is the source of our sense of the real.

VI Whence the great importance of early education. *Early years are critical.* Error or truth.
Text 7 The early years are critical (I,167/t.57):

The most dangerous period in human life lies between birth and the age of twelve. It is the time when errors and vices spring up, while as yet there is no means to destroy them; when the means of destruction are ready, the roots have gone too deep to be pulled up.

Importance, in Cartesian sense, of initial notions.

VII Stress the role ascribed to things. Rousseau not to be interpreted according to our current terminology. An original, *even if paradoxical idea.*
Things are instructive because addressed to the imagination; they are striking, simply and forcefully perceived. *Means of avoiding abstraction. Tools which are useful and complementary.*
For Rousseau all this is true. But a deeper reason. Things are instruments of culture. Not a way of offering assistance. Only from them that moral action can come. They fashion man.
Get down to the essential. Moral law is a wall of brass which stops man. The yoke is salutary. Immorality if will is capricious. Contact with nature can be useful here. Hence sciences contribute to moral education. Feeling of necessity, of the *resistance of things.* Superior to will. It is this pre-moral education that is at issue.

B. Application of the principle to moral life

I To be strictly accurate, there is no moral education as such. *No human relations; so no morality.* Any feeling of obligation to give him moral ideas necessarily implies a departure from the rule; also, that man is intervening between things and children. *A bad introduction.*

188

An example: lies. (1) In relation to the past. Child has every reason to state what is since he has need of his fellow men in order to become adapted. To deceive is simply to do injury to himself. He lies because he has received a command. (2) Making a promise one has no intention of keeping. But the child is ignorant of social convention. Exists only in the present.

Text 8 Lies (I,195/t.66):

Children's lies are therefore entirely the work of their teachers, and to teach them to speak the truth is nothing less than to teach them the art of lying.

II Yet this is impossible in practical terms. Contact with men; not a complete vacuum. Essential notions. But (1) at a later date. (2) Sentient. The present.

Text 9 Necessity for moral initiation (I,180/t.61):

I think it impossible to train a child up to the age of twelve in the midst of society, without giving him some idea of the relations between one man and another, and of the morality of human actions. It is enough to delay the development of these ideas as long as possible, and when they can no longer be avoided to limit them to present needs, so that he may neither think himself master of everything nor do harm to others without knowing or caring
. . . but there are also stormy dispositions whose passions develop early; you must hasten to make men of them lest you should have to keep them in chains.

Is Rousseau about to violate his principle? No. No commands or prohibitions. *Education must come from reality,* from the spectacle of the forces at work in it. *Tutor will do no more than direct and manipulate them. Action of educator and doctor compared.*

III Yet tutor must conceal his action so that pupil is not aware of it. Otherwise, effect will misfire. A product of will, not of things. So some acting is essential.

IV How to set about it? Two sides to moral life. Rights and duties. Rights must come first. The only feeling the child experiences is self-love. It is this motive that must be exploited.

Text 10 Rights and duties (I,181/t.61):

189

All our instincts are at first directed to our own preservation and our own welfare. Thus the first notion of justice springs not from what we owe to others, but from what is due to us. Here is another error in popular methods of education. If you talk to children of their duties, and not of their rights, you are beginning at the wrong end, and telling them what they cannot understand, what cannot be of any interest to them.

V But what rights? People? Things? People can defend themselves. *They act by themselves. No threats.*

Different with things. *'Therefore the first idea he needs is not that of liberty but of property'* (I,182/t.62).

Why? *Artificial.*

VI Then what of his right of property? By what means? *The lessons of things. Let him witness the birth of his right, let him experience how it feels.* Create the circumstances which gave rise to this institution.

Toys excluded, and clothes. For property is not primitive.

VII What this right implies originally. (1) Work. (2) Right of first occupant. *'The notion of property goes back naturally to the right of the first occupier to the results of his work'* (I,188/t.63). Two elements. (1) Work. (2) Privilege of the first occupant by force.

VIII Whence, to respect for the property of others. Contract. The broken windows. Child locked up. Agreement. Commitment. First obligation. First social tie. The individual is caught.

Text 11 Social tie (I,191/t.64):

The naughty little fellow hardly thought when he was making a hole for his beans that he was hewing out a cell in which his own knowledge would soon imprison him.

We are now in the world of morals, the door to vice is open. Deceit and falsehood are born along with conventions and duties ... The sorrows of life begin with its mistakes.

Stop here.

IX Another principle. Imitation. *'Man imitates, as do the beasts. The love of imitating is well regulated nature'* (I,202/t.68).[15] An inferior process; all the more appropriate.

Text 12 Imitation (I,202/t.68):

> I know that all these imitative virtues are only the virtues of a
> monkey . . . But at an age when the heart does not yet feel any-
> thing, you must make children copy the deeds you wish to grow
> into habits, until they can do them with understanding and for
> the love of what is good.

But remains true to the principle. All social motives excluded.
One act which itself summons forth another. No exhortations or
appeals to the desire to shine.

The first, non-definitive draft of the fourth lecture

A. The concept of negative education

I Summary: (1) Imitation of nature. (2) All beings limited; a
condition of harmony. (3) Limited by what? Things. *Only they can
convey the impression of necessary limits:* invincible and legitimate.

Hence the child must live surrounded by things. Only they can
educate. *Tutor through them. If he acts by himself, must imitate
the action* of things, and rooted in the nature of things.[16]

II In that case, how is this education to be described? Positive,
in so far as it implies intervention for the purposes of transmitting
ideas, sentiments, etc. Tutor remains aloof. Observes from a distance. Offers no information. Thus negative. (Texts)[17]

III Term negative accurate in a sense. For something has been
eliminated: man, society. Excluded. *Human opinions.* (Text)
Morality. (Text)

IV But this negative morality also has a positive value. It is the
essential part of morality. (Text) Why? Man in the natural state
lives in innocence. What this means. Men far removed from one
another. No evil. Negative morality. Thus morality *par excellence.*
*Apply this point of view to the social sphere. Men not doing wrong
to each other or encroaching.* No fusion; negative relations.

Method of voting.

V In more general terms, the action of things is positive. It pre-
forms. It imprints upon the mind certain specific attitudes which
will crop up again and again. The essential part of all education.
(Text)

Why? Because man in the natural state is the basis of social man
and everything depends on the foundations. The one modelled on
the other. *Turn back to the two kinds of education.*

Whence great importance of early education. *This is the source
of our sense of the real.* Once this is completed, man is formed.
Early years are critical. (Text)

VI Stress the role thereby ascribed to things. Rousseau not to be
interpreted according to our own ideas and terminology. An
original idea, even if paradoxical and false. Things are instructive
because addressed to the imagination; they are striking, more
simply and forcefully perceived. Means of avoiding abstraction.
Tools which are useful and complementary. For Rousseau, things
are instruments of culture. Of course, *the child understands best
that which is tangible; but there are some, essential lessons that can
only come from things.* They fashion man.

B. Application of the principle to moral life

I If one observes the principle to the letter, there is no moral
education as such. No human relations. No place for either morality
or immorality. *Any feeling of obligation to give him moral ideas*
implies a departure from the rule. It means that man is intervening
between things and children. A bad introduction.

An example. Lies. (1) *In relation to the past.* Child has every
reason to state what is, since he has need of his fellow men in order
to become adapted to things. *To deceive is simply to do injury to
himself.* He lies because he has received a command. (2) Making
a promise one has no intention of keeping. But commitment, social
convention. Child cannot commit himself: exists only in the present.
(Text)

II Yet this is impossible in practical terms. Not a complete vacuum.
Contact with men. Some moral ideas or feelings are essential. (Text)

Is Rousseau about to violate his principle? No. *The desired result* should be obtained with neither commands, nor prohibitions, nor punishments. Education must come from reality, from life, from the forces at work in life.

Tutor will do no more than manipulate and direct them. *Art of educator and doctor compared.*

Yet tutor must *conceal his action* so that pupil is not aware of it, so that he does not mistake the processes of things for the product of an arbitrary will. Whence necessity for acting.

III How to set about it? Two sides to moral life. Rights and duties. Rights must come first. *Only sentiment child experiences is self-love.* It is this that must be exploited. Hence rights. (Text)

IV But what rights? Of people? Of things? Those which threaten him the most are dangerous.[18] People can defend themselves. So no threats. Different with things. *'Therefore the first idea he needs is not that of liberty but of property'* (I,182/t.62).

His right must come first. But how? *No teaching.* The lessons of things. Let him witness the birth of his right, let him experience how it feels. (Refer back to beginning.) *Create artificially the circumstances which gave rise to the institution of property.*

Hence toys excluded. For property is handed on, not acquired by him.

V What right of property implies originally: (1) Work. (2) The right of first occupant. *'The notion of property goes back naturally to the right of the first occupier to the results of his work.'* Whence the fable in two acts. (1) Work. (2) Privilege of first occupant. Resistance of force.

VI Thence, to respect for the property of others. Contract. The broken windows. They are mine. Commitment. First obligation. This is the social tie. *The individual is caught.* (Text)
  Stop here.

VII Another principle: imitation. *'Man imitates, as do the beasts. The love of imitating is found in well-regulated nature.'*[19] An inferior process. All the more appropriate.

But remain true to the principle. All social motives excluded. It is seeing the act which summons forth the act. No explanation or appeal to the desire to shine, to be applauded.

VIII Not an exhaustive list. Vice. No treatment of the consequences. Let him feel what is abnormal in him. (I,178)

Notes

1 [The article is that by Durkheim published posthumously the year before in the *Revue de métaphysique et de morale* (XXV, pp. 1–23 and 129–61) entitled 'Le "Contract social" de Rousseau' (1918b). It was reproduced later in *Montesquieu et Rousseau, précurseurs de la sociologie*, with a foreword by A. Cuvillier and an introductory note by G. Davy (1953a). The book was translated into English by R. Manheim as *Montesquieu and Rousseau: Forerunners of Sociology*, with a foreword by H. Peyre (1960b). – W.S.F.P.]

2 (For this third expanded version of the Second Lecture, see the Third Lecture, and particularly in the Definitive Draft, the first paragraph under the heading: Dependence on Things. – Xavier Léon.)

3 (The text indicated is missing: it is clearly Text 6 of the Third Lecture. – Xavier Léon.)

4 (Text missing, but obviously it is also Text 6 of the Third Lecture.—Xavier Léon.)

5 (Text missing: most probably *Émile*, I, pp. 155 and 164. – Xavier Léon.)

6 (Cf. *Revue de métaphysique et de morale*, XXV, p. 21. – Xavier Léon.)

7 [This refers to an illustration of the point that the tutor should not be overtroubled by an ill-tempered child, advising the tutor not to complain immediately about any inconvenience he is caused. See t.64. – W.S.F.P.]

8 [Translation should read: 'everything about him', not 'everyone about him'. – H.L.S.]

9 [The last sentence has not been translated by Foxley. – H.L.S.]

10 (For texts turn to the first paragraph of the Fourth Lecture (Definitive Draft). – Xavier Léon.)

11 (For texts, see preceding draft of this lecture. – Xavier Léon.)

12 (For texts, see Definitive Draft of the Fourth Lecture, paragraphs A and B. – Xavier Léon.)

13 (Allusion to Robinson Crusoe. – Xavier Léon.)

14 (Allusion to the vote of the sovereign people and to the expression of the general will. – Xavier Léon.)

15 [Translation by H.L.S.; text unclear. See also the same quotation on p.193. – H.L.S.]

16 [Text unclear. – H.L.S.]

17 (For texts, see preceding draft of this lecture. – Xavier Léon.)

18 [French text is unclear. It has been emended to: 'Ceux qui le menacent le plus dangereux.' – H.L.S.]

19 [See n.15 above. – H.L.S.]

Bibliography

(See Notation and bibliographies, p. ix, and Abbreviations, p. x)

Morals

Durkheim on morals

1885b   Review. 'Fouillée, A., *La Propriété sociale et la démocratie*', *RP*, XIX, pp. 446–53.

1887c   'La Science positive de la morale en Allemagne', *RP*, XXIV, pp. 33–58; 113–42; 275–84.

1893b   *De la Division du travail social: étude sur l'organisation des sociétés supérieures*, Alcan, Paris. (See especially Introduction.)

t.1933b   from 2nd ed. 1902b, with Introduction, by G. Simpson, *The Division of Labour in Society*, Macmillan, New York.

1895a   *Les Règles de la méthode sociologique*, Alcan, Paris.

t.1938b   by S. A. Solovay and J. H. Mueller, *The Rules of Sociological Method*. Edited, with an introduction by G. E. G. Catlin, University of Chicago Press, Chicago, and (1950) Free Press, Chicago.

1897a   *Le Suicide: étude de sociologie*, Alcan, Paris.

t.1951a   by J. A. Spaulding and G. Simpson, *Suicide: A Study in Sociology*. Edited, with an introduction by G. Simpson, Free Press, Chicago, and (1952) Routledge & Kegan Paul, London.

1898a(ii)   'La Prohibition de l'inceste et ses origines', *AS*, I, pp. 1–70.

t.1963a   with an introduction by E. Sagarin, *Incest. The Nature and Origin of the Taboo by Émile Durkheim*, Lyle Stuart, New York.

1898c   'L'Individualisme et les intellectuels', *RB*, 4th series, X, pp. 7–13.

t.1969d   by S. and J. Lukes, 'Individualism and the intellectuals', *Political Studies*, XVII, pp. 19–30.

t.1973a   by M. Traugott, 'Individualism and the intellectuals', in R. N. Bellah (ed.), *Émile Durkheim on Morality*

	and Society. University of Chicago Press, Chicago and London, pp. 43–57.
1899a(ii)	'De la Définition des phénomènes religieux', *AS*, II, pp. 1–28.
t.1975a	by J. Redding and W. S. F. Pickering in W. S. F. Pickering (ed.), *Durkheim on Religion*, Routledge & Kegan Paul, London and Boston, pp. 74–99.
1899c	Contribution to: 'Enquête sur l'introduction de la sociologie dans l'enseignement secondaire', *RIS*, VII, p. 679.
1900a(7)	Review. 'A. Asturaro, "La scienza morale e la sociologia generale" ', *AS*, III, p. 330.
1901a(i)	'Deux Lois de l'évolution pénale', *AS*, IV, p. 65–95.
t.1973b	by T. Anthony Jones and Andrew Scull, 'Durkheim's two laws of penal evolution', with an introduction, *Economy and Society*, 2, 3, pp. 278–308.
1901a(iii)(6)	Review. 'Ross, Edward Alsworth, *The Genesis of Ethical Elements*', *AS*, IV, pp. 308–9.
1901a(iii)(45)	Review. 'Fouillée, Alfred, *La France au point de vue moral*', *AS*, IV, pp. 443–5.
1902a(iii)(13)	Review. 'Dumont, Arsène, *La Morale basée sur la démographie*', *AS*, V, pp. 320–2.
1902a(iii)(14)	Review. 'E. Westermarck, "L'elemento morale nelle consuetudini nelle leggi" ', *AS*, V, pp. 326–7.
1904a(5)	Review. 'Lévy-Bruhl, L., *La Morale et la science des moeurs*', *AS*, VII, pp. 380–4.
t.1979a	in this volume.
1905b	Contribution to: 'La Morale sans Dieu: essai de solution collective', *La Revue*, LIX, pp. 306–8.
t.1979a	in this volume.
1906a(10)	Review. 'Hoeffding, Harold, *On the Relation between Sociology and Ethics*', *AS*, IX, pp. 323–4.
1906a(11)	Review. 'Bayet, Albert, *La Morale scientifique: essai sur les applications morales des sciences sociologiques*', *AS*, IX, pp. 324–6.
t.1979a	in this volume.
1906b	'La Détermination du fait moral', *BSFP*, VI, pp. 169–212. (Reproduced in 1924a.)
t.1953a	see 1924a.
1906d	'Le Divorce par consentement mutuel', *RB*, 5th series, V, pp. 549–54.

1906e   Lecture on Religion and Morality delivered in the École des Hautes Études in the winter of 1905–6. Summary by A. Lalande in 'Philosophy in France (1905)', *PR*, XV, pp. 255–7.

1906f   Examination of thesis. M. Aslan, *La Morale de Guyau*, *RMM*, XIV, supplément, July, p. 14.

t.1968e   by S. Lukes 1968. (Reproduced in Lukes 1972, pp. 636–8.)

1907a(3)   Review. 'Fouillée, Alfred, *Les Éléments sociologiques de la morale*', *AS*, X, pp. 354–61.

1907a(4)   Review. 'Belot, Gustave, "En Quête d'une morale positive"', *AS*, X, pp. 361–9.

1907a(5)   Review. 'Landry, Adolphe, *Principes de morale rationelle*', *AS*, X, pp. 353–4.

1907a(9)   Review. 'Richard, G., "Les Lois de la solidarité morale"', *AS*, X. pp. 382–3.

1907a(10)   Review. 'Westermarck, Edward, *The Origin and Development of the Moral Ideas*', *AS*, X, pp. 383–95.

t.1979a   in this volume.

1908a(2)   Contribution to discussion: 'La Morale positive: examen de quelques difficultés', *BSFP*, VIII, pp. 189–200.

t.1979a   in this volume.

1910b   Contribution to discussion: 'La Notion d'égalité sociale', *BSFP*, X, pp. 59–63; 65–7; 69–70.

t.1979a   in this volume.

1910c(1)   Examination of thesis. M. Pradines, *Principes de toute philosophie de l'action*, *RMM*, XVIII, supplément, January, pp. 29–31.

t.1968e   by S. Lukes 1968. (Reproduced in Lukes 1972, pp. 643–6.)

1911b   'Jugements de valeur et jugements de réalité', in *Atti del IV Congresso Internationale di Filosofia*, Bologna, 1911, vol. I, pp. 99–114, *RMM*, XIX, pp. 437–53, and in 1924a.

t.1953b   see 1924a.

1912a   *Les Formes élémentaires de la vie religieuse. Le système totémique en Australie*, Alcan, Paris.

t.1915d   by J. W. Swain, *The Elementary Forms of the Religious Life: A Study in Religious Sociology*, Allen & Unwin, London; Macmillan, New York.

t.1975a   (certain sections) by J. Redding and W. S. F. Pickering in W. S. F. Pickering (ed.), *Durkheim on Religion*, Routledge & Kegan Paul, London and Boston.

1912c　Examination of thesis. M. Terraillon, *L'Honneur, sentiment et principe moral*, *RMM*, XX, supplément, July, p. 31.

t.1968e　by S. Lukes 1968. (Reproduced in Lukes 1972, pp. 653–4.)

1913a(ii)(15)　Review. 'Deploige, Simon, *Le Conflit de la morale et de la sociologie*', *AS*, XII, pp. 326–8.

1914b　Contribution to discussion: 'Une nouvelle position du problème moral', *BSFP*, XIV, pp. 26–9; 34–6.

1915c　*L'Allemagne au-dessus de tout: la mentalité allemande et la guerre*, Colin, Paris.

t.1915f　*'Germany Above All': German mentality and the War*, Colin, Paris.

Published posthumously

1920a　'Introduction à la morale', with an Introductory note by M. Mauss, *RP*, LXXXIX, pp. 79–97.

t.1979a　in this volume.

1922a　*Éducation et sociologie*. Introduction by P. Fauconnet, Alcan, Paris.

t.1956a　by S. D. Fox, *Education and Sociology*. Introduction by S. D. Fox and Foreword by T. Parsons, Free Press, Chicago.

1924a　*Sociologie et philosophie*. Preface by C. Bouglé. Alcan, Paris. (Reproduces 1906b and 1911b.)

t.1953b　by D. F. Pocock, *Sociology and Philosophy*. With an introduction by J. G. Peristiany, Cohen & West, London.

1925a　*L'Éducation morale*. Introduction by Paul Fauconnet, Alcan, Paris.

t.1961a　by E. K. Wilson and H. Schnurer, *Moral Education: A Study in the Theory and Application of the Sociology of Education*, with an introduction by E. K. Wilson, Free Press, New York.

1937a　'Morale professionelle', with a note by M. Mauss, *RMM*, XLIV, pp. 527–44; 711–38. (Reproduced in 1950a.)

1938a　*L'Évolution pédagogique en France*, with an introduction by Maurice Halbwachs. 2 vols, Alcan, Paris.

t.1977a　by Peter Collins, with a translator's introduction, *The Evolution of Educational Thought*, Routledge & Kegan Paul, London and Boston.

1950a   *Leçons de sociologie: physique des moeurs et du droit.*
Foreword by H. N. Kubali. Introduction by G. Davy.
L'Université d'Istanbul, Istanbul, Presses Universitaires
de France, Paris.

t.1957a   by C. Brookfield, *Professional Ethics and Civic Morals*,
Routledge & Kegan Paul, London.

1955a   *Pragmatisme et sociologie. Cours inédit prononcé à la
Sorbonne en 1913–14 et restitué par Armand Cuvillier
d'après des notes d'étudiants*, Vrin, Paris.

t.1960c   lectures 1–5, 13 and 14 by C. Blend in K. H. Wolff (ed.),
*Émile Durkheim 1858–1917: A Collection of Essays,
with Translations and a Bibliography*, Ohio State
University Press, Columbus, Ohio.

1960a   'Les Raisons d'être. Morale de la société en général',
Annales de l'Université de Paris, no. 1, pp. 54–6
(presented by Raymond Lenoir).

1968a(1–12)   'De l'Enseignement de la morale à l'école primaire'.
Notes made by R. Lenoir of a series of lectures by
Durkheim. In Lukes 1968, vol. 2, pp. 147–241.

1968c   'La Morale'. Notes made by G. Davy, probably at the
1908/9 lecture course. In Lukes 1968, vol. 2,
pp. 248–60.

1968d   'La Morale'. Notes of lectures made by A. Cuvillier.
In Lukes 1968, vol. 2, pp. 261–97.

On Durkheim and morals

ALPERT, H. 1939 *Émile Durkheim and his Sociology*, Columbia University Press, New York.

ARON, R. 1967a *Les Étapes de la pensée sociologique*, Gallimard, Paris.

ARON, R. 1967b *Main Currents of Sociological Thought*, 2 vols. Translation of *Les Grandes Doctrines de sociologie historique*, Basic Books, New York. (1968 Weidenfeld & Nicolson, London.)

BAYET, A. 1905 *La Morale scientifique: essai sur les applications morales des sciences sociologiques*, Alcan, Paris. (Cf. Durkheim 1906a(11).)

BAYET, A. 1925 *La Science des faits moraux*, Alcan, Paris.

BELLAH, R. N. (ed.) 1973 *Émile Durkheim: On Morality and Society*, selected writings, edited with an Introduction by R. N. Bellah, University of Chicago Press, Chicago and London.

BELOT, G. 1905–6 'En quête d'une morale positive', *RMM*, XIII, pp. 39–74; 561–88; and XIV, pp. 163–95. (Cf. Durkheim 1907(a)(4).)

BELOT, G. 1907 *Études de morale positive*, 2 vols, Alcan, Paris.

BOUGLÉ, C. 1922 *Leçons de sociologie sur l'évolution des valeurs*, Colin, Paris. (English translation *The Evolution of Values*, New York, by H. S. Sellars, 1926.)

CANTECOR, G. 1904 'La Science positive de la morale', *RP*, LVII, pp. 225–41; 368–92.

CANTECOR, G. 1907 'Revue de philosophie. La morale sociologique', *Année psychologique*, 13, p. 459–76.

COHEN, J. 1975 'Moral freedom through understanding in Durkheim', *ASR*, 40, pp. 104–6. (See also comments by T. Parsons and W. Pope which follow.)

DAVY, G. 1920 'Durkheim: II – l'oeuvre', *RMM*, XXVII, pp. 71–112.

DEPLOIGE, S. 1911 *Le Conflit de la morale et de la sociologie*, Dewit, Bruxelles. (English translation *The Conflict between Ethics and Sociology*, Herder, St Louis and London, by C. C. Miltner, 1938.) (Cf. Durkheim 1913a(ii)(15).)

FAUCONNET, P. 1904 'La Morale et la science des moeurs', *RP*, 57, pp. 72–87.

FOUILLÉE, A. 1905 *Les Éléments sociologiques de la morale*, Alcan, Paris. (Cf. Durkheim 1907a(3).)

GIDDENS, A. 1978 *Durkheim*, Fontana, London.

GINSBERG, M. 1951 'Durkheim's ethical theory', *BJS*, 2, pp. 210–18.

GODDIJN, H. P. M. 1976 'De ontwikkeling van Durkheim's moraalsociolozie', *Bijdragern*, 37, pp. 304–19, 391–403.

GURVITCH, G. 1937a 'La Science des faits moraux et la morale théoretique chez É. Durkheim', *Archives de philosophie du droit et de sociologie juridique*, VII, pp. 18–44 (reproduced in G. Gurvitch, *Essais de Sociologie*, 1938, and *La Vocation actuelle de la sociologie*, 1950).

GURVITCH, G. 1939 'The sociological legacy of Lévy-Bruhl', *Journal of Social Philosophy*, 5, pp. 61–70.

GURVITCH, G. 1963 *Traité de sociologie*, vol. II (ch. III), P.U.F., Paris.

HART, H. L. A. 1967 'Social solidarity and the enforcement of morals', *University of Chicago Law Review*, 55, pp. 1–13.

HAYWOOD, J. E. 1960 'Solidarist syndicalism: Durkheim and Duguit', *SR*, n.s. 8, pp. 17–36; 185–202.

HENRIOT, J. 1967 *Existence et obligation*, P.U.F., Paris (part 2, ch. 1).

KARADY, V. 1970 'La Morale et la science des moeurs chez Durkheim et ses compagnons', *Revue universitaire de science morale*, XII–XIII, pp. 85–114.

KÖNIG, R. 1976 'Émile Durkheim. Der Soziologe als Moralist'. In D. Käsler (ed.), *Klassiker der Soziologie*, Beck, Munich.

LACAPRA, D. 1972 *Émile Durkheim: Sociologist and Philosopher*, Cornell University Press, Ithaca and London.

LACROIX, B. 1976 'La Vocation originelle d'Émile Durkheim', *RFS*, XVII/2, pp. 213–15.

LADD, J. 1957 *The Structure of a Moral Code*, Harvard University Press, Cambridge, Mass.

LANDRY, A. 1906 *Principes de morale rationnelle*, Paris. (Cf. Durkheim 1907a(5).)

LENOIR, R. 1918 'Émile Durkheim et la conscience moderne', *MF*, LXXVII, pp. 577–95.

LÉVY-BRUHL, L. 1903 *La Morale et la science des moeurs*, Alcan, Paris.

(English translation *Ethics and Moral Science*, Constable, London, by E. Lee, 1905.) (Cf. Durkheim 1904a(5).)

LUKES, S. 1968 'Émile Durkheim: an intellectual biography', D.Phil. thesis, University of Oxford.

LUKES, S. 1972 *Émile Durkheim: his life and work, a historical and critical study*, Harper & Row, New York. (1973 Allen Lane, London.)

MAUCHASSAT, G. 1928 Sur les Limites d'interprétation sociologique de la morale', *RMM*, XXXV, pp. 347–79.

MAUSS, M. 1925 'In memoriam, l'oeuvre inédite de Durkheim et de ses collaborateurs', *AS*, n.s. 1, pp. 7–29.

MAYS, W. 1974 'Popper, Durkheim and Piaget on moral norms', *Journal of the British Society for Phenomenology*, 5 (3), pp. 233–42.

OUY, A. 1926 'L'Éducation morale', *RIS*, XXXIV, pp. 199–206.

OUY, A. 1939 'Les Sociologues et la sociologie: Deuxième partie, le sociologisme, Émile Durkheim', *RIS*, XLVII, pp. 245–75.

PARODI, D. 1910 *Le Problème moral et la pensée contemporaine*, Alcan, Paris.

PARSONS, T. 1937 *The Structure of Social Action*, Free Press, Chicago.

RAUH, F. 1904 'Science et conscience à propos d'un livre récent', *RP*, LVII, pp. 358–67.

RICHARD, G. 1905 'Sur les lois de la solidarité morale', *RP*, LX, pp. 441–71.

RICHARD, G. 1911 'Sociologie et métaphysique', four articles, *Foi et vie*, June–July, 1911.

RICHARD, G. 1925a 'Sociologie religieuse et morale sociologique. La théorie solidariste de l'obligation', *RHPR*, 1925, pp. 244–61.

RICHARD, G. 1925b *L'Évolution des moeurs*, Doin, Paris.

SAHAY, A. 1976 'The Concepts of Morality and Religion. A Critique of the Durkheimian world-view', *Sociological Analysis and Theory*, 6, pp. 167–85.

SIDGWICK, H. 1886 *History of Ethics*, London. (Enlarged edition 1931, London.)

TIRYAKIAN, E. A. 1964 'Introduction to a bibliographical focus on Émile Durkheim', *Journal for the Scientific Study of Religion*, vol III, no. 2, pp. 247–54.

TRAUGOTT, M. 1978 Introduction to *Émile Durkheim on Institutional Analysis*, edited by M. Traugott, University of Chicago Press, Chicago and London.

WALLWORK, E. 1972 *Durkheim: Morality and Milieu*, Harvard University Press, Cambridge, Mass.

WOLFF, K. H. (ed.) 1960 *Émile Durkheim 1858–1917: A Collection of Essays, with Translations and a Bibliography*, Ohio State University Press, Columbus, Ohio. (Republished in 1964 as *Essays in Sociology and Philosophy*, Harper & Row, New York.)

Education

Durkheim on education

1901i   'Rôle des universités dans l'éducation sociale du pays', in *Congrès international de l'éducation sociale, 26–30 September, 1900*. Alcan, Paris.

t.1976a   by George Weisz, 'The role of universities in the social education of the country', with introductory notes by George Weisz, *Minerva*, XIV, 3, pp. 380–88.

1903b   'Pédagogie et sociologie', *RMM*, XI, pp. 37–54. (r.1922a)

1904a(40)&(41)   Review. 'Durkheim, "Pédagogie et sociologie" in *Revue de métaphysique et de morale*, 1903, and Paul Barth, "Die Geschichte der Erziehung in soziologischer Beleuchtung", *Vierteljahrschrift für wissenschaftliche Philosophie und soziologie*, 1903', *AS*, VII, pp. 683–6.

t.1979a   in this volume.

1905f(2)   Examination of thesis. L. Gockler, *La Pédagogie de Herbart*, *R de P*, 6, pp. 608–16.

t.1968e   by S. Lukes. (Reproduced in Lukes 1972, pp. 629–35.)

1906c   'L'Évolution et le rôle de l'enseignement secondaire en France', *RB*, 5th series, V, pp. 70–7. (r.1922a)

1909a(2)   Contribution to discussion: 'L'Efficacité des doctrines morales', *BSFP*, IX, pp. 219–31.

t.1979a   in this volume.

1910c(2)   Examination of thesis. P.-J. Mendousse, *Du Dressage et l'éducation*, *RMM*, XVIII, supplément, March, pp. 31–2.

t.1968e   by S. Lukes 1968. (Reproduced in Lukes 1972, pp. 646–9.)

1911a   Contribution to discussion: 'L'Éducation sexuelle', *BSFP*, XI, pp. 33–8; 44–7.

t.1979a   in this volume.

1911c   Articles: (1) 'Éducation', pp. 529–36, (2) 'Enfance', pp. 552–3 (with F. Buisson), (3) 'Pédagogie', pp. 1538–43, in *Nouveau Dictionnaire de pédagogie et d'instruction primaire* publié sur la direction de F. Buisson, Hachette, Paris. ((1) and (3) r.1922a.)

t.1979a   (2) in this volume.

1912b   Contribution to discussion: 'Sur la culture générale et la réforme de l'enseignement', *Libres entretiens*, 8th series, pp. 319–20; 322; 332.

t.1979a   in this volume.

1916c   Contribution to: 'La Grandeur morale de la France: L'école de demain', *Manuel général de l'instruction primaire. Journal hebdomadaire des instituteurs et des institutrices*, 83 (17), 8 January 1916, pp. 217–18.

t.1919c   'The School of Tomorrow'. In F. Buisson and F. E. Farrington (eds.), *French Educational Ideals of Today. An Anthology of the Molders of French Educational Thought of the Present*, World Book Co., Yonkers-on-Hudson, New York, pp. 188–92.

t.1979a   in this volume.

Published posthumously

1919a   'La "Pédagogie" de Rousseau', *RMM*, XXVI, pp. 153–80.

t.1979a   in this volume.

1922a   *Éducation et sociologie*. Introduction by P. Fauconnet, Alcan, Paris. (Reproduces 1911c(1), 1911c(3), 1903b, 1906c.)

t.1956a   by S. D. Fox, *Education and Sociology*. Introduction by S. D. Fox and Foreword by T. Parsons, Free Press, Chicago.

1925a   *L'Éducation morale*. Introduction by Paul Fauconnet, Alcan, Paris.

t.1961a   by E. K. Wilson and H. Schnurer, *Moral Education: A Study in the Theory and Application of the Sociology of Education*. Edited, with an introduction, by E. K. Wilson, Free Press, New York.

1938a   *L'Évolution pédagogique en France*, 2 vols, Alcan, Paris.

t.1977a   by Peter Collins, *The Evolution of Educational Thought*. Introduction by Maurice Halbwachs, translator's Introduction by Peter Collins, Routledge & Kegan Paul, London and Boston.

1968a(1–12)   'De l'Enseignement de la morale à l'école primaire.' Notes made by R. Lenoir of a series of lectures by Durkheim. In Lukes 1968, vol. 2, pp. 147–241.

On Durkheim and education

ALPERT, H. 1939 *Émile Durkheim and his Sociology*, Columbia University Press, New York.

ARON, R. 1967b *Main Currents of Sociological Thought*, 2 vols. Translation of *Les Grandes Doctrines de sociologie historique*, Basic Books, New York. (1968 Weidenfeld & Nicolson, London.)

AYKROYD, P. 1941 Review. '*L'Évolution pédagogique en France de la rénaissance à nos jours*, by Émile Durkheim, Alcan, Paris', *Sociological Review*, 33, pp. 192–5.

BANTOCK, G. H. 1963 *Education in an Industrial Society*, Faber & Faber, London.

BANTOCK, G. H. 1965 *Education and Values*, Faber & Faber, London.

BARNES, G. M. 1977 'Durkheim, É. Contribution to Sociology of Education', *Journal of Educational Thought*, 11, pp. 213–23.

BAYET, A. 1926 Review. 'Émile Durkheim: *L'Éducation morale*', *RP*, 102, pp. 304–9.

BERNSTEIN, B. 1967 'Open schools open society', *New Society*, 10, pp. 351–3.

BERNSTEIN, B. 1973–5 *Class, Codes, Control,* 3 vols, Routledge & Kegan Paul, London.

BOOCOCK, S. S. 1973 'The school as a social environment for learning', *Sociology of Education*, 46, pp. 15–50.

BOUGLÉ, C. 1938 *Humanisme, sociologie, philosophie: remarques sur la conception française de la culture générale*, Hermann, Paris.

BREMBECK, C. S. 1966 *Social Foundations – a Cross-Cultural Approach*, Wiley, New York.

BUISSON, F. and FARRINGTON, F. E. (eds) 1919 *French Educational Ideals. An Anthology of the Molders of French Educational Thought of the Present*, World Book Co., Yonkers-on-Hudson, New York.

CASE, C. M. 1924 'Durkheim's educational sociology', *Journal of Applied Sociology*, 9, pp. 30–3.

CLARK, T. N. 1973 *Prophets and Patrons*, Harvard University Press, Cambridge, Mass.

COLLINS, P. 1977 Introduction to Durkheim, *The Evolution of Educational Thought* (English translation of 1938a), Routledge & Kegan Paul, London and Boston.

COSER, L. 1971 *Masters of Sociological Thought*, Harcourt Brace, New York.

CHERKAOUI, M. 1976 'Socialisation et conflit: les systèmes éducatifs et leur histoire selon Durkheim', *RFS*, XVII, 2, pp. 197–212.

CHERKAOUI, M. 1977 'Basil Bernstein and Émile Durkheim: two theories of change in educational systems', *Harvard Educational Review*, 47, pp. 556–64.

CRITTENDEN, B. S. 1964 'Sociology of knowledge in Durkheim and Mannheim and its bearing on educational theory', Ph.D. thesis, University of Illinois.

CURTIS, S. J. 1958 *An Introduction to the Philosophy of Education*, University Tutorial Press, London.

DEBESSE, M. 1966 'Preface' to Durkheim, É., *Éducation et sociologie*, 2nd ed., P.U.F., Paris.

DORE, R. P. 1965 *Education in Tokugawa Japan*, Routledge & Kegan Paul, London.

DREEBAN, R. 1968 *On What is Learned in School*, Addison & Wesley, Reading, Mass.

FAUCONNET, P. 1922 Introduction to Durkheim, *Éducation et sociologie*, Alcan, Paris.

FILLOUX, J.-C. 1978 'Sur la Pédagogie de Durkheim', *Revue française de pédagogie*, 44, pp. 83-98.

FLOUD, J. E. 1962 'Teaching in the affluent society', *BJS*, XIII, 4, pp. 299-308.

FORSTER, P. J. 1973 'Discussion', *Sociology of Education*, 46, pp. 92-8.

DE GAUDEMAR, P. 1969 'É. Durkheim, sociologue de l'éducation', *Annales de la Faculté des Lettres et Sciences Humaines de Toulouse,* V, 4, pp. 129-42.

GERDY, D. F. 1969 'Implications of three selected sociological theories of Émile Durkheim for the goals of contemporary American public education 1969', Ph.D. thesis, Michigan State University.

GIDDENS, A. 1978 *Durkheim*, Fontana, London.

HALBSWACHS, M. 1938 Introduction to Durkheim, *L'Évolution pédagogique en France* (1938a/t.1977a).

HUESO, V. 1911 *La educación moral en la escuela primaria, segun Durkheim*, vol. 18, Anales, Junta para Ampliación de Estudios é Investigaciones cientificas, Madrid.

KARABEL, J. and HALSEY, A. H. 1977 'Educational research: a review and an interpretation' in J. Karabel and A. H. Halsey (eds), *Power and Ideology in Education*, Oxford University Press, New York.

KARADY, V. 1976 'Durkheim, les sciences sociales et l'université: bilan d'un semi-échec', *RFS*, XVII, 2, pp. 267-311.

KAY, W. 1975 *Moral Education: a sociological study of the influence of society, home and school*, Allen & Unwin, London.

KOHLBERG, L. 1968 'Moral development', in *International Encyclopedia of the Social Sciences*, Macmillan and Free Press, New York.

LEAR, E. N. 1961 'Émile Durkheim as Educator', *Journal of Educational Sociology*, 34, 5, pp. 193-204.

LEVITAS, M. 1974 *Marxist Perspectives in the Sociology of Education*, Routledge & Kegan Paul, London.

LOUREAU, R. 1969 'La Société institutrice (Durkheim et les origines de la science de l'éducation)', *Les Temps modernes*, 24, pp. 1648-64.

LUKES, S. 1968 'Émile Durkheim: an intellectual biography', D.Phil. thesis, University of Oxford.

LUKES, S. 1972 *Émile Durkheim: his life and work, a historical and critical study*, Harper & Row, New York. (1973, Allen Lane, London.)

MAC KENSIE, J. S. 1925 Review. 'L'Éducation morale d'Émile Durkheim', *Litteris*, 2, 3, pp. 185-96.

MAUSS, M. 1925 'In memoriam, l'oeuvre inédite de Durkheim et de ses collaboratuers', *AS*, n.s. 1, pp. 7-29.

205

BIBLIOGRAPHY: **Education**

MAYS, J. B. 1967 *The School in its Social Setting*, London University Press, London.

MITCHELL, M. M. 1931 'Émile Durkheim and the philosophy of nationalism', *Political Science Quarterly*, 46, pp. 87–106.

MORRISH, I. 1967 *Disciplines of Education*, George Allen & Unwin, London.

MUSGROVE, F. 1964 *Youth and the Social Order*, Routledge & Kegan Paul, London.

OTTAWAY, A. K. C. 1955 'The educational sociology of Émile Durkheim', *BJS*, 6, pp. 213–27.

OTTAWAY, A. K. C. 1968 'Durkheim on Education', *British Journal of Educational Studies*, 16, pp. 5–17.

OUY, M. 1926 'L'Éducation morale', *RIS*, 34, pp. 199–206.

PARSONS, T. 1959 'The school class as a social system: some of its functions in American society', *Harvard Educational Review*, 29, pp. 297–318.

PIAGET, J. 1932 *Le Jugement moral chez l'enfant*, Paris. (Translated as *Moral Judgement of the Child*, Kegan Paul, Trench & Trubner, London, 1932.)

PIAGET, J. 1971 *Science of Education and the Psychology of the Child*, translated by D. Coltman, Longman, London.

PIAGET, J. 1974 *The Child and Reality, Problems of Genetic Psychology*, translated by A. Rosin, Muller, London.

RICHMOND, W. K. 1975 *Education and Schooling*, Methuen, London.

SCHONFIELD, W. R. 1976 *Obedience and Revolt. French Behaviour towards Authority*, Sage Library of Social Research, 22, Beverly Hills, California and London.

WALLER, W. 1965 *The Sociology of Teaching*, Wiley, New York.

WALLWORK, E. 1972 *Durkheim, Morality and Milieu*, Harvard University Press, Cambridge, Mass.

WEISZ, G. 1976a 'Émile Durkheim on the French universities', *Minerva*, XIV, 3, pp. 377–9.

WEISZ, G. 1976b 'The academic élite and the movement to reform French higher education, 1850–1885', Ph.D. thesis, State University of New York at Stony Brook.

WHITE, P. 1972 'Socialization and education', in R. F. Dearden, P. H. Hirst, and R. S. Peters (eds), *Education and the Development of Reason*, Routledge & Kegan Paul, London and Boston.

WILSON, E. K. 1961 Introduction to Durkheim, *Moral Education: A Study in the Theory and Application of the Sociology of Education* (English translation of 1925a), Free Press, New York.

ZEITLIN, I. M. 1968 *Ideology and Development of Sociological Theory*, Prentice-Hall, New York.

Name index

(Excluding names in the Bibliographies)

Subject index

(Where recognized translations have been made, Durkheim's books, articles and reviews are given according to the English title.)

213